THE CENTER FOR CHINESE STUDIES

at the University of California, Berkeley, supported by the Ford Foundation, the Institute of International Studies (University of California, Berkeley), and the State of California, is the unifying organization for social science and interdisciplinary research on contemporary China.

PUBLICATIONS

Schurmann, Franz. *Ideology and Organization in Communist China.* 1966.
Wakeman, Frederic, Jr. *Strangers at the Gate: Social Disorder in South China, 1839–1861.* 1966.
Townsend, James R. *Political Participation in Communist China.* 1967.

CAPITALISM AND THE CHINESE PEASANT

CAPITALISM AND THE CHINESE PEASANT

SOCIAL AND ECONOMIC
CHANGE IN A
HONG KONG VILLAGE

Jack M. Potter

UNIVERSITY OF CALIFORNIA PRESS

BERKELEY AND LOS ANGELES, 1968

HN
761
·H62
P6

University of California Press
Berkeley and Los Angeles, California

Cambridge University Press
London, England

To Barbara

Preface

This book is the result of anthropological field research carried out in Ping Shan, a traditional Chinese lineage in Hong Kong's New Territories, over a period of eighteen months, from August, 1961 until January, 1963. In all frankness, this study represents the work of a frustrated anthropologist who would have preferred to write a book based on first-hand investigation of a Chinese commune. But given the present political situation, the New Territories were as close to China as I could get. Anthropologists specializing in Chinese studies are probably more frustrated over the inability to enter China than other social scientists because the hallmark of our trade is the intensive study of a living, on-going community through participant observation. It is more difficult for anthropologists to study China from a distance than it is for historians, economists, and political scientists who are more accustomed to working from documentary materials. Like other students of China, I hope that conditions will someday improve to the point that we can cease studying communes through refugee interviews or by peering at them through binoculars across the Sham Chun river. Until then, I am afraid that anthropologists studying China will remain "fish out of water," and will either have to learn the techniques of documentary research or be content with the study of Chinese in Hong Kong, Taiwan, or other overseas Chinese communities.

One of the main objections to this book and to all such studies of Chinese society on Taiwan or in Hong Kong will be that these places are not China and have little relevance for the understanding of either traditional or modern Chinese society. I am fully aware, almost painfully so, that the New Territories are not China. But even so, I firmly believe that if caution is exercised and allowances are made for the limiting and special circumstances that affect the Chinese in these areas, much can still be learned about Chinese social, cultural, and economic patterns that will increase our knowledge of traditional China and help to furnish a base line for the study of some aspects of Communist China.

Many people had a part in making this book possible. The Ford
Foundation Foreign Area Training Fellowship Program (now called
the Foreign Area Fellowship Program and now under the auspices of
the Social Science Research Council and the American Council of
Learned Societies) sponsored my field work in Hong Kong. They,
of course, do not necessarily agree with the opinions and conclusions
expressed in this book. The Center for Chinese Studies at the University of California, Berkeley, supported my graduate training program in Chinese studies. Professors Wolfram Eberhard and Franz
Schurmann gave me advice and support during the course of my research in Hong Kong; and Professor Theodore D. McCown super-
vised the writing of an earlier version of this work in the form of
a Ph.D. dissertation. Professor Maurice Freedman, whose book, *Lineage Organization in Southeastern China,* first stimulated my interest
in the New Territories, and Professor Eugene A. Hammel read an
earlier draft of the book and made valuable suggestions for its re-
vision. Mr. John Service of the Center for Chinese Studies read over
the final draft and helped prepare the Glossary. James L. Watson and
Wilhemina Stocking helped in the preparation of the manuscript for
publication. Professor Robert F. Murphy, now of Columbia University, supported me through many years of undergraduate and
graduate work in anthropology. To all of these persons, I express
my sincere appreciation.

It would be a gross ingratitude not to mention the kind and
friendly assistance of the villagers of Ping Shan who welcomed my
wife and me into their society and made our stay there both memora-
ble and profitable: Chinese villagers are among the finest people
anywhere. I am also indebted to the officers of the Hong Kong Government, particularly the staff of the Yuen Long District Office, for
encouragement and assistance that went far beyond the call of duty.

Miss Lynda Spence of the University of California Press performed
the difficult editorial task of making this book as intelligible and
readable as it is. With dedicated persistence she improved both style
and substance and stubbornly insisted that I clarify turgid prose and
untangle complicated statistics. Much of the credit for this book belongs to her.

Acknowledgment is gratefully given to the Hong Kong University
Press for permission to reproduce material from *The Cost of Living
in Hong Kong* by Edward F. Szczepanik; to the M. I. T. Press for permission to quote from C. K. Yang's book *A Chinese Village in Early
Communist Transition;* and to The University of Chicago Press for
permission to use material from *Earthbound China: A Study of Rural
Economy in Yunnan* by Fei Hsiao-tung and Chang Chih-i. The map

of Hong Kong, Kowloon, and the New Territories that appears in this book is based upon a Crown-copyrighted map, reproduced by permission of the Hong Kong Government.

Most of all, I thank my wife Barbara, who helped with the field work and assumed the burden of typing the manuscript.

Aside from place names and other Cantonese terms commonly used in Hong Kong, the Chinese terms have been romanized in mandarin, using the Wade-Giles system. Exceptions are the names of villagers (all pseudonyms) and village ancestral halls, which have been romanized following the Chao system of Cantonese romanization (see Chao, 1947).

All monetary figures in the book are in Hong Kong dollars, unless otherwise indicated. The exchange rate in 1961–1963 was about HK$5.6 to US$1, and this figure has been used in conversions.

Some statistical columns in the book do not add up to 100 per cent because the figures have been rounded off, sometimes to one decimal place and sometimes to the nearest whole number.

J. M. P.

Contents

TABLES

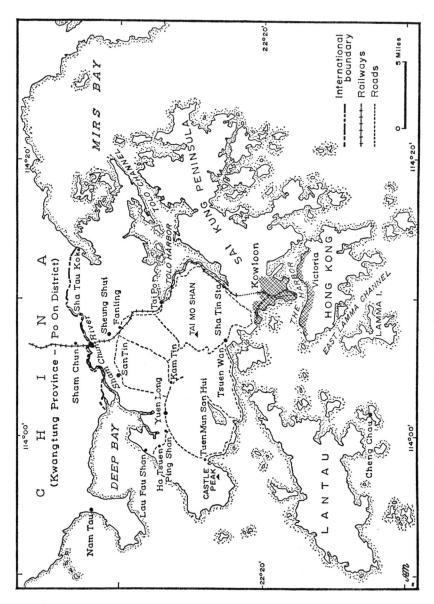

MAP 1. Hong Kong, Kowloon, and the New Territories.

Introduction

This is a study of the changing economy of Hang Mei, one of the eight villages that together comprise the Tang lineage of Ping Shan, located near the market town of Yuen Long in Hong Kong's New Territories. In it I describe the economy of the village as it existed in 1961–1963 and, as far as limited historical data allow, review the complex forces that have changed it over the past half-century. Since Hong Kong was founded as the first Western treaty port on the coast of China in 1841, the colony has grown and prospered from its role as a great entrepôt in the China trade. After World War II, the colony successfully carried out an industrial revolution, adding a flourishing industrial sector to its traditional commercial economy. In recent years, Hong Kong has become one of the most prosperous areas in East Asia.

The problem of analyzing and explaining the economic development and industrialization of the colony in its larger aspects, however, must be left to the economist, for the anthropologist is not equipped to study large-scale economic systems. Just as social anthropology can be characterized as a form of "micro-sociology" when compared to traditional sociology (Firth, 1951:3), economic anthropology is distinguished from traditional economics in that its characteristic approach is one of "micro-economics."

The anthropologist deals preferably with small-scale economic systems, where he can study economic behavior first-hand and in detail. He studies these small-scale systems from a holistic point of view, emphasizing the interrelationship between economic behavior and other aspects of the concrete social and cultural framework within which economic action takes place. The anthropologist operates under the assumption that this approach to the study of one small unit within a larger socio-economic system gives insights that cannot be gained by the methods and the theoretical approach of the economist. He deals with "people" rather than with highly abstract "primary in-

1

dustries." The responsibility for analyzing the macro-economy is left to the economist while the anthropologist concentrates on the task of interpreting the effect of national economic programs or processes on his small unit and the reciprocal effect of economic decisions made in the small community on the larger economic system. The large-scale analysis and the small-scale analysis are complementary; the anthropologist's contribution is collaborative and not definitive.

This study concentrates on one small aspect of the process of economic development in Hong Kong—the effects of industrial development and commercial expansion on the economy of a small village in the rural hinterland of the colony. In brief, I attempt to show that the effects of economic development within a capitalist framework have on the whole been beneficial to the rural villages of the colony. The villages of Ping Shan, and to a lesser degree most other New Territories' villages, were in 1962 remarkably prosperous by Asian standards. This statement needs no elaborate proof for it is obvious to even the casual visitor to the villages and towns of the New Territories. In the market towns, theaters and teashops are filled to capacity, and hawkers' stands sell the best Washington apples and California oranges. In the villages, one sees electric lights, Japanese fans and radios, and not a few automobiles. In the eyes of the refugees from Communist China, the New Territories, no less than the urban centers of the colony, are indeed "heaven" (the term by which refugees frequently refer to Hong Kong). A central purpose of this study will be to explore in detail the reasons the villagers have prospered from their participation in the general industrial and commercial expansion of the colony.

In addition, this study will also be concerned with the more general theoretical problem of the nature of a peasant economy and the way it changes in the process of economic development. This involves setting up a model of a traditional peasant-type economy and specifying how the parts are modified as it changes to a modern economy. The peasant village is not a completely self-sufficient economic unit. It is a "part-economy" in that it is involved in a wider economic network that includes not only other villages, but also rural markets, towns, and even cities. As George Foster puts it: "Peasants are primarily farmers, and sometimes artisans as well. They produce much of their food and are able to make many of the material items they need for life such as clothing and tools. But they depend on town markets to sell surplus produce and to buy items which they cannot make themselves" (1962:46).

Peasant economy can be conceived as consisting of two "halves." One half is the subsistence-oriented sector, which is not completely differentiated from the social and ritual relations that exist within the traditional peasant community. This nonmarket sector of a peasant economy is relatively self-contained and allows the peasant to "hold the market at arm's length" (Redfield, 1956:46). The external economic relations with markets, towns, and cities comprise the second half of the economy. It is here that the peasant sells part of his produce and purchases goods and services that he needs but does not himself produce. The economic system of a peasant community is not as self-contained as an ideal-type "primitive economy," such as that found in an isolated Pacific island society; yet it is more self-sufficient and less involved in wider market relations than is a rural community in a modern industrialized nation such as the United States. On an ideal-type continuum, peasant economy falls approximately midway between a "primitive economy" at one pole, and a completely differentiated, market-dominated economy at the other pole.[1]

The industrialization of a traditional peasant society decreases the self-sufficiency of the peasant community and intensifies its external economic relations with markets, towns, and cities. Market relations extend into the peasant village, and economic activities become fully differentiated from the traditional social and ceremonial relations to which they were once tied. This has a disruptive effect on the traditional social relations that govern the peasant's ties to kinsmen and to fellow villagers. Particularistic ties such as kinship, real or fictive, are transformed into more impersonal, universalistic relationships. A "collectivity orientation" of the traditional kind, which stresses the obligation of the individual to such groups as the extended family, the lineage, and the village as a whole, gives way to an "individualistic orientation" where the economic interests of the individual become more important than his obligation to the collectivity. Traditional means of validating status in the community, such as redistributing personal wealth at marriages, funerals, and other such ritual or ceremonial occasions, become less important. This form of "economic irrationality" becomes subordinated to the "economic rationality" of individual self-interest.

The market mentality penetrates what once was the peasant's closed social universe, and the market is no longer "held at arm's length." The quality of interpersonal relations is transformed; diffuse types of traditionalistic economic relations give way to more functionally specific relations, and status gives place to contract. The old social framework that was suited to the traditional peasant economy is gradually forced to give way to a new social framework created by the new economic relations. A society is a functionally interrelated system

---

[1] See the discussions of economic relations in peasant societies in Diaz (1967) and Wolf (1966, chapter 2).

composed of mutually interdependent variables. Once one part of the system changes, other parts of the system must change and adapt themselves to the new conditions. The industrialization and commercialization process transforms the traditional peasant social and cultural framework, as well as the economy.

Industrialization's initial effects on the peasant village are most clearly seen in the occupational structure. Those members of the community originally engaged in nonagricultural occupations move into new occupations created by the expansion of industry and commerce, and the "peasant," whose agricultural activities are mainly oriented towards growing subsistence crops, is changed into a "farmer" or agricultural businessman, who operates his farm as a business enterprise and is primarily oriented towards producing cash crops for the market (Wolf, 1955:454). The participation in occupations of a nontraditional type, once firmly established, eventually leads to a readjustment of the peasant family and other social groupings. Usually, the change in occupation necessitates a change in residence, with peasants moving out of the village and into the town and city. Here, in an urban milieu, they are exposed to new ideas and new values, and they bring these novelties back into the village. Young men and women who go to work in the city are free from the social-control mechanisms of parents, kinsmen, and fellow villagers. Modern ideas, such as those of romantic love and free marital choice, subvert the traditional structure of the extended family. In all these ways, changes in the occupational pattern of peasant villagers represent the first step in the complete transformation of the traditional peasant economy, society, and culture.

In this study, I relate in detail this "depeasantization process" as it has occurred in the villages of Ping Shan over the past half-century. By presenting this detailed case history of the effects of industrial and commercial development on a Chinese village, I hope to contribute to the understanding of the worldwide process through which traditional peasant villages are becoming part of the modern industrial world.[2]

In addition, this study is intended as a contribution to the understanding of the economic and social effects of Western treaty port cities on adjacent areas of rural China, an important but little-understood phase of modern Chinese history (see Fairbank, Eckstein, and Yang, 1960:25–26). In the final chapter of the book, I argue that the results of this study, together with historical evidence from other parts of China, contradict the orthodox interpretation of the effects of treaty port industry and commerce on the rural Chinese economy during the

[2] For a more general discussion of the modernization of peasant societies, see Potter, 1967.

modern period. I argue that this orthodox interpretation is not strongly supported by the available evidence and that it is in some respects oversimplified and misleading. Treaty port industry and commerce, imperialistic or not, was not as detrimental to the rural Chinese economy as most previous writers have believed.

I
The Setting

THE COLONY

The colony of Hong Kong, a total land area of 398 square miles with a total population, in 1961, of about three million,[1] lies on the south coast of China at the head of the Pearl River Delta, ninety miles south of Canton and thirty-five miles east of Macao. It is separated from Kwangtung Province of the People's Republic of China by the Sham Chun River, which forms the colony's northern boundary (see Map 1).

Three major areas comprise the colony—Hong Kong Island, Kowloon, and the New Territories. Hong Kong Island, the original place of settlement in the colony when it was founded in 1841, has an area of approximately nine square miles and lies about one mile off the mainland. On the north side of the island, facing Kowloon, is Victoria, a city of about one million. The peninsula of Kowloon juts into Victoria Harbor across from the city of Victoria and, together with its surrounding area, had a population of about one and one-half million in 1961. The New Territories includes the area on the mainland between Kowloon and the Sham Chun River. In 1961, the New Territories contained a population of 409,945[2] and included a land area of 365 square miles (Hong Kong Government, 1962:319).

The colony lies within a region of tropical South China which Cressey (1955:212) has called "The Canton Hinterland." The area is hilly and mountainous with level land amounting to less than 10 per cent of the total area. Hong Kong itself is extremely mountainous with a rugged coastline that falls precipitously into the sea. Only about 14 per cent of the total land area of the colony is suitable for agricultural purposes and most of this is located in valleys in the northern and western parts of the New Territories (Blackie, n.d.:5).

[1] By 1965 the population had grown to 3,823,200 (see Hong Kong Government, 1966:235).
[2] The population of the New Territories had increased to about 675,000 by 1965 (see Hong Kong Government, 1966:267).

This region of China has a monsoonal climate with hot, wet summers and cool winters. The winters are colder than those found in most tropical areas, giving some seasonal variation in climate. The summer months are hot and humid, with frequent rainfall. The autumn months with their warm and sunny days are the most pleasant period of the year. The winter months are damp, overcast, and somewhat chilly (Tregear, 1955:17).

The average annual temperature is about 72 degrees F., with a mean monthly temperature of 59 degrees F. in February and 82 degrees in July (Blackie:5). In winter the temperature rarely falls below 40 degrees F. and the maximum temperature in the summer is often over 90 degrees (Tregear, 1955:23). Humidity is highest in the summer months, when it averages more than 80 per cent; and lowest in the short winter season, when it falls to 70 per cent (Tregear, 1955:23–24).

Average annual rainfall in the colony is about 84 inches (Tregear, 1955:18). Of this, 25 per cent comes in the spring months, 50 per cent in the summer months of June, July, and August, 20 per cent in the fall, and only 5 per cent in the winter months of December, January, and February (Blackie:4). These seasonal averages are, however, subject to great yearly fluctuations, adding to the problems of the colony's farmers, who depend on the early spring rains for planting their first rice crop. Quite often the spring rains do not come in time and the first rice crop cannot be planted except in those limited areas where irrigation is available. Typhoons are not uncommon in the fall and sometimes, as in 1962, cause serious crop and property damage throughout the colony.

The tropical climate permits a growing season of 365 days a year. The agricultural cycle in this area has traditionally consisted of two rice crops, grown from spring to fall, with an additional winter catch crop of sweet potatoes. Tea and silk are important products in the areas surrounding Canton, but are of limited importance in the New Territories. Fish ponds are widespread in the countryside and fish farming is a major industry.

The Canton hinterland has long been one of the most commercially developed areas of China. This is at least in part because this region has had commercial contact with the West ever since the establishment of the Portuguese at Macao in 1557. (Cressey, 1934:136–138, 363–366).

The colony of Hong Kong was founded in 1841 as a result of the Opium War between England and China. It was intended to serve as a secure base from which English merchants could carry on trade with China, free from the stifling restrictions imposed by the Chinese government which had disturbed and limited trade at Canton. Initially, the colony consisted only of Hong Kong Island, then a rocky, barren place inhabited only by a few fishermen and pirates. The total population of Hong Kong Island when the British took possession was about fifteen hundred (Tregear, 1955:4).

Fires and typhoons caused setbacks in the early years of the colony, and malaria decimated the European population. Chinese, attracted by employment opportunities, began to arrive in considerable numbers, however, and by 1844 the population had increased to 19,000 (Hong Kong Government, 1961:309). The growth and development of the colony was further aided by the great wave of Chinese emigration (1849–1851) to Southeast Asia, America, and Australia, for which Hong Kong served as the embarkation port (Hong Kong Government, 1962:340).

In 1860, as a result of the Second Anglo–Chinese War, Kowloon peninsula was ceded to Great Britain and soon became an integral part of the expanding colony. Extensive dock facilities were started and Kowloon began to develop, following Victoria, as the second great urban area of Hong Kong. Thirty-eight years later, in 1898, the Chinese government leased the New Territories to Great Britain for a period of 99 years (from 1898 to 1997). This large section of rural Chinese countryside was an important addition to the older areas of Hong Kong Island and Kowloon.

The inhabitants of the New Territories did not wish to be incorporated in the British colony and, in tacit cooperation with the Chinese government, organized armed resistance to the British occupation. The undisciplined local troops had no chance, however, against the British troops; resistance crumbled after a few skirmishes, allowing the British to take over the area in about two weeks.

The history of Hong Kong since 1898 is in large part a story of migrations of Chinese, who were driven into the colony by the unsettled social and economic conditions that prevailed within China during the first half of the twentieth century. After the Chinese Revolution of 1911 there was a large influx of refugees. Another inflow from the mainland occurred in 1938, after Canton had fallen to the invading Japanese army. It has been estimated that 100,000 Chinese entered Hong Kong in 1937, 500,000 in 1938, and 150,000 in 1939, bringing the colony's population to a prewar high of one and one-half million (Szczepanik, 1958:25).

An important episode in the history of the colony began in December, 1941, when the Japanese invaded Hong Kong from the mainland. After a spirited defense by a handful of British defenders, the colony was forced to surrender to the Japanese on Christmas Day, 1941, thus beginning almost four years of Japanese occupation. The period of Japanese occupation was one of economic dislocation and near starvation for many residents of the colony. British residents were interned in detention camps and many of the Chinese residents went home to their native villages in China.

After the Japanese surrender in 1945, the British resumed control of the colony, and former Chinese residents began to return. Szczepanik (1958:27) estimates that about 700,000 Chinese came into the colony in the immediate postwar period, from 1945 to 1948. With the start of the civil war on the mainland, another and more momentous wave of refugees, fleeing the southward advance of the Chinese Communist armies, escaped to the colony. By 1951 the population had increased to two million (Hong Kong Government, 1962:25). Another group of about 140,000 refugees entered Hong Kong in 1955–1956. After this there were no further mass immigrations, but natural increase and a continuing trickle of immigrants, most of them illegal, brought the population in 1961 to the relatively astronomical figure of just over three million. The refugees from the mainland who have entered Hong Kong since the war have virtually swamped the colony and have created the social and economic "refugee problem." [3]

Until the war with Japan, most of the Western trade with South China flowed through Hong Kong's famous seaport, and much of the financing of the trade with China was supplied by the large banking institutions of the colony. After the end of the war, and especially after the Communist take-over on the mainland in 1949, trade between the West and China declined, and the colony was forced to adapt to new economic conditions to remain economically viable. In the eighteen years since the war, an astonishing industrial development has taken place which has more than made up for the reduced trade with China. Hong Kong has changed from a trade-based to an industry-based economy. Because of this, it has been able to absorb the tremendous mass of refugees by creating employment and economic prosperity for the residents of the colony as a whole (Szczepanik, 1958:13).

Economic prosperity, increased population, and the important tourist trade have transformed the cities of Victoria and Kowloon into major metropolitan areas. Acculturation to the Western pattern of urban life had been characteristic of the colony's urban Chinese since its founding and has accelerated in the years since the war. Increasingly, in the last decade Western cultural and social influences have affected the rural areas of the colony, which are at present experiencing rapid social and cultural changes.

Hong Kong is notable as a place of many striking contrasts. The

[3] For a discussion of Hong Kong's refugee problem, see Hambro, 1955.

European upper class that dominates the colony, both politically and socially, inhabits the "Peak" area on the island, with height above sea level corresponding quite closely to the family's wealth and social position. The commercial and administrative center of the colony is in the city of Victoria, where the central district contains the government offices and the old prestigious commercial institutions long famous in the history of Western contact with China, such as Jardine Matheson and the Hongkong and Shanghai Banking Corporation. West of this modern and highly cosmopolitan area is the Chinese area of Wanchai, where shop-lined streets are filled to capacity with lower-class and middle-class Chinese residents.

Across the harbor from Victoria, on the tip of the peninsula, is the Tsim Sha Tsui section of Kowloon, where luxurious Western-style hotels, restaurants, and modern shops cater to the needs of the thousands of tourists who visit the colony each year. Further north on the peninsula is the traditional Chinese part of Kowloon with thousands of shops, artisan workshops, and apartment houses like those found in Canton or in other Chinese cities.

On the outskirts of Kowloon is the area known as New Kowloon. Here are located most of the new light-industrial plants and factories that have been responsible for the economic development of the colony in the last two decades. Also on the outskirts of the city stand tier upon tier of large concrete apartment houses or "resettlement blocks," which now house most of the refugees who once lived in wooden shacks on the surrounding hillsides. Large Chinese families occupy one small room, about 10 by 12 feet, which serves as living and sleeping quarters; and each family shares cooking and water facilities with other families on their floor. The impression given here is one of extreme congestion but not of extreme poverty. Many of the workers employed in the new factories are inhabitants of these government resettlement blocks.

Passing north out of Kowloon and into the New Territories, one quickly leaves behind the tremendous congestion and noise of the city and enters an area of green countryside, rice paddies, and Chinese villages that date back to the Sung Dynasty. Until after World War II, the New Territories was a peaceful rural countryside; the new four-lane highway running out from Kowloon is symbolic of the rapid transformation of this area in the last twenty years.

THE NEW TERRITORIES

The New Territories are under the control of a District Commissioner, who, under the authority of the Governor of the colony, is

responsible for administering the entire area. Under the Commissioner
are four District Officers, who are the chief governing officials in the
four administrative areas into which the New Territories are divided
—Tai Po, Yuen Long, Tsuen Wan, Sai Kung and Islands (Hong
Kong Government, 1964:273). Each district is divided in turn into
rural township units, which usually include from ten to thirty villages.
In Yuen Long District, these smaller administrative units are called
hsiang. In each *hsiang*, a Rural Committee to assist the District Officer
in village matters is elected from the Village Representatives, one or
two of which are elected by each village. The Chairmen and Vice Chairmen of the 27 Rural Committees in the New Territories, together with
other prominent local Chinese, form the Hsiang I Chü, or Rural
Consultative Council, that serves as an advisory body to the Commissioner and acts as a spokesman for local opinion (Hong Kong Government, 1966:267–268).

By far the largest part of the New Territories, both on the islands
and on the mainland, is mountainous and barren. The eastern half of
the mainland portion of the New Territories, the Tai Po District and
the Sai Kung Peninsula, is extremely hilly, with village settlements
found only in small valleys along the coast and on small inland
plateaus. The soils in this area are not so fertile or deep as soils in the
Yuen Long Valley, where most of the villages are found.

Before the recent immigration, there were four ethnic groups in the
New Territories: Cantonese (Penti) peasants, Hakka peasants, Tanka
or "boat people," and Hoklo. The Hakka are a non-Cantonese Chinese group, originally from north and central China, who are linguis-
tically and culturally somewhat distinct from the Cantonese but who,
like them, are peasant farmers (see Pratt, 1960). The Hakka came into
this area after the Cantonese settlement; consequently, they occupy the
poorer mountain regions in the eastern part of the New Territories.
They are in almost exclusive possession of the two large eastern
peninsulas and are the dominant group in the areas surrounding the
market towns of Tai Po and Sha Tin (see Map 1). The Tanka boat
dwellers (see Anderson, 1967; and Ward, 1954, 1959, 1965) have inhabited the South China coast from time immemorial and were
probably one of the non-Chinese ethnic groups that inhabited the area
before Chinese settlement. The Hoklo are also boat people, who
originally came from Fukien Province, but some of them have settled
ashore, combining agriculture with fishing.

Cantonese peasants began to settle this southern outpost of China
early in the Sung Dynasty, although Chinese influence had been
present in Canton much earlier. The Cantonese, who have traditionally been the dominant group in the area, look down on the other

ethnic groups and until recently refused to intermarry with the "boat people," although some intermarriage with the Hakka has taken place. They occupy the richest agricultural land in the northern and western section of the New Territories, which lies in the Yuen Long Valley, and own most of the other good land throughout the New Territories, which over the centuries has gradually been settled by peasant farmers from elsewhere in Kwangtung. These early settlers founded lineages that today have grown into sizable villages or clusters of villages. The older established lineages had prior claims to most of the best land; consequently, the later arrivals settled marginal land or became tenants of the established lineages. Most of the New Territories exhibits a local pattern of one long-established, powerful, landowning lineage surrounded by tributary tenant villages descended from later arrivals to the area.

Until its incorporation into the colony in 1898, the New Territories were part of Po An Hsien (changed to San On Hsien after the 1911 Revolution). The *hsien* administrative seat, the headquarters of the district magistrate, was located in the city of Nam Tau, northwest of the New Territories across Deep Bay (see Map 1). Before the British occupied Hong Kong, the villagers of the area were oriented north and west to Nam Tau and Canton, since at that time the Kowloon–Hong Kong area was relatively unimportant except for the small walled city of "Old Kowloon," which contained a minor garrison of imperial troops.

The history of the New Territories from 1898 to the beginning of the Japanese occupation in 1941, is one of slow change as the approximately 600 rural villages and towns were incorporated into the economic and administrative system of the colony. Immediately after the British occupation, an administrative system was established which has not changed essentially since that time. Police stations were set up to maintain law and order and District Offices were established as seats of local government. Soon after 1900, a land survey in the New Territories established the ownership of land for tax purposes; deeds of ownership were issued and Crown Rent Rolls drawn up (Topley, 1964). In the first decade of the century, a rudimentary road network was extended from Kowloon to the major market towns in the New Territories, and the Kowloon–Canton Railroad was built through the eastern part of the New Territories, passing through the market town of Tai Po. In the first few decades, attempts were made to establish elementary schools in the rural areas, but progress in education was slow until after the war. The market towns of the New Territories began to develop better transportation facilities as trade with the city increased. All these factors led to some changes in the culture and

economy of the rural villages, but this progress was slow and gradual
and not nearly so abrupt as the changes that were to occur after the
war.

Since the Communist Revolution in 1949, many refugees from the
mainland have settled in the New Territories on small plots of land
rented from the older village inhabitants. On these rented fields the
refugees have built small wooden houses and have made their living
by growing vegetables and raising chickens and pigs for the city
market. They have been economically quite successful, and shacks of
the refugee farmers now dot the countryside between the original
peasant villages.

In the last fifteen years, and especially in the last decade, the excess
population from the overcrowded cities has begun to spill over into
the New Territories. Large numbers of lower-class Chinese have
moved into some of the older villages that are conveniently located
near transportation facilities and near the market towns. Some of the
newcomers have found employment in the towns, but most of them
leave their families in the village and continue to work in the cities,
establishing a "suburban" pattern of living. Most of the men reside
more or less permanently in the cities and visit their families only on
weekends or on the major Chinese holidays. The move to the villages
is popular because living conditions in the country are better and
more economical, and also because primary education for the children
is much cheaper in the village schools.

Recently, industrial and commercial firms from the city have begun
to set up small branches and factories in the rural areas of the New
Territories, thus increasing employment opportunities for the villagers. Industry and commerce have also stimulated the development
of better transportation facilities. Road networks, and with them
electricity and piped water, are being extended into rural areas;
villages that once were isolated even from the market towns are now
connected to the city by bus and taxi service, and some have telephones and street lights. Since the war, modern elementary schools
supported by the government have been established in almost all the
rural villages and many private middle schools have been set up near
the market towns. Medical facilities in the market towns have also
been improved. These factors—outsiders resident in or near the
villages, improved transportation facilities, commercial and industrial
development, and improved social services—have precipitated a process
of rapid social, cultural, and economic change in the New Territories
that has begun to alter fundamentally the older traditional patterns of
the villages.

There are several large market towns in the New Territories, in addition to the several hundred old-established villages, the scattered homesteads of vegetable farmers, and the fishing villages along the coast. On the south coast, not far from Kowloon, is the new industrial town of Tsuen Wan, which, before the war, was a sleepy country market town of traditional Chinese shops and businesses. In the postwar years Tsuen Wan has been transformed into an industrial center and now contains large factories, a flourishing business district, and many resettlement blocks for the factory workers. The other major market towns in the New Territories are Yuen Long in the northwest plain, with a population of over 33,000; Tai Po, on the east coast, with a population of 17,000; and, in the northeast, the towns of Sheung Shui, population 26,332, and Fanling, with 26,282 inhabitants. In addition to these sizable market towns, there are lesser markets scattered throughout the New Territories along the main roads (District Commissioner of the New Territories, 1961:16).

The rural social and economic network in the New Territories, as in most of China, has a cell-like structure, consisting of a market town and its surrounding tributary villages.[4] The market towns are extremely important political, social, recreational, and economic centers with clearly defined areas; most villagers travel frequently to their own towns, but seldom if ever to other markets or to the city. As Hong Kong's economy continues to develop, the larger towns like Yuen Long are becoming small cities, and the markets, in turn, are becoming good-sized towns.

THE VILLAGES OF PING SHAN

On the northwest rice plain of the New Territories, close to the main road, about two miles west of Yuen Long and twenty-six from Kowloon, there lies a cluster of eight villages which are known collectively as Ping Shan (see Map 1). Because these eight villages were all established by descendants of one branch of the Tang family (Teng in mandarin), they are referred to as the Tang lineage of Ping Shan. The field study here reported was concerned with this lineage. However, it was concentrated particularly on one village, Hang Mei, which is considered the principal village of the lineage.

The convenient geographical location of Hang Mei and the other Ping Shan villages has been an important factor in the lives of the villagers, for it has enabled them to have easy access not only to the nearby market town of Yuen Long, but also to bus and taxi facilities leading to Kowloon. Social, cultural, and economic change has pro-

---

[4] For a discussion of the market town network, see Skinner, 1964.

ceeded much faster in villages like Hang Mei, which are close to the main roads, than it has in the more isolated villages. Hang Mei, then, is representative of the larger, older, established villages of the New Territories that are close to the market towns and to transportation facilities.

Hang Mei village (the name means "the tail of the stream") faces northwest towards Nam Tau Peninsula, about ten miles away across Deep Bay. Behind it, the ground slopes up to a small, tree-covered hill. In front of it lie several *mow* (one *mow* equals one-sixth of an acre) of rich vegetable gardens which are intensively cultivated by village gardeners throughout the year. Beyond the gardens are several large fish ponds. In 1962 the village consisted of about one hundred houses, one village temple, and four ancestral halls, all built of grey brick on foundations of cut stone.

To the north, separated from Hang Mei only by two large common ancestral halls which belong to all the Ping Shan villages, is the village of Hang Tau ("head of the stream"), which in 1961 had a population of approximately 667. The front part of Hang Tau village is occupied by Hang Mei people who, because of lack of space in their own village, built their houses on the north side of the central ancestral halls. Their houses can easily be distinguished from those of the Hang Tau people, who live at the rear of the village, by the distinctive shape of their house tops. About fifty yards north from Hang Tau is the Hang Tau village temple.

One hundred yards northwest of Hang Tau, separated from the two villages of Hang Mei and Hang Tau by the fish ponds, some vegetable gardens, and a few chicken and pig sheds, is the small walled village of Sheung Cheung Wai which faces south (see Map 2). The villagers say that this village was built to keep the *feng-shui* (geomantically imbued luck or fortune; See Freedman, 1966b:118–154) of Ping Shan from being swept away by the small river that used to flow in front of the village towards Deep Bay. The Ping Shan pagoda, located a few hundred yards north of Sheung Cheung Wai, was reputedly also built for the same magical purpose. Beyond Sheung Cheung Wai is the large and fertile rice plain, the richest agricultural region of the colony, which stretches north and west to the coast of Deep Bay and directly north to the Sham Chun River and Communist China.

South of Hang Mei, separated by the Ping Ha Road which runs between the two villages, is the village of Tong Fong, which, like Hang Mei and Hang Tau, faces to the northwest. Tong Fong village (population 289) is also mostly inhabited by Hang Mei people who built houses and an ancestral hall there, partly because there was no

or otherwise) with natural leadership abilities who belong to a powerful branch of the lineage (Freedman, 1966a:10–11).

The Ping Shan lineage has territorial unity in that the eight villages are clustered close together and are clearly separated from the villages that belong to other lineages. It has a unity derived from kinship because all male members of the lineage are descended in a direct line from a common ancestor and consider themselves collectively to be *hsiung-ti* ("brothers"). It has a ritual unity in that all members belong to a common "church," in the Durkheimian sense, centered around the ancestor cult. Ideally, the men of Ping Shan also form a solidary group that protects its own against any person or group outside its boundary. Furthermore, the lineage is a corporate group in that it holds common property, and is a legal and political entity which makes decisions on matters that affect the lineage as a whole. Finally, there is a unity in the sense that all members share in the high social position, derived from power, numbers, and wealth, that the lineage enjoys in the rural society of the New Territories. Thus it is not surprising that the outside world regards Ping Shan as a single unit. If a villager is identified to another person, he will be introduced as a "Ping Shan *jen*," ("a man of Ping Shan"), and ordinarily no mention will be made of the particular village or sublineage to which he belongs.

Internally, of course, the lineage is highly differentiated, because wealth, prestige, and power are not distributed equally either among villages or among the various subgroups within each village. The lineage contains extremely wealthy men as well as extremely poor peasant farmers, and it has always been so. Conflict, jealousy, and competition are prevalent within the lineage and within each village. Lineage segments are not equal in numbers and do not own equal amounts of collective property, so that there is a continual imbalance rather than the theoretically "balanced segmentary opposition" that prevails in the lineage systems of nondifferentiated societies. Within the lineage, some villages are more powerful, dominating the lesser ones. This process is repeated within villages, where powerful sublineage segments dominate. To the external world, Ping Shan presents a common front, but within the lineage this unity is a prevailing fiction which the members employ to hold the group together.

HANG MEI VILLAGE

Of all the villages of Ping Shan, Hang Mei is the largest, wealthiest, and most prestigious, and has the strongest voice in determining policy for the lineage as a whole. Indeed, the prominent position held by Ping Shan in the Yuen Long Valley is due mainly to the wealth and prestige of Hang Mei, which are derived from the fact that the Tangs were one of the earliest groups to settle in the area and thus had first claim to some of the best land. Through the centuries this position has been maintained because Hang Mei produced officials and merchants who brought the village not only official connections and prestige, but also wealth in the form of great ancestral landholdings, which stretched at one time as far as the eye could see.

In 1962 Hang Mei had a population of approximately 820. This figure includes those who work and reside most of the time in the town or city, but who have families living in the village, return frequently, and consider the village their home. This figure does not, however,

TABLE 1

LENGTH OF RESIDENCE OF OUTSIDER HOUSEHOLDS (1962)

Number of Years	Number of Households
Less than 1	16
From 2 to 5	11
From 6 to 10	11
From 11 to 15	5
From 16 to 20	3
Over 20	1
Not known	1
Total	48

include those who have moved permanently into town with their families, even though they may return occasionally to the village, nor does it include several members who have gone abroad or to the mainland and have not returned for several years.

The largest population group in 1962 was the Tangs. The population also included the Ha Fu (a serflike group attached to the Tangs) and a large resident group of outsiders from the crowded cities.

Outsiders

In 1962, 257 members of the village were "outsiders" (wai jen) who had resided in the village for periods varying from thirty years for one household, to only a few days. The length of residence of outsider households is shown in Table 1.

Before 1949, few outsiders lived in the village. Since that time, however, and especially during the last few years, greater numbers of outsider families from the city have arrived to rent houses from the villagers. This trend will probably continue, because the population of the New Territories is growing and the Tangs are rapidly building houses to rent to the outsiders.

Most of these outsiders are originally from the districts in Kwangtung Province around the city of Canton, with a substantial number coming from the Sey Iap *(ssu-i)* area southwest of Canton. Some are from the area between Hong Kong and Canton, and a few are from places in China outside Kwangtung Province.

The outsider population is socially just what the name implies; they live in the village but do not belong to it in a social sense. The outsiders have very little to do with the original village inhabitants (the *pen-ti jen* or "native inhabitants") , and they establish few close social bonds among themselves. In this respect, they are very much like some of the isolated and anonymous households in Kowloon where no one knows his neighbors or cares to know them. They are of very diverse social origin. In 1962, there was a total of twenty-seven surnames among the outsiders and few were related by kinship or occupational ties to more than one other household of the group. Thus the outsiders are isolated from each other and from the rest of the village community.

Pen-ti Jen

The 563 *pen-ti jen,* or original inhabitants of the village, are divided into two main groups. In addition to the dominant Tang group, who are the "owners" of the village and inhabit the middle and front parts of the village, there are 19 non-Tang, Ha Fu households who occupy smaller houses at the rear of the village. Ha Fu (mandarin, Hsia Fu) is a derogatory term used in this area to refer to subordinate, lower-class, client groups which serve the dominant lineages in powerful and wealthy villages.[5]

In the distant past, members of the dominant lineage bought boys from poor families in far-away villages. They acted as servants in the master's household, where their special duty was to attend the young sons of the master's family. When these servant boys became of marriageable age, they were married to servant girls of approximately the same social status and were given small houses at the rear of the village in which to set up their households. They were also assigned lands to farm as tenants of the patron household and in return had to perform certain traditional tasks. On occasions such as marriages or funerals among the Tangs, for example, the Ha Fu had to serve as carriers, and

---

[5] The terms used to refer to this group vary in other parts of the New Territories and Kwangtung Province. (I am indebted to Mr. Hugh Baker for this information.) See the discussion by Chen Han-seng (1936:54–58) .

they also served as warriors in the intervillage feuds that were common in traditional days. They were addressed by their first names by members of the Tang group, the absence of a kinship term emphasizing their lowly status. To further stress their subordinate position, the Ha Fu were allowed to use only kinship terms reserved for women when they addressed the Tangs.

Formerly the Ha Fu population in the village was much larger, but as new employment opportunities opened up in the city and overseas before and after the war, the Ha Fu gradually left the village to escape their social stigma. This exodus is evidenced by the large number of small mud-brick houses in the Ha Fu area of the village which are now empty or rented to outsiders.

The 19 Ha Fu families who remain in the village are doing quite well and are sharing in the general prosperity of the villagers. Many of the men have found well-paying jobs outside the village as truck drivers, and those who are still farmers have prospered by growing vegetables for the city market. Most of the Ha Fu families have been able to purchase their house sites from the Tangs, and several of them have even been able to build new houses.

The Ha Fu–Tang relationship has gradually changed since the British assumed control of the New Territories and as the Ha Fu's economic circumstances improved. The Ha Fu have become so independent that they now refuse to perform their traditional duties for the Tangs, who resent this but are unwilling to force the issue for fear of action by the government in support of the Ha Fu. Old attitudes die hard, however, and the old class distinctions are still present in the village; the Tangs continue to look down on the Ha Fu with ill-disguised disdain and contempt, and the Ha Fu attitude towards the Tangs is one of bitterness, resentment, and even hatred.

The remaining 75 households in Hang Mei Village are those of the Tangs. In addition, there are 18 Tang households in Hang Tau and 12 in Tong Fong that belong to the Hang Mei branch of the Ping Shan lineage and identify themselves socially as "Hang Mei *jen*" ("people of Hang Mei"). Hang Mei has a social meaning as well as a territorial one, and the two usages do not coincide exactly. Socially, the Tang sublineage of Hang Mei would include the "Hang Mei *jen*" residing in the two villages adjacent to Hang Mei, because for the Tangs the principle of lineage relationship is more important, for almost all purposes, than territorial contiguity. The Tang households both in Hang Mei and those of the Hang Mei branch in the two adjoining villages have been included in this study. This is a compromise between the treatment of Hang Mei village as a social group defined by ties of descent and as a spatially defined administrative unit. It would have been artificial to exclude those members of the lineage who did not reside in the village, just as it would have been inexcusable to omit the outsiders and the Ha Fu from consideration. The group which serves as the main basis for this study is shown in Table 2.

TABLE 2

PERSONS INCLUDED IN STUDY

	Number of Households	Number of Persons
Outsider (Hang Mei)	48	257
Ha Fu (Hang Mei)	19	109
Tang (Hang Mei)	75	454
Tang (Hang Tau)	18	99
Tang (Tong Fong)	12	65
Totals	172	984

THE TANG LINEAGE

The Tang lineage, as I have noted, has inhabited the Ping Shan area since the Sung Dynasty and are thought to be among the very earliest settlers of the New Territories, with historical roots that even predate the establishment of Ping Shan. The first ancestor of the Tangs in the New Territories, as related by the lineage genealogy, was an official from Kiangsi Province who, after his retirement, built a house in the Yuen Long Valley near Kam Tin. The grave of this founding ancestor is still worshipped by all the Tangs in the New Territories.

The founders of the Tang lineages in the New Territories were three brothers, grandchildren of the first ancestor. One brother founded the Ping Shan branch of the New Territories Tangs; the second brother founded the Kam Tin branch, which is located about five miles from Ping Shan to the east of Yuen Long; and the third founded the Tai Po branch. After seven generations, the Kam Tin lineage split, and a powerful new lineage was founded at Ha Tsuen, about two miles west of Ping Shan, near the coast (see Map 1).

As we have seen, the Tangs for centuries have been the dominant group in the New Territories because of their economic resources, political power, and high social prestige. Ping Shan, like the other

Tang lineages, is surrounded by a group of smaller villages of tenants who settled in the area with the permission of the Tangs. These smaller villages acted as satellites of Ping Shan and supported them in feuds with other powerful lineages in the New Territories, receiving in return the protection of the Tangs. Before the British occupied the New Territories, it is probable that the tenant villagers paid their taxes (on any lands that they owned) to the Tangs, who in turn transmitted these taxes to the government. In early centuries, and even up to the British take-over, the Tangs wielded great power in the New Territories region and their influence reached into the adjacent counties farther north within China, where other strong branches of the clan are located (see Balfour, 1941).

The present-day villagers of Ping Shan are well aware of their glorious past and are extremely proud of their family history and traditions. The people of Ping Shan, particularly the members of the more wealthy subbranches in Hang Mei, look back with nostalgia on the "golden age" when their ancestors had great wealth and prestige; in their eyes, the present compares unfavorably with the past. As one of my elderly friends in the village told me, "In the old days you could climb the hill back of the village, and as far as you could see, the lands all belonged to Ping Shan. When my great-grandfather went out, he was carried in a sedan chair by his servants. In those days we didn't have to work because we could live well off the rent from our lands. Now we have sold our lands and we have to struggle and work hard just to make a living and educate our sons." This is a view of past times held by many of the villagers from the wealthier segments of the lineage but, in fact, the past was probably not so glorious as it now appears through nostalgic eyes, and their present economic circumstances are not nearly as bad as some villagers would have them appear.

Over the centuries that have elapsed since the first Tang settled near Hang Tau village, the lineage has undergone a process of elaborate segmentation. At various times in the past, men moved out from Hang Tau to settle the other seven villages of Ping Shan and to form sublineages. The lines of Hang Tau and Hang Mei separated when a member of the seventeenth generation of Ping Shan moved over from Hang Tau to found Hang Mei village and the Hang Mei subbranch.

The internal structure of Hang Mei village is much too complex to describe here in detail. The major segments of the lineage are defined in relation to collectively owned ancestral property and this is of central importance for our discussion of the economy.

It was the custom in traditional times for a member of the lineage who became wealthy through business or through an official career to leave a large part of his accumulated property in trust for his sons and their descendants. These corporate ancestral landholdings were owned collectively by the direct male descendants of the wealthy ancestor and were supposed to be used (1) to educate his descendants so that they could compete for official positions in the imperial examinations, (2) to finance the yearly ancestor-worshipping ceremonies, and (3) as direct income by his descendants. Only rich men could afford to leave sizable ancestral estates in trust for their descendants. The wealth and prestige of any subbranch of the lineage can easily be determined by the number and size of the branch ancestral halls and/or ancestral estates which it owns.[6]

Ancestral property, theoretically, could be left by any one of the lineage ancestors, at any point in the genealogy stretching back through twenty-seven generations. The crucial points of lineage segmentation, in reference to which subsegments of the lineage are formed, are those points at which sizable ancestral property is located. The important corporate subsegments of the Hang Mei lineage are formed in relation to these sizable holdings of ancestral property. Sublineage A separates itself from sublineage B because sublineage A has rights in the ancestral property and the branch ancestral hall left in the name of the ancestor of group A. Sublineage B, in turn, is separated from other groups in the village because its members are a corporate group holding ancestral property B in common.

The three major sublineage segments in Hang Mei are those groups which own the three largest ancestral estates of the village. They are, in order of wealth, Lok Ka ("Six Families"; mandarin, Liu Chia), Wai Shan Hall (mandarin, Wei Hsin T'ang), and Yat T'ai Hall (mandarin, I T'i T'ang). The genealogical relationship between these three groups is shown in Figure 1, which is simplified and telescoped for clarity.

Almost all the Tangs in Hang Mei are descended from the man in whose name Yat T'ai Hall was built. Thus almost everyone in the village has a share in the ancestral hall and property left in this man's name. There are three major branches (*fang*) descended from the three sons of the Yat T'ai ancestor. Wai Shan Hall was built in the name of one of these three sons, and his male descendants in the direct line of descent have a share in the large property holding attached to the hall. The descendants of the Wai Shan ancestor's two brothers have no such share, since they are collateral lines and not in the main line of descent.

Wai Shan Hall is divided into three branches, which are descended from the three sons of the founder of the hall. One of the three sons,

---

[6] See Freedman, 1958, for a discussion of the structure of the Southeastern Chinese lineage.

Jui T'ai, became very wealthy and left an enormous amount of property in his ancestral estate, which is called Chap Ng Tsoh (mandarin, Chi Wu Tsu). All the direct descendants of Jui T'ai have a share in the Chap Ng Tsoh lands. As a corporate group, this sublineage segment is known as the "Six Families," because they are internally divided into six subbranches, descended from the six sons of Jui T'ai. The Six Families are distinguished from the other two branches of Wai Shan Hall, descended from Jui T'ai's two brothers; as collateral lines, these branches have no share in Chap Ng Tsoh.

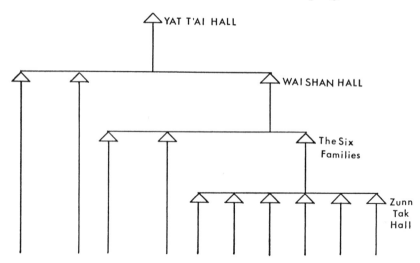

FIGURE 1

Each of the Six Families is differentiated from the others by having its own separate ancestral property or separate ancestral hall, or both. The most powerful family is known as Zunn Tak Hall (mandarin, Ch'ung Te T'ang), a subbranch of the lineage which occupies a large, walled compound of buildings at the southwest corner of the village. It is from this branch that the political leader of Ping Shan has come in the last three generations. The prestige of Zunn Tak Hall is indicated by a scroll which hangs in the central hall of their large gentry-type house; it was, according to members of the group, written by Sun Yat-sen, who spent a night in the house in the early part of this century.

The Six Families is not only the dominant group within the village of Hang Mei, it is also the dominant group in the eight villages of Ping Shan, and the most powerful group in the thirty-three villages in the adjacent countryside which comprise Ping Shan Hsiang, a rural administrative unit. It is largely due to the Six Families that Ping

Shan has traditionally had such high social and political position in the Yuen Long Valley. The members of the poorer branches of the Tang lineage of Ping Shan, who are not blessed with the large ancestral properties of the Six Families, have a somewhat ambivalent attitude towards them. As "people of Ping Shan," the poorer branches share the general glory of the Six Families in relations with the outside world, but, as a price for this, they are dominated by them in most internal affairs.

The segments and subsegments of the lineage and the shares in ancestral estates are not mutually exclusive units within Hang Mei village. A villager may have a share in many ancestral landholdings at different levels and may be a member of many corporate kin groups at the same time. At the lowest level of lineage segmentation, a person shares with his brothers in the ancestral estate left by his father. If he is a member of a highly differentiated and elaborately subsegmented group like Zunn Tak Hall, he has a share not only in his father's estate but also in the property of Zunn Tak Hall, at a higher level. He also has a share in Chap Ng Tsoh property and is a member of the Six Families. Since Chap Ng Tsoh is, in turn, one of the three branches of Wai Shan Hall, he will also have a share in the ancestral properties of the Wai Shan ancestor and be a member of that kin group. And, since Wai Shan Hall members are all descended from one of the three sons of the Yat T'ai Hall ancestor, the members of the Six Families also have a share in this hall and are a part of the group composed of all male descendants of the Yat T'ai ancestor. Hang Mei village, as a whole, is one branch of the Ping Shan lineage, and thus the villagers have a share in the central ancestral hall of Ping Shan, which is dedicated to the memory of the founding ancestor of the entire lineage. Finally, the Ping Shan lineage, together with the other maximal lineages of the Tangs in the New Territories, such as Kam Tin, Ha Tsuen, and Tai Po, has a share in the common ancestral lands held in the name of the ancestors of all the Tangs in the New Territories, and is a member of this Tang clan, which includes all the Tangs in the New Territories.

The social structure of the village, then, is basically a localized corporate patrilineage divided into sublineage segments which are differentiated by the ownership of large ancestral estates. In many ways this lineage organization is similar to the unilineal descent group model defined by Fortes (1953). The principal difference between the lineage organization of Ping Shan and Fortes' lineage model is that the Chinese lineage has existed for centuries in a highly differentiated society with an elaborate class structure (Freedman, 1958). Marked differences in wealth, status, and power have always existed within the

Ping Shan lineage. Even in traditional times, the Six Families group contained officials, scholars, merchants, and landlords, whereas most of the other branches were made up of small merchants or poor peasant farmers. In other words, the internal segments of the lineage were never equal, and one group, because of superior wealth, power, and status was usually able to dominate the village.

The Ping Shan lineage performed many important functions in traditional Chinese society before the area was incorporated into the colony of Hong Kong. It was a corporate unit that competed for prestige and power with the other sizable lineages of the New Territories. It was also an important landholding unit—a corporation that regulated jural rights over the land and the inheritance of land. Furthermore, it was an important legal, political, and military unit on the lower levels of Chinese society that existed beneath the imperial bureaucracy. The lineage regulated sexual activity and marriage and functioned as a ritual unit in the important ancestral cult. The ancestral ritual symbolized the social divisions within the lineage at every important point of lineage segmentation and was also an important device to bind together the members of the various groups in ascending levels within the lineage hierarchy.

At the lowest level, the basic unit of the village social structure is, of course, the family. As in the rest of China, the family types present in the village include extended families, polygynous families, and stem families, with nuclear families predominant numerically. This family organization has been so well described elsewhere [7] that it is not necessary to repeat these descriptions here.

The minimal effective agnatic unit at the lowest level of lineage segmentation is the *su-po hsiung-ti*, or the group of males descended from a common grandfather. In Ping Shan, and probably in Kwangtung Province as a whole, the *su-po hsiung-ti* unit, and not the *wu fu*, or "circle of mourning relatives" as in many parts of China,[8] is the unit in which the members have frequent and intimate obligations to each other. They attend all celebrations, such as marriages or funerals, of one of the member households without having to be formally invited. They also have the responsibility of arranging for the marriage of one of the young men of the group if his father is dead. The relations of the *su-po hsiung-ti* group are close and intimate, in contrast to the often more formal relations with distant agnatic kin in the lineage. Affinal ties with the families of one's mother, wife, and

---

[7] For descriptions of the Chinese family, see Yang, 1959*a*; Levy, 1949; Lang, 1946; Hsu, 1948; and Lin, 1948.

[8] For a discussion of the "circle of mourning relatives" (*ng fok* in Cantonese; *wu fu* in mandarin), see Hu, 1948:17, and Freedman, 1958:41.

daughter's husband are of some importance in individual families; as a rule, however, they are not nearly so important as one's ties within the lineage.

As in most Chinese villages, nonkin associations, such as the village guard and crop-protection association, burial associations, money-lending associations, religious associations, and extra-village political associations, are of importance in the social organization of the village and in the "countrywide network" that binds the village to other persons and groups in the rural society. Institutionalized friendships and business partnerships are of special importance to those villagers who engage in business or political activities outside the village, in the wider society that includes the town and the city.

The religious system of the village is especially rich and varied. In addition to the ancestral cult centering around the lineage organization and the household ancestral cult centering around the family, there is an elaborate system of temple cults, a complex cycle of yearly festivals within the village, and an extremely complex magical system involving astrology and geomancy. The various deities in the village temple and in other local temples are worshipped mainly to ensure the health and well-being of the family and to ensure the success and fortune of the male members of the family in economic activities. Magical practices of all kinds, including divination, fortune telling, and the like, are quite common in the village, even among the younger people. The belief in *feng-shui,* or the influence of the configurations of the earth on human fortunes, is widespread among the villagers. Spirit mediums are prominent in village religion, functioning mainly to cure children of illness caused by soul loss or soul theft by the malignant *kuei* (evil "spirits" or "ghosts"). The traditional belief in the *kuei* and *shen* (good "spirits" or "ghosts") is still widespread, even among some of the younger educated people. The local *nan–wu hsien–sheng,* or "Taoist priest," continues to fulfill his functions in the religious system, acting as director of funerals, housebuilding, exorcisms, and other activities in the traditional religious system. This tremendous variety of religious and magical elements in supplemented by an extremely rich mythology.

The religious beliefs of the villagers are relevant for our purposes chiefly because religion for the villagers is intimately connected with economic activity. The main focus of religious and magical beliefs and practices is to ensure success and wealth in this world for the heads of village families. The villagers are great believers in the importance of luck and fortune in determining the success of their worldly activities, especially in the business world. A person becomes wealthy because he is "lucky"; a person remains poor throughout his life because this is his fate. Even though, theoretically, a person's fate in life is determined at birth, the villagers spare no efforts to change bad luck to good fortune. This desire to attain success and wealth in this world is perhaps the central value orientation of the villagers, and the religious system is centered around aiding the villagers in attaining these goals.

Politically, the village is part of a formal administrative organization which was established by the British in 1898, and has not been changed in essential respects since that time. Because Hang Mei is a large village, it elects two Village Representatives to work with the District Officer on matters that concern the village. As might be expected, the most prominent Village Representative, is a young man from Zunn Tak Hall of the Six Families, who is assisted by a second elected representative from the second branch of Wai Shan Hall. The able young man, Tang Lai-ming (a pseudonym), is also the Chairman of the Rural Committee of Ping Shan Hsiang and a member of the Hsiang I Chü. As such, he is a very influential and powerful man in the Yuen Long area and is a notable political figure in the entire New Territories.

Ping Shan Hsiang is one of the seven *hsiang* that make up Yuen Long District, which is under the control of a British District Officer, with headquarters near the village. The District Office also contains the Land Office, where the villagers pay their taxes and attend to such matters as land sales and building permits. Tang Lai-ming works closely with the Chinese subordinates employed in the District Office and sees that any matter concerning one of the villagers is speedily attended to. The great strength of his position is that he is effective in representing the villagers' interests in government affairs.

This formal political system is superimposed on the political system of the lineage. Within the lineage, formal leadership is held by the Clan Elder and other elders, heads of the various lineage segments, selected on the basis of kinship seniority. These are often poor and uneducated men with no leadership abilities, and their power is extremely limited, restricted mainly to ritual duties and the management of the ancestral lands. The real leaders of the village are able and wealthy men who operate effectively in the world outside the village. This was true even in traditional times; the educated men who had passed the imperial examinations and were able to deal on a basis of equality with the *hsien* magistrate really ran village affairs and did not allow lineage elders chosen solely on the basis of kinship seniority to challenge their authority. The present generation of village leaders are comparable to the old gentry-scholar-official group; they are "gentry" of a new type, able to operate in a changing society.

The educational system of the village, which until the late 1930's remained largely classical in character, has changed markedly since 1945. Ping Shan, like almost all the other groups of villages in the New Territories, has a modern, government-supported primary school with well-educated teachers. Almost all the children of primary-school age are now in school and will receive at least a primary education. This is a revolutionary change; before the war, only the sons of wealthy families had an opportunity to receive more than two or three years' schooling. There is also a government middle school in Yuen Long and many private middle schools in the vicinity, so that most of the village children will be able to get the equivalent of a high school education. Although Hong Kong University is out of the question because of the expense involved, there are many private Chinese colleges in Kowloon where the wealthier children can receive a college education, and a few privileged sons have gone to college in Taiwan with scholarship support from the Nationalist Government. This increase in education, the opportunities for which are much more accessible than they were in the years before World War II, has led to a bifurcation of the village into traditionally-oriented parents and modern-minded young people. It is likely that as the older generation passes, the cultural and social patterns will change to conform more closely to the modern urban Chinese pattern, which serves as a model for the younger generation. The older generation, however, is fully cognizant of the importance of educating their children, and this is one of their major concerns. With government assistance, the people of Ping Shan have raised sufficient funds to construct a second primary school near their villages which, in 1962, was nearing completion.

Literacy is widespread among the wealthier members of the older generation and is almost universal among the younger generation. A number of village families subscribe to daily newspapers from the city, and radios are common in village households, so there is no lack of news of the outside world. A few of the villagers can even talk knowledgeably about international affairs, although most people are concerned primarily with local affairs in the colony or with events affecting China.

The material accruements of modern life have come into the village on a large scale during the postwar years. Most households have electricity, running water, and some appliances. One of the village shopkeepers and one of the Village Representatives have installed telephones. Most of the younger men and some of the older men who frequently go to the market town and the city on business have adopted Western clothes. There are also three or four automobiles, owned by the more wealthy residents.

Health services, both public and private, are available in the market town at a reasonable cost, and most of the villagers seek Western-style medical help in addition to the traditional Chinese medicines. Since the war, most babies of the village have been born in the government hospital located near Yuen Long.

In short, since the war, most aspects of village society and culture have undergone a process of rapid change. The rate of change is astounding when compared to the much slower rate that had been characteristic of the prewar period. By 1962, the lives of the villagers included a curious mixture of the old and the new existing side by side in a mosaic that was confusing to the anthropologist, if not to most of the villagers. On the one hand, there were the traditional social and cultural patterns still adhered to by the older generation; on the other hand, there were the new, urban patterns followed by most of the younger people and the outsiders in the village. The contrast between old and new was evident in every aspect of village culture, from hair styles to marriage.

Many, if not most, of the changes that have occurred in village social and cultural patterns in the last two decades have, of course, been closely connected with rapid and drastic changes in the economic life of the village. These changes in the economic system are the result not only of external commercial and industrial influences, but also of internal developments in the agricultural sector of the village economy. Because it is in a transitional state, the economic system of the village is extremely complex, with old and new levels existing simultaneously. To be understood, this system must be shown as it existed in the past, as it is today, and as it is developing for the future.

THE VILLAGE ECONOMY IN HISTORICAL PERSPECTIVE

The base line for the study of economic changes is the system as it existed around 1898, just prior to the time the village became part of the colony. A longer historical perspective, dating from the time of first Western influence on the village, would be preferable, but little reliable information on this area before 1898 was available to me. From this base line, then, the economic system of the village has passed through three distinguishable periods. The first, from 1898 to 1940, begins with the incorporation of the New Territories into the colony and ends with the outbreak of World War II. The second, from 1941 to 1945, is the period of Japanese occupation. The third is the period from 1945 to 1962, the year this study was made.

The Traditional Economy in 1898

Historical documentation on the economy of the New Territories villages at the time of the British take-over is not complete.[9] In formulating my reconstruction of this period, I have used two major sources: (1) information remembered by villagers in 1962; and (2) reports written by British officials at the time of incorporation.[10]

According to some of the older villagers, in the "old days" the lands of Ping Shan were rented to tenant farmers. Rice, sugar cane, and peanuts were the major crops. Some farmers grew limited crops of vegetables that were consumed by their own families and sold in the village market, but vegetables were not grown commercially to the extent that they are at present. A few of the wealthier village families owned small stone mills, operated by buffalo power, which were used to press locally grown sugar and peanut oil; these old-fashioned mills have not been used for thirty years or more.

Before the British came to the New Territories, there were no roads to Kowloon or even to the market town of Yuen Long. To get from the village to Kowloon, one had to walk to Castle Peak, a difficult journey in the rainy season, and then take a boat to the city. Goods were transported to Yuen Long by carrying pole, with the villagers following paths that bordered the paddy fields. Some of these narrow flagstone paths, leading to temples in isolated areas of the New Territories, are still visible.

In those days the market in Yuen Long belonged to an ancestral hall of the Kam Tin branch of the Tang clan. Markets were traditionally held on every 3, 6, or 9 day of the month (that is, the 3rd, 6th, 9th, 13th, 16th, 19th, and so forth). The villagers sold their surplus rice and vegetables, as well as their pigs, in the market town and purchased articles such as plows, pottery utensils, and wooden buckets, and foodstuffs such as cooking oil, salt, wine, and the like. Even in traditional times the economy of the village consisted of two sectors: a self-

[9] The following discussion of the history of the economy of the village and the New Teritories is provisional until more historical information is uncovered. The historical records for the New Territories available to me in the Colonial Secretariat Library of Hong Kong were sketchy and incomplete. Maurice Freedman tells me that more records are available in government archives in London, and he suspects that there is more historical data available in out-of-the-way places in Hong Kong itself. Many of the records of the New Territories Administration were destroyed at the time of the Japanese invasion. See his discussion in 1966b:viii. Fortunately, there is an indication that more information on this area will be available in the future. A new book by Wakeman (1966) is an excellent study of one aspect of the history of this area.

[10] For a description of life in the New Territories at the time of its incorporation into the colony, based on government reports and his own observations, see Hayes, 1962:75–105; see, also, Lockhart, 1900.

sufficient sector that depended upon two-crop rice agriculture, and one that depended upon the market town. In 1898, the self-sufficient sector was apparently as important as the market sector, since large-scale commercialization was as yet unknown.

This picture of the village economy in traditional times given by some of the older villagers is remarkably similar in most respects to the descriptions of the New Territories' economy written by some of the British officers who visited the area just before and after its incorporation into the colony. In 1898, J. H. Stewart Lockhart was appointed as Special Commissioner to visit and report on the area that was soon to be leased to Great Britain. In his ensuing report, Lockhart described the economic situation in the New Territories. The report is such a valuable historical source that it is worth quoting in some detail.

Lockhart wrote that in 1898 rice was the major crop grown in the New Territories. The quality of the New Territories' rice was so good that "a quantity of it is exported to San Francisco for the use of the Chinese residents there." At that time, the water supply appeared to be excellent, and "sufficient water to raise two crops a year seems always to be available throughout the district" (1900:38). Lockhart also saw large areas of land planted in "sugar cane, indigo, hemp, peanuts, potatoes of different varieties, yam, taro, beans, sesamum, pumpkins and vegetables of all knds." He wrote, "In almost every village is carried on the rearing of pigs, large numbers of which are exported annually," and adds that "poultry breeding, and fruit growing for the Hong Kong market form lucrative occupations for many villagers" (1900:43).

Lockhart reported that "although the population is chiefly occupied in the cultivation of the soil," there are "large fisheries in which many persons are engaged in the bays surrounding the territory." The fish were "sorted, salted, and sundried and exported to various markets." This trade in dried fish impressed Lockhart because of the large numbers of people thus engaged. In addition to salt water fish, "the rearing of fresh water fish in ponds for the Hong Kong market and elsewhere" occupied the villagers near Yuen Long. Lockhart added that pearl fisheries were found in Tolo Harbor, in the eastern part of the New Territories (1900:42–43).

Lockhart also mentioned lime burning, the manufacture of bricks, quarrying, pottery making, salt manufacture, indigo dyeing, boat building, the making of ropes and nets from locally grown hemp, and the manufacture of joss sticks, as industries of some importance in the New Territories. (1900:42–43).

Lockhart summed up his impressions of the economic conditions of the New Territories in 1898 as follows: "Taken as a whole the inhabitants may be regarded as an industrious, frugal, and well-behaved people. . . . The inhabitants, though by no means wealthy, seem to be, as a rule, comfortably well off, and able to earn an honest livelihood without difficulty. Few signs of anything approaching destitution were seen, and only a few beggars were met" (1900:42).

A source of information on the New Territories' economy just after the British take-over is a report by Sir Arthur Henry Blake, the first governor of the colony, written after his first visit to Ping Shan. Blake (1900) wrote:

On the 4rth Instant I proceeded to Castle Peak Bay by launch and then by chair to Ping Shan, which is situated in a flat and most carefully cultivated valley about seven miles from Castle Peak Bay. The crops are rice and sugar cane, the latter apparently of not very good quality. Here I met over one hundred committee men, who struck me as being somewhat better class than those in the Taipo-Hui District, and more wealthy. . . .

I learned from them that the sugar canes have never been changed, and that they use the primitive rough stone mills for expressing the juice. I have promised to get a better quality canes for them and to try to procure a few Chattanooga Steel Mills. . . .

The valley is typical of all the large valleys in the New Territories, the population may broadly be said to depend upon rice cultivation, two crops of rice being grown in the year, the crops pay well in good seasons, but like the potato in Ireland before the famine, it involves the danger that being the sole resource of the mass of the people, if it fails there is nothing behind it.

As the limited historical information suggests, the New Territories' economy in 1898 was basically a two-crop rice economy, coupled with some handicraft industries and supplementary industries such as pig and fish raising. As such, it conforms well to the model "peasant economy" previously mentioned. There is no doubt that there were some commercial relations between the New Territories' villages and Kowloon in 1898; however, this trade was limited when compared to the commercial ties that presently exist.

It is useful to consider the economic changes that have taken place in the New Territories, and particularly in Ping Shan, over the past half-century in the context of Rostow's formulation of the stages of economic growth that occur in the transformation from a "traditional society" to a modern industrial society. What anthropologists have termed "peasant economy" is equivalent, on the village level, to Rostow's "traditional society" (1960:5). In Rostow's terms, the economy of the traditional society is characterized by limited production functions based on a pre-Newtonian science and technology. Because a ceiling exists on the productivity of such an economy, a high proportion of resources is devoted to agriculture. Family and clan play an important role in the society, and values are geared to the assumption that the opportunities available to one's descendants would be about the same as those available to one's ancestors (1960:5). In other words, the peasant economy is basically static or slow-changing. This, then, is the type of economy that existed in Ping Shan at the turn of the century, and it is from this general base line that we must view the changes that began to take place.

The Preconditions for
Economic Development—1898–1941

The first period of economic change in the New Territories and in the village lasted, as we have said, from 1898 until the beginning of the Japanese occupation. During this forty-year period, what Rostow (1960:17–35) calls the "preconditions for economic growth" began to appear in the New Territories.

It is certain that trade and market relations between the New Territories' villages and Kowloon increased when the Kowloon–Canton Railroad was built through the New Territories. The railroad was started in 1906, and by 1915 it was completed as far as Sham Chun, a market town within China, across the Sham Chun River. It was not until 1924 that the full 112 miles to Canton was completed (Tregear, 1955:50). The railroad ran through Tai Po and Sha Tin in the eastern part of the New Territories, and it is probably in this area, and not in the Yuen Long area, that the increased contact with the city first began to affect the peasant economy.

In 1900 the main road from Kowloon to Tai Po was started, and about thirteen miles of the road was completed before the end of 1901. By 1913 this road was extended to Fanling. Meanwhile, the section from Tsuen Wan along the coast to Castle Peak had been finished, and soon the full fifty-two mile circuit was completed with the extension of the western section from Castle Peak to Yuen Long and then to Fanling (Tregear, 1955:51). These first roads were very primitive affairs as shown by the specifications of Ormisby, the government engineer. The only really good road was from Kowloon through Tai Po to Sham Chun. This was a second-class carriage road, twelve feet wide, reinforced with gravel and permanently bridged. The other roads to Yuen Long and Ping Shan were only "bridle paths" for horses (Lockhart, 1900:56).

It seems clear that transportation from the Ping Shan area to Kowloon, almost thirty miles away, over a horse trail, was not conducive to extensive commerce, because almost all goods would have to be transported by human carrier. Since the establishment of Kowloon as a major urban area in 1861, the vegetable gardening belt has gradually extended outward in a concentric circle into the New Territories. One source from the early 1930's suggests, however, that at that time vegetable gardening activities in the New Territories were still concentrated mainly in the villages near the city of Kowloon (Gibbs, 1931:132–134). It was not until after World War II, when transportation facilities were greatly improved, that vegetable growing for the city market became very important to the villagers of Ping Shan, although it is likely that vegetable growing on a large scale may have started much earlier in those areas in the eastern part of the New Territories that border the railroads.

Another source for information on the economy of the New Territories during this period is an unpublished and undated manuscript by a Mr. Wong, a resident of Yuen Long and the father of one of the principals of a private Yuen Long primary school. Mr. Wong notes in this manuscript that several of the old-style sugar crushing mills were still operating in the 1930's, and that there were many local factories making dried bean curd. By the late 1930's some modern factories, built by outside interests and producing such goods as bricks, beer, and chinaware for export abroad, had already appeared in Tsuen Wan, a market town near Kowloon.

The two most populous market towns in the '30's were Yuen Long and Tai Po. Mr. Wong writes that in 1914 the "old market" in Yuen Long was replaced by a "new market" built nearby by a corporation known as Hop Yick Company, which was formed by a number of villagers in the Yuen Long area. In time the new market was enlarged so that it reached what is now the main street of Yuen Long, and in 1935 the Hop Yick Company expanded again, purchasing a large area of land in Yuen Long from the government. Forty-eight new buildings were erected on this property and were rented out as shops to market-town merchants and hawkers.

In 1935, according to Wong's account, the total population of Yuen Long was about three thousand, and there were more than one hundred buildings in the market town. Most of the shops sold rice, vegetables, pork, fresh fish, groceries, and foreign goods. There were also a pawn shop and a few restaurants. A large peanut-oil-pressing factory, founded by one of the Tangs from Kam Tin, was quite successful. Also, a Western-style motion picture theater was opened in Yuen Long in the late '30's.

Wong also mentions that in 1925 the government began to encourage the New Territories' farmers to grow vegetables. This government program grew out of a strike by the Hong Kong workers in 1925, which prevented the importation of vegetables and other foodstuffs from the mainland. According to Wong, the government, realizing that it was risky to depend solely on the mainland for essential food-stuffs, tried to make the colony more self-sufficient. If Wong's statements are accurate, then it is possible that vegetable growing for the city market was important in the villages before the war. However, I have no information on the extent of this government program or on whether it affected Ping Shan. The village farmers insist that truck gardening was not important before the war, although some vegetables were undoubtedly grown for the city market in other areas of the New Territories.

From Wong's account, it is clear that commercial and industrial influences had begun to penetrate the New Territories on a small scale by the late 1930's. Factories had been built in Tsuen Wan, and market towns like Yuen Long had grown considerably since 1898. The growth of the market town is one of the key indicators of increased commercial relations between the Yuen Long area and Kowloon. Another indicator is Mr. Wong's statement that pig raising was an increasingly important factor in the village economy.

In this same period, several village men, taking advantage of new employment opportunities in the city job market, began to work in Kowloon and Hong Kong. A few of the villagers even went abroad to Europe, and some of the village men began to work on British ships. This marked the beginning of the villagers' participation in the city economy and resulted in a broadening of their economic horizons. The growth of Hong Kong's urban areas and the gradual improvement in communication and transportation facilities between the village and the city brought further changes in the stationary village economy, with the village gradually becoming a part of the commercial network and the market economy which, by 1941, had extended to the rural areas.

These changes, however, should not be overemphasized, because only some of the villagers were able to take advantage of the new economic opportunities in the town and city. The farmers continued to earn a living from their rice crops, supplemented by peanuts, cane, sweet potatoes, and a few vegetables, and this pattern was only slightly altered by the beginnings of commercial vegetable growing. The wealthier men of the village from the large landholding branches of the lineage did not participate much in the new occupational market. They were too proud to accept low-class jobs in the city and did not have the education and language skills necessary for a better position. They usually did nothing but live off their land rents, and their income from the ancestral lands was sufficient to maintain most of them in the traditional style of the gentry class. Some of the wealthier families maintained themselves and paid for their sons' education by selling their meager private landholdings to merchants from the city or to local landlord-money-lenders. Others who had a little capital tried to take advantage of the expanding economy by opening shops or restaurants in the market town, but almost every one went bankrupt and thus used up most of their savings.

The Economic Effects of the
Japanese Occupation—1941–1945

The economic effects of the Japanese occupation on the economy of the colony as a whole have already been mentioned. The effects of the occupation on Hang Mei village were just as traumatic. In telling of the Japanese occupation period, the villagers emphasize the extreme hardships they suffered owing to the lack of employment opportunities and the shortage of food. One villager described the economic conditions in the village in the following way:

During the Japanese occupation all village people worked very hard. They seldom had enough money to buy meat. Usually we ate salted fish and vegetables only. Each family had a ration card to buy rice from the government once in five days, but each person was able to buy only 6.4 ounces per day which was only enough for one meal per person. It was possible to buy rice from the black market, but this was very expensive. Those people who had no money to buy on the black market had to eat rice gruel. Sugar and cooking oil were also in short supply. Most village people lived on rice gruel, sweet potatoes, taro, and some very poor people, towards the end of the war, even began to eat the seeds of grass which they gathered on the hillsides. Many people were ill from malnutrition and if the Japanese occupation had continued for another year, many villagers would undoubtedly have died.

During the occupation, all ritual functions such as marriages and funerals, which are usually occasions for validation of family status by elaborate displays of wealth, were pared to the bare essentials. Very few marriages took place during this period because there was no money to give the customary banquets; if a couple had been engaged before the invasion, they were married quickly in a very simple fashion. The same situation prevailed for funerals. If a poor person died during this period, there was not even a coffin, and only close kinsmen participated in the burial.

Those hardest hit by the economic difficulties of the Japanese occupation were poor villagers engaged in nonagricultural occupations. Since all commerce came to a standstill, the nonfarmers were thrown out of work and were hard pressed to find enough to eat. Particularly affected in this way was the Ha Fu group. Many of the wealthy people of the village were also hard hit. Prior to the occupation, most of them had supplemented their incomes from the ancestral land rents by engaging in small-scale commercial ventures; these opportunities were eliminated by the general economic failure, however, and many of the landholders were forced to sell off their valuables, including clothing.

The only villagers who really benefited from the economic conditions during the occupation were the farmers, who not only had plenty to eat but also got a good price for their rice on the black market. Some wealthy landlords took back rented ancestral land from their tenants and began to farm it either by themselves or with the help of hired labor. Thus one result of the occupation was the levelling of classes in the village—the farmers became almost as wealthy as the landowning segment of the village population.

The poverty and starvation that prevailed during the years of the Japanese occupation affected every aspect of village life. Social, cultural and economic patterns were severely disrupted, and traditional values were weakened to such an extent that the village was extremely susceptible to the new forces of change that developed after the war. This disruption of the old patterns of rural society undoubtedly took place in villages all over China during this period and paved the way for change.

The Postwar Period—1945–1962

In contrast to the gradual changes that had taken place in the prewar period, the changes in the village economy in the seventeen years between 1945 and 1962 were rapid and far-reaching. Village contact with the market town and the cities became more intimate than it had ever been before. This increase in contact is the result of the participation of the rural areas of the colony in the "takeoff" period (Rostow, 1960:36) of Hong Kong's economic development.

II

The Occupational Structure

Hang Mei has never been primarily a village of small peasant farmers, for many of the villagers have always depended upon land rent for their livelihood. The secure economic base of rental income from ancestral and private lands allowed many of the villagers, even in traditional times, to engage in commercial and business ventures in the hope of making a fortune in the world outside the village. In the earlier decades of this century, and probably even in earlier times, there was a well-developed network of trade between the New Territories and Canton. Sugar cane and peanuts grown by the farmers were processed into sugar and oil in local mills. These were then transported by boat to Canton, where they were exchanged for silk, wine, and other articles that would be sold in local market towns. Many of the wealthier men of the village are said to have owned small cane mills which they would rent to the farmers in return for a share of the sugar produced. Some of the mill-owners used hired labor to farm extensive holdings of cane and peanuts, and thus supplied their own raw materials.

Some villagers did business not only in Canton, but also in the market towns in Kwangtung Province or in the nearby market town of Yuen Long. A few villagers, it is said, became successful merchants, but most of them went bankrupt and eventually returned to the village in their old age to live off the ancestral lands. Some of the villagers attempted to go into business in Kowloon or Hong Kong after the New Territories became part of the colony, but most of these attempts failed and at present there is only one villager who owns a going business concern in the urban area. Other villagers, in the past half century, became minor officials in the Chinese government or policemen in cities like Canton. Some of the men from wealthier families became Chinese doctors or traditional scholars. In any case, few men from the wealthier branches of the village were farmers. As has been noted above, most of the farmers were from the poorer and weaker segments of the lineage.

There are two major types of villages in the New Territories. One type, represented by Hang Mei, is the old, large, established, wealthy, landlord village, which contains many merchants and scholars, with only the weaker and poorer branches engaging in agriculture. The second type, comprising most of the villages in the New Territories, is the small, weak, poorer village that is composed almost entirely of small peasant farmers.

The reaction to economic change in the wealthier villages has been quite different from that in the smaller agricultural ones. Not only have the wealthy lineages been able to provide their sons with Western education, the key to social mobility in the new society, but they have also had more contact with Western patterns. The peasant farmers, on the other hand, are the most conservative part of the population, and their customs are slow to change. The commercially oriented population travels frequently to the local market town and to the city in search of business contacts and opportunities. The farmer is tied down to the village, where he works in his fields from morning till night every day of the year; he has little time or opportunity to come into contact with new goods and new ideas, and little money to educate his sons. This difference between the farming and nonfarming population is evident in the following analysis of the occupational structure and economic activities of the village in 1962.

ECONOMIC ACTIVITY IN THE VILLAGE

In 1962, out of a total population of 984, 187 men and 87 women were employed full time in income-producing activities. This is 28 per cent of the total village population. The rest, 72 per cent of the population, including children under 6 years of age, students attending schools at all levels, the unemployed, the retired, and housewives, were not engaged full time in income-producing activities (see Table 3).

Within the student sector of the village population, some of the children of farm families helped their parents with chores after school, but a surprising number did not help their parents at all. This lack of participation in work on the family farm reflects the attitude of many parents that education is so important that the children should devote themselves entirely to their studies. It also reflects a distaste for farm work on the part of middle-school-age adolescents of the village, who look forward to better jobs. In almost all families the girls helped with child care and household chores and in general had less freedom after school than the boys. However, most of the students, especially the boys, did absolutely nothing besides go to school and play.

Among the 129 women in the village who were primarily housewives

TABLE 3

ECONOMIC ACTIVITY OF VILLAGE POPULATION

Degree of Economic Activity	Male	Female	Total	Per Cent
Economically fully active:	187	87	274	28
Economically partly active:				
Housewives:				
Who also raise pigs		32		
Who also farm		17		
Who help husbands in other ways		10		
Total		59		
Students who help farm	20	20		
Retired persons working part-time	5	17		
Total	25	96	121	12
Economically inactive:				
Under six years	95	89		
Six to fourteen, not in school	16	16		
Over fourteen years, not working or seeking work	7	6		
Students	142	117		
Housewives		70		
Unemployed	2	2		
Retired	10	17		
Total	272	317	589	60
Totals	484	500	984	100

not engaged in full-time work, 59 carried on substantial income-producing activities in addition to their housework. Thirty-two of these women raised pigs for sale (a major source of income for village families), 17 farmed part time, and 10 engaged in various other activities, such as helping in the family store, selling candy from small village stands, or helping their husbands in various handicraft industries.

Moreover, in their spare time many of the women of the village strung plastic beads, fitted plastic flowers together, or embroidered gloves. This minor piecework was obtained from jobbers who represented some of the new factories in the city. The work was not very remunerative, nor was it always available; but it did help to fill some of the leisure time of the housewives, and it enabled them to make some pocket money for gambling, the most frequent activity of unemployed housewives.

Some of the older people of the village worked part time. The older women helped with housework and child care, especially in the farm families where the daughter-in-law worked in the fields with her husband. The older men took care of village and kin-group affairs, and some of the older retired farmers helped with the management of their farms, which were worked mainly by their sons. Most of the older men sat around the village store or the ancestral halls in the evenings exchanging gossip, and many spent their days visiting the tea shops in Yuen Long. The leisure of the older retired people of the village depended largely upon the family's wealth: if the family was well off the older people did nothing; if the family was poor, the older people continued to work as long as they could.

An estimated 40 students helped farm; 59 housewives were partly active; and 22 older retired people did at least some work, making a total of 121 villagers who were engaged part time in productive economic activity. This figure, added to the 274 who worked full time, gives a total of 395 villagers, or 40 per cent of the population, who were fully or partly working in income-producing activities. Five hundred eighty-nine villagers, or 60 per cent of the village population, were economically inactive. Of the 191 men of the village between the ages of 20 and 60 years, 187, or 98 per cent, were working full time. Of of 195 women in the same age group, 87, or 45 per cent, were employed full time.

These figures show what is immediately evident to any observer—that the villagers as a whole are an extremely energetic and hardworking group of people. In the daytime the village is deserted; the farmers are in their fields, the children are in school, and the workers are at their jobs outside the village. The total picture is one of dynamism, and the economy of the village can in no way be considered stagnant or the people without the will to work. Economic gain is perhaps the central value of the village culture and a major goal for every individual. In fact, desire for wealth is the driving force of the society, as it has probably always been. The money-making opportunities presented by the economic development of the colony in the postwar years have intensified this acquisitive attitude and business acumen. In 1962, every villager, with few exceptions, was a potential businessman or shopkeeper on a large or small scale, and no money-making opportunity was overlooked or failed to be exploited, if the means to exploit it were at hand. Economic development has not meant a change in the basic motivations and values of the villagers; rather, it has created the conditions in which traditional motivations and values can be more fully realized than ever before.

THE DISTRIBUTION OF VILLAGE OCCUPATIONS

The occupations of the villagers are presented in tables 4 and 5. The striking thing about this occupational distribution is its extreme variety, representing almost the entire economic spectrum. It is also surprising that there are so few people engaged in agriculture. Such a diversified occupational picture would be expected more in urban Kowloon than in the rural areas of the colony. There are, however, important differences between the village and the urban distributions, which will be discussed below.

With the exception of agriculture, which accounts for only about one-sixth of the male workers, there is no one occupational class or category in which most of the other villagers are employed. The next

TABLE 4

VILLAGE OCCUPATIONS (MALE), 1962

Category	Number Employed	Category	Number Employed
General broker	7	Butcher	7
Hop Yick Co. officer	4	Government official	1
Travel agency owner	1	Chicken hatchery owner	1
Chauffeur (private)	1	Telephone repairman	1
Retail clerk	8	Taxi and bus caller	3
Draftsman	1	British Army employee	3
Store proprietor	7	Shipyard worker	1
Moneylender	2	Vegetable wholesaler	1
Auto mechanic	3	Duck raiser	1
Office clerk	6	Village guard head	1
Restaurant proprietor	1	Street sweeper	1
Hawker	10	Coolie	6
Farmer	29	Bus washer	4
Cook	2	Carpenter	1
Pig raiser	2	Ivory craftsman	2
Factory worker	15	Barber	1
Policeman	6	Gardener	2
Gambling worker	6	Chicken farm owner	1
Teacher	3	Agricultural laborer	1
Kindergarten owner	1	Broom-maker	9
Doctor (Western medicine)	1	Village handicraftsman	4
Chinese Doctor	3	Brick layer	1
Waiter	4	Pig injector (vet.)	1
Bus ticket collector	1	Curio dealer	1
Driver (bus, truck, taxi)	6	Total	187
Veterinarian	1		
Architect (village houses)	1		

largest category, that of factory worker, contains only 15 men, a very small proportion of the total. The participation of village men in the nonagricultural sector of the economy, which has been expanding steadily since the war, is not concentrated in one area, but is scattered.

TABLE 5

VILLAGE OCCUPATIONS (FEMALE), 1962

Category	Number Employed
Retail shop clerk	1
Proprietress of grocery store	1
Farmer	25
Librarian	1
Nurse	2
Coolie	15
Amah (servant)	14
Teacher	2
Seamstress	2
Hawker	5
Textile factory worker	8
Local factory worker	4
Spirit medium and curess	2
Opera singer	1
Seller of school supplies	1
Waitress	1
Teahouse clerk	1
Medicine-shop clerk	1
Total	87

Table 6 sets forth the distribution of the villagers' occupations grouped in broad economic categories and stratified by sex. Of the fully active village population, 62, or 22.6 per cent, were employed in agricultural occupations; 57, or 20.8 per cent, were engaged in service occupations as waiters, cooks, servants, policemen, and the like; 54, or 19.7 per cent, were employed in commercial activities, ranging from hawkers to shopkeepers and general brokers; 44, or 16.0 per cent, worked in manufacturing industries, ranging from small handicraft broom factories in the village to textile factories in Kowloon and Tsuen Wan; 27, or 9.9 per cent, were employed in transportation and communications, primarily as truck, bus, and taxi drivers; 18, or 6.6 per cent, worked in construction; and 12, or 4.4 per cent, were employed in utilities.

The male working force of the village was distributed almost evenly

TABLE 6

OCCUPATIONS OF HANG MEI VILLAGERS GROUPED INTO BROAD ECONOMIC CLASSES AND COMPARED WITH THE OCCUPATIONAL DISTRIBUTION OF THE NEW TERRITORIES AND THE COLONY AS A WHOLE

Economic Sector	Villagers				New Territories	Colony
	Male	Female	Totals	Per Cent	(Per Cent)	(Per Cent)
Manufacturing industries	31	13	44	16.0	29.0	40.0
Construction and engineering	3	15	18	6.6	8.3	8.4
Utilities	12		12	4.4	0.9	1.6
Commerce	42	12	54	19.7	8.5	11.0
Transportation and communication	27		27	9.9	3.0	7.3
Services	35	22	57	20.8	17.3	22.3
Agriculture, forestry and fishing	37	25	62	22.6	29.9	7.4
Unclassified					2.0	1.4
Mines and quarries					1.2	0.8
Totals	187	87	274	100.0	100.1	100.2

SOURCE (for the New Territories and Colony figures): *Hong Kong Report on the 1961 Census*, Vol. III, pp. 26 and 28, tables 239 and 242. The figures have been rounded off to the nearest decimal place.

Fifteen of the villagers, 11 men and 4 women, or 6 per cent of the village workers, hold professional, managerial, or technical positions. This group includes a Western–style physician who works for the government, 3 teachers, an official in the water department of the government, a government-employed veterinarian, a prominent political leader and broker, an architect, 2 nurses, a librarian, and 4 officers of Hop Yick Co., which controls most of the market town of Yuen Long. This is a fairly large percentage of high-status occupations for a New Territories village and is probably higher than the average, most likely because Hang Mei is a wealthy and established landowning village.

Within Hang Mei village, most people with such occupations are from the Six Families branch of the lineage; there are no professional people among the outsiders or among the poorer branches. This is because the Six Families people not only have sufficient wealth to give their sons and daughters a higher education, but they also have the wide social connections necessary to get good jobs in the highly competitive Hong Kong job market, in which qualified applicants usually outnumber available positions. The other sections of the village population cannot afford to educate their children beyond middle school and lack social influence as well.

Two examples will make clear how disparate occupational opportunities are for the various segments of the village population. One of the families of Zunn Tak Hall, the most prestigious branch of the "Six Families," consists of nine members—father, mother, five sons, and two daughters. The head of this family is a well-known Chinese physician, who as a young man went to Singapore to study Chinese medicine. Upon his return to Hong Kong, he became a doctor in one of the best-known Chinese hospitals in Kowloon, where he practiced for a few years before retiring to the village. He is now the best educated man in the village in the classical Chinese literary style. Although he is by no means wealthy, he has been able to give his children a Western education that is better than that received by the other village children. The eldest daughter, twenty-eight years old, graduated from a nursing school in the city and is now a professional nurse in a New Territories hospital. She helped to educate her two oldest brothers, and they, in turn, will help with the education of their younger brothers. The eldest son graduated from the government-operated English-language middle school in Yuen Long and then attended Taiwan National University, where he earned a degree in veterinary medicine. Upon his return to the village in 1961, he obtained a position in the Agriculture and Forestry Department of the Hong Kong Government. The second son of the family is studying medicine at a Taiwan university and will become a Western doctor upon graduation, while the third son, in his early twenties, is studying in middle school and will probably go on to college. The youngest daughter dropped out of middle school after two years and is working in a Kowloon factory to help pay for the education of her younger brothers.

A Ha Fu family of the village serves as a contrast to the family of Zunn Tak Hall. The Ha Fu family has six members—father (a widower), two sons (aged 23 and 21), and three unmarried daughters (17, 15, and 11). The father is a successful farmer, but he is illiterate, or barely literate, and characteristically spends most of his leisure time gambling. His two sons graduated late from the six-year primary school in the village because they had to help with farm chores and consequently were not able to start school at the normal age. After graduation they obtained jobs in Kowloon, one as a bus mechanic and the other as a bus washer. The two unmarried teen-age daughters, who had only a primary-school education in the village, are now helping on the farm while awaiting marriage, probably into another farm family. Since there was no family tradition of scholarship and no financial resources to enable the children to obtain an English middle-school education (the requirement for a good position in Hong Kong), the sons have moved into very low-status occupations and the daughters will either get married or go to work in the textile factories in the city.

Although these families represent extremes, the first is in general characteristic of the Six Families branch of the Tangs, and the second is characteristic of the poorer families in the Ha Fu group. The other branches of the Tangs would fall somewhere in between. The situation was quite similar in traditional times, when only the wealthier families could afford to educate their sons for the imperial examinations. This differential motivation and opportunity for social mobility, based upon class and wealth distinctions, has persisted in the new society.

It is too soon to tell what occupations the children of the outsiders will fill because most outsiders are middle-aged couples and their children are still quite young. These children will probably show considerable social mobility, because many outsiders are from well-educated, urban families and encourage their children in their studies. The outsider children, as a general rule, do much better in school than the village children and seem to have more motivation for academic achievement.

An important aspect of the village occupational structure is the large number of villagers who work in the urban areas of the colony, most of them factory workers, coolies, craftsmen, and shop clerks. As can be seen from Table 8, 66, or about one-fourth of the village workers are employed in the city. Most of the men who work in Kowloon or Hong Kong live in the city, returning to their families in the village only weekly, monthly, or on the major Chinese holidays, depending upon the nature of their jobs. Few commute daily from the village to the city because salaries are usually so low that the two-dollars-per-day transportation cost is prohibitive. Some of the employers in the city provide living quarters for their employees, but many villagers working in the city have to seek private accommodations, which are usually expensive and of very poor quality.

TABLE 8

VILLAGE WORKERS WHO HAVE PERMANENT JOBS IN THE CITY AND
ONLY OCCASIONALLY RETURN TO THE VILLAGE

Village Group	Male		Female		Total
	Married	Unmarried	Married	Unmarried	
Six Families	5	9	2	3	19
Wai Shan Hall	3	3	0	3	9
Yat T'ai Hall and					
Hang Mei	5	3	2	1	11
Ha Fu	1	7	0	1	9
Outsiders	12	4	1	1	18
Totals	26	26	5	9	66

Of these 66 workers, 52 are men and only 14 women. Only 5 of the 14 women are married. One is the second wife of a village man who operates a grocery store; one is a childless first wife who works as a servant; one is a widow who also works as a servant; one is an amah whose husband has gone abroad; and one is a Chinese opera singer. It would be considered improper for a married woman other than a widow or a cast-off childless first wife to work in the city, and, until recently, married women were not even allowed to work outside the village.

Of the 9 unmarried girls who work in the city, 5 are workers in textile factories and 4 are employed as servants. It is becoming more and more common for unmarried girls of poorer families to go to the city to work between graduation from primary school and marriage. Many of these girls marry fellow workers whom they meet in the city, and these marriages are invariably of modern style with free marital choice and courtship.

Of the 52 village men who work in the city, 26 are married and 26 are single. It is an accepted practice for the young unmarried men to go to the city to work after leaving school. Both young men and women appear to welcome the opportunity to get out on their own, away from the restrictive atmosphere of village public opinion and parental surveillance. Most of the young men who go to the city to work and who marry there bring their wives back to the village to live, not only to maintain family and community ties through residence in the village, but also because living conditions are better and cheaper there.

Villagers are attracted to outside jobs because they offer a monthly salaried income which may not be large, but which is more regular and dependable. Of the fully active village working population, 145, or 53 per cent, are salaried workers; 126, or 46 per cent, are self-employed; and 3 workers, or 1 per cent, are apprentices (see Table 9). The income of the self-employed people, who range from farmers and petty hawkers to affluent real estate brokers, is irregular at both the lower and upper economic levels. At the lower levels, the income from

TABLE 9

SOURCES AND TYPE OF INCOME OF VILLAGE WORKERS

Employment Type	Male	Female	Total	Per Cent
Salaried employees:				
Permanent monthly rate	88	37	125	
Permanent daily rate		4	4	
Piece rate		1	1	
Casual or temporary	4	11	15	
Total	92	53	145	53
Apprentices	3		3	1
Self-employed	92	34	126	46
Totals	187	87	274	100

pig raising and vegetable gardening—the main income-producing agricultural occupations—is dependent upon the imponderables of the market and the uncertainties of the weather. At the upper economic levels, a broker may close a big deal and make a small fortune; on the other hand, he may go for long periods without having any income at all. Commercial or brokerage ventures may lead to wealth or, more frequently, to bankruptcy. However, many of the villagers, especially the wealthier people of the Six Families, choose to try their luck instead of settling for a small but steady income. This drive to "strike it rich" is so intense that many of the men who have regular positions carry on additional speculative business ventures after their working hours.

There is then an "irrational" sector in the villagers' economic activities, a kind of economic adventurism quite different from the Western pattern of regular salaried labor. Nonetheless, the attraction of a regular and dependable income has led many villagers to engage in a more "rational" type of economic activity and, in 1962, about half the village workers held salaried jobs. It is probable that as economic development continues in Hong Kong and more regular positions are created, the percentage of salaried employees will increase. This seems to be a necessary process in the development of a bureaucratically organized capitalist economy. The shift to regular salaried occupations has had an important effect on the patterns of expenditure and savings of the village population and will be discussed in a later chapter.

According to information gathered from 69 Hang Mei men on the occupations of their fathers and grandfathers, during the past two generations about 15 out of 69 families have switched from agriculture to other occupations. However, 3 men whose fathers were not farmers have taken up farming, reducing the net loss in the farming population to 12.

Not only has there been a shift in the occupational structure away from agriculture, but there has also been a marked change in the character of nonagricultural occupations. The occupations most frequently mentioned for the fathers and grandfathers of the Six Families men were merchant, shopkeeper, scholar, and broker. For the most part, however, these men engaged in extremely small-scale commercial enterprises. The brokerage business, for example, was not as good then as it is at present, since the price of land and the volume of land sales were so much lower. A number of the men of the village, particularly those from lineage branches with sizable collective landholdings, formerly engaged in no productive enterprise, leading a life of leisure and living on the rent from the ancestral lands. In any event, very few of the village men who were nonfarmers engaged in professional or wage-earning occupations, as they are now beginning to do.

In the old days there was little knowledge of Western patterns. Until after the war, education for most of the villagers was mainly in the old classical tradition. The Western-style schools that were available were too expensive for any but the wealthiest villagers, and thus most of the villagers did not have the linguistic and technical competence to take advantage of the jobs available to educated Chinese in the colony. The classical Chinese education and the traditional ideals that led men to seek a life of leisure, to have few wants, and to live slightly above the subsistence level did not generate the dynamic and disciplined orientation that is required for success in a rapidly changing industrial economy. Among the Six Families, at least, there was a clinging to the old patterns; among the rest of the villagers, there was not so much an active resistance to change as there was a lack of knowledge of the new opportunities and the means to take advantage of them.

The importance of these traditional attitudes, however, should not be overemphasized. If the majority of the villagers failed to participate in the new urban-oriented economy before the war, it was simply because this economy, not yet fully developed, offered the villagers limited opportunities. In the postwar years, however, there has been tremendous industrial and commercial development in the colony, and the villagers have adapted to the new economic situation with remarkable speed, as is clearly indicated by the present occupational structure of the population. The traditional values and the traditional social and cultural patterns of the villagers have not been important impediments to their participation in the modern economic life of the colony.

III

From Peasants to Farmers

The revolutionary changes in the occupational structure of the village have been paralleled by equally far-reaching changes in agricultural practices. The agricultural system of Hang Mei and the adjoining villages of Ping Shan is in a state of rapid transition, with the older subsistence-oriented rice-growing economy giving way to a market-oriented vegetable-growing economy.

The traditional system of agriculture in Ping Shan was based on two-crop rice agriculture. Rice was grown on the low-lying paddy fields where water was usually available; sweet potatoes, sugar cane, peanuts, and various varieties of beans were grown on highland fields that lacked a dependable water supply. If a farmer grew only rice, he would have a cash income twice a year, after each rice harvest. Most farmers, however, had at least a few highland fields devoted to the cultivation of crops such as peanuts and sugar cane, which furnished them with a supplementary cash income. A large percentage of the rice produced was used by the farmer for his own family's consumption; the surplus rice, along with the peanuts and sugar cane, was sold in the market town for cash, which the farmer used to purchase commodities that he did not produce himself. Even in the traditional agricultural system, the farm economy was not completely self-sufficient; the farmer had to sell part of his crop in the market to get cash for his other needs.

Sweet potatoes could be grown either on the highland fields or as a winter catch crop on the paddy fields. Sweet potatoes were sometimes sold in the market town, but more often they were used as food by the farmer near harvesttime when his supply of rice ran low. If there was a surplus of sweet potatoes, it was used as food for the farmer's pigs.

On some highland fields, peanuts were planted in March and harvested in June or July, followed usually by a crop of sweet potatoes. On other highland fields, sugar cane was planted in the spring and could be harvested for three to five years in succession, but since the cane did not yield a good harvest after the second year, many farmers replanted every year or two (Tregear, 1955:40).

In the traditional system of agriculture, subsistence farming was much more important than farming for the market. Some farmers grew a few vegetables, but these were mainly for personal consumption. As one farmer said, "Farming in the old days was not like doing business. No one paid much attention to markets and prices." Under this agricultural system, the farmers were poor. They made just enough to live on, and what little surplus they did manage to accumulate was siphoned off to pay for periodic rituals, such as marriages and funerals. According to their own testimony, the farmers have done considerably better in the years since the war. As one farmer reported, "Before, we poorer people ate one-third sweet potatoes and two-thirds rice; now no one has to eat sweet potatoes."

The first major change in this traditional pattern of agriculture actually began in the 1930's, when urban interests, local landlords, and a few wealthy Chinese returning from overseas began to buy land in the New Territories, on which they built houses and established farms. At this time, most of the Ping Shan villagers considered the highland fields to be of little value compared to the lowland fields on which rice was grown, so that some were willing to sell these fields at extremely low prices. In the immediate postwar years, land sales proceeded at an even more rapid pace. With the growth of population in the colony and the beginning of industrial development, the value of land, particularly of that near the roads and market towns, greatly increased. Some of the villagers, with little foresight, sold land at prices that seemed attractive at the time, but which were only a small fraction of its later value.

By 1962, many highland fields owned privately by the villagers had already been sold. Members of the Six Families group sold land to finance commercial ventures, to educate their children, or simply to maintain their traditional style of life. The sale of highland fields and the conversion of much of it for building naturally reduced the land available for the farmer to plant cash crops. This might have damaged the farm economy had not the transition from rice agriculture to vegetable farming, stimulated by the colony's economic growth, begun in the immediate postwar period.

Before the war, only 20 per cent of the vegetables consumed in the colony were grown locally, with the balance imported mostly from China via the Kowloon–Canton Railroad. By 1954, however, about 50 per cent of the vegetables consumed in the colony were grown in the New Territories, the balance coming from China. This represented a tremendous increase in vegetable production within a relatively short period.

The shift to vegetable growing by the village farmers can be attributed to several factors. Just after the war, refugees from China settled near Yuen Long and began to grow vegetables for the Hong Kong market. These refugees came from villages near urban areas in China (particularly Canton) where there was a long tradition of vegetable growing for city markets, and they were well versed in the skills and techniques of the truck-gardening business. Gradually, the outsiders passed these skills along to the *pen-ti* farmers, who also took up commercial vegetable growing. Another factor was that the mainland was more isolated economically from the colony in the years after 1949, and this increased the need for the farmers of the New Territories to supply food for the expanding urban population. A third factor was the creation by the government of two marketing organizations that were designed to bring about the self-sufficiency of the colony in foodstuffs by encouraging vegetable production.[1] Each of these organizations sought to make vegetable growing profitable for the farmer by eliminating the middlemen who, under the system of marketing that had existed before the war, had received a large portion of the farmers' profits. The first of these organizations, the Vegetable Marketing Organization established in 1946, was concerned with controlling the urban markets, and legislation enacted by the government made it compulsory for all vegetables marketed in the urban markets to be sold through the Vegetable Marketing Organization or its licensed brokers. The second organization was actually a group of agricultural cooperatives developed on the local level to help the farmers of the New Territories market their produce. Collection depots to which the farmers could bring their produce were established along roads throughout the New Territories. The Vegetable Marketing Organization sent out a fleet of trucks daily to collect the vegetables and transport them to the wholesale market in Kowloon. This has made it more convenient for the farmer to market his produce: he need only carry it from the field, in standardized baskets furnished by the local cooperatives, to a collecting station on the road near his fields. Here the vegetables are weighed, loaded on a truck, and taken to the city market. At the time his produce is weighed the farmer is given a receipt which, after two days, he can present to his local cooperative office and receive payment. A small commission is deducted from the selling price to cover the operating costs of the marketing organization

---

[1] For a discussion of the traditional marketing procedures in the New Territories and the development of the government Vegetable Marketing Organization, see Topley, 1964:179–182.

and to pay for the fleet of trucks that was initially furnished by the government. Marketing costs are reduced and the farmer is saved the inconvenience of personally marketing his produce. This government program has been remarkably effective: since the end of the war, the volume of vegetables sold in the Kowloon wholesale market has increased every year, and at present almost 50 per cent of the land in the New Territories that was once planted in rice is devoted to truck gardening.

This shift did not occur suddenly in Ping Shan; the process, as yet not fully completed, has passed through several distinguishable stages. After the war, the villagers first began to experiment with commercial vegetable growing on a small scale. At first, the village farmers gradually introduced vegetable crops into older agricultural patterns. Instead of growing sweet potatoes on the fields during the winter months after the second rice crop had been harvested, they began to plant a catch crop of winter vegetables. The first experiments were so successful that the farmers began to increase the area of land in winter vegetables, bringing into cultivation paddy land that had formerly been plowed under to lie fallow during the winter months. As the farmers discovered the sizable profits that could be made from vegetables, they switched increasing amounts of land from rice to vegetables. In fact, some rice fields that were suitable in soil quality and water supply were changed over to the year-round cultivation of vegetables.

The switch to vegetables is attractive, not only because of the greater profits, but also because the income is continuous throughout the year, in contrast to the twice-yearly income from rice. Vegetable crops, on the whole, mature rapidly, and some can be sold one month after planting. Also, many of the slower-growing crops can be cut again and again after an interval of one or two days. The farmers themselves are now very aware of the economic advantages of vegetable growing as compared to rice.

Since they had sufficient capital, land, and farm equipment, the *pen-ti* farmers tended initially, and to some extent even now, to plant slow-growing vegetable crops that did not require as much labor as the fast-growing ones. In the last few years, however, because of the greater income possible, they have been gradually switching to the faster-maturing vegetables that require less capital, less land, and more labor.

At present vegetable production in the New Territories is not mainly dependent upon the *pen-ti* farmers. Most vegetables are still grown by refugee farmers from China, who have settled in the New Territories in ever-increasing numbers since 1949. These refugees came into the colony with literally nothing but the shirts on their backs and rented small plots of land on which they built wooden shacks.[2] Because they did not have the land, the capital, or the equipment of the *pen-ti* farmers, they specialized in the year-round production of the fastest-maturing vegetable crops which brought the highest market prices. They expend intensive labor on their small plots and make considerable profits, growing four, six, or even eight crops a year. Living close to their gardens, they can tend them carefully every day and protect their crops against theft. The fast-growing vegetables require great amounts of fertilizer and water. Where irrigation is not available, the farmers must carry water to the gardens in old kerosene cans that have been converted into large sprinklers. Vegetable growing has proved very successful for the refugees, and their shacks now dot the countryside in areas close to the major roads and the market towns.

The trend of the last few years for *pen-ti* farmers to abandon rice and to concentrate solely on growing vegetables will probably continue into the future because it is a simple economic fact that the profits from growing rice do not compare with those from vegetables. Eventually, most New Territories farmers will probably be engaged in this type of agriculture, since this is the current direction of the process of change.

The changes that have taken place in the agricultural practices of Ping Shan since 1898 can be broken down into four stages, all of which were still present in the farm economy of the village in 1962:

1. *The traditional system* of two-crop rice agriculture combined with cash crops of sugar cane, peanuts, and sweet potatoes grown on the highland fields. This system was primarily oriented towards subsistence, with some produce sold to meet the farmers' other needs. Some vegetables were grown, mainly for family consumption, although a limited amount was sold in the village and in the market town.

2. *The system of two-crop rice agriculture plus a winter catch crop of vegetables,* usually of the slow-maturing type. This was the stage of initial experimentation with vegetable growing for the market in the late prewar or early postwar years.

3. *Large-scale vegetable growing,* in which the winter catch crop of vegetables was extended, and one or more of the rice crops was replaced by slow-maturing vegetable crops. Some land was devoted to vegetables throughout the year, and although rice was still grown, vegetables gradually became more important than rice in the farm economy.

[2] See Topley (1964) for a discussion of refugee vegetable farmers in the New Territories.

4. *The system of intensive vegetable growing similar to that practiced by the refugee farmers.* This is the stage in which the *pen-ti* farmers are switching almost entirely to vegetable gardening and giving up rice agriculture. Fast-maturing crops of vegetables commanding good market prices are grown throughout the year on small farms that require the intensive application of labor.

THE FARM ECONOMY IN 1962

This analysis of the farm economy is based on a survey, carried out in the fall of 1962, of 42 farms in Ping Shan.[3] The sample of 42 farms consists of 24 operated by people from Hang Mei village (a 100 per cent sample), plus 15 in the adjacent villages of Tong Fong, Hang Tau, and San Tsuen. In addition to these farms, all run by *pen-ti jen,* I have included 3 farms of refugee vegetable farmers near Ping Shan. The farms from adjacent villages were included to increase the size of the sample and to make it more representative of the farm economy of Ping Shan as a whole.

The measures used in this discussion require some explanation. The *dau–chung* [mandarin, *tou-chung*] is the traditional local unit of land measurement and is supposed to be equivalent to the area that can be planted by 1 *dau* measure of rice (1 *dau* of rice is 10 catties, or about 13.3 pounds). The *dau–chung* is usually equivalent to 0.134 acres, but varies in size according to the fertility of the land and between highland fields and rice fields. The farmers use the *dau–chung* unit as an equivalent of the more widespread Chinese measure of land area—the *mow* (0.166 acres). A *mow* is slightly larger than 1 *dau–chung,* but according to local usage both equal approximately one-sixth acre. The *dau–chung* unit is used here because the farmers habitually use this measure in discussing land units. The figures used in this study are based on the farmers' own estimates of the sizes of their fields and are only rough approximations.

Size of Farms

Altogether, the 42 farms surveyed comprise a cultivated area of 311 *dau–chung* (hereafter, d.c.). This gives an average farm size of 7.4 d.c. The largest farm in the sample is 36 d.c. and the smallest is only 1 d.c. Eighteen out of 42 farms are under 5 d.c., or less than 1 acre, in size. An almost equal number (16 out of 42) are from 6 to 10 d.c. Al-

[3] This survey was carried out by me and my assistants. Mr. Chen served as my research assistant, language tutor, and interpreter for the first twelve months of field work; my other assistant was a village farmer. I am satisfied with the general accuracy of the findings in this survey, but statistical material, particularly on farm income, should be regarded as only approximate.

together, 34 of the 42 farms, or 81 per cent of the farms surveyed, are 10 d.c. or less in size. Only 8, or 19 per cent, are larger than 10 d.c. The distribution of farm size is shown in Table 10.

TABLE 10

SIZE OF PING SHAN FARMS IN 1962

Farm Size (in d.c.)	Number of Farms	Percentage of Total Number of Farms in Survey
1–5	18	43
6–10	16	38
11–15	5	12
16–20	2	5
21 and over	1	2
Totals	42	100

The size of farms in Ping Shan can be usefully compared to the size of those in Nanching, a village near Canton which is described by C. K. Yang (1959b: 35-36):

Nanching shared a common feature of the rice region of China, namely, the minute scale of farm operation. The majority of the farms were from five to ten mow (about 0.83 to 1.66 acres). Fairly common were farms over ten but under fifteen mow. Less common but still found in good numbers were farms above fifteen but under twenty mow. But farms over twenty mow were few. There was only one large farm, that of Wong Yung, who operated about seventy mow, somewhat less than twelve acres, in 1949.

As this passage indicates, the distribution of farm size in Nanching is similar to that in Ping Shan. Although an exact comparison is difficult because Yang's figures for Nanching were reproduced from memory, it appears that Ping Shan farms are, on the whole, slightly smaller. This is probably because commercial vegetable growing had proceeded further in Ping Shan in 1962 than it had in Nanching in 1949, where only one-fourth of the land was devoted to truck gardening (C. K. Yang, 1959b:27).

Ping Shan farms were not always as small as they were in 1962. In prewar days and in traditional times, the farms apparently were larger since they included a number of highland fields. The trend toward decreased size began about 30 years ago with the sale of these fields to outsiders. The results of the farm survey clearly show a continuation of this trend in the years since the war, with many village farmers giving up rice fields and growing vegetables on 4 or 5 d.c. of their best land near the village. Of the 31 farmers who were able to supply such information, 9 reported no change in the size of their farms; 1 reported an increase; and 21, or 50 per cent of the total sample, reported a decrease.

Of the 21 farmers whose farms had decreased in size, 15 reported a loss of land on which they had grown rice; 4, a loss of field-crop land (cane, potatoes, and sweet potatoes) ; and 2 reported a loss of vegetable-growing land. There was a total loss of 58 d.c. of rice land, 24 d.c. of field-crop land, and 4 d.c. of vegetable land since the war. This adds up to a total decrease of 86 d.c., or 28 per cent of the total area of the farms sampled; since farms were larger in the prewar years, the decrease over the past 35 years must have been even greater. As I have mentioned previously, this decrease is closely related to the change from rice agriculture to vegetable gardening. Whereas the average size of village farms growing both rice and vegetables is 11.3 d.c., the average for farms devoted solely to vegetable cultivation is only 4.2 d.c., which is about the maximum area that can be tended by an average family growing vegetables intensively throughout the year.

Only one farmer in the sample devoted his farm entirely to rice agriculture (see Table 11) ; this was a small farm of only 6 d.c. Nineteen farmers grew a combination of rice and vegetables, while 22 grew vegetables only. In 1962, then, Ping Shan farmers were about equally divided between those who grew both rice and vegetables and those who grew only vegetables. This, however, does not mean that an equal

TABLE 11

CROPPING PATTERNS OF PING SHAN FARMS

Crops Grown	Number of Farms	Percentage of Total Number of Farms
Rice only	1	2
Rice and vegetables	19	45
Vegetables only	22	52
Totals	42	99

area of crop land was devoted to rice and vegetables. Table 12 shows that of the 311 d.c. total farm land in the sample, only 65 d.c. (21 per cent) were devoted solely to rice cultivation. Thirty-eight d.c. (12 per cent) were devoted to growing both rice and winter vegetables, and 208 d.c. (67 per cent) were devoted to vegetable growing only. These figures indicate the overwhelming importance of truck gardening in the farm economy.

TABLE 12

AREA DEVOTED TO RICE AND VEGETABLES ON PING SHAN FARMS

Crops Grown	Area (in d.c.)	Percentage of Total Area
Rice only	65	21
Rice and winter vegetables	38	12
Vegetables only	208	67
Totals	311	100

Number of Fields per Farm

The distribution of the number of fields per farm in Ping Shan is shown in Table 13. Out of a total sample of 34 farms (this information was not available for 8 of the farms), which altogether had a total area of 258 d.c., the crop land was divided into 355 fields. This gives an average of about 10 fields per farm. The average size field in Ping Shan was only about 0.7 d.c., which is quite small. The distribution of number of fields per farm closely parallels the distribution of farm size, with 22 out of 34 farms having from 1 to 10 fields. The average farm in Ping Shan, then, has about 10 fields and is about 7 d.c. in size.

TABLE 13

NUMBER OF FIELDS IN PING SHAN FARMS

Number of Fields in Farm	Number of Farms
1–5	11
6–10	11
11–15	6
16–20	3
21–25	2
over 25	1
Total	34

As in most of China, the fields of one farm in Ping Shan are almost never concentrated in one area; they are usually scattered in at least two localities some distance apart. Some of the fields owned by the villagers are close to the village, but most are about one-half mile distant, and a few are as far as a mile or two away. The fields owned by Ping Shan villagers that are situated quite far from the village are usually rented out to farmers in villages adjacent to the fields. Most of the fields farmed by Hang Mei farmers are about fifteen minutes from the village by foot, or five minutes away by bicycle, the usual means of transportation.

In the last few years, village farmers have built small wooden houses and animal sheds near their fields where they store farm equipment and keep pigs and cows, and which they sometimes use as temporary dwelling quarters. This follows the pattern established by the refugee vegetable farmers and not only saves time for the farmer but also allows him to keep a close watch over his valuable vegetable crops.

Types of Crops Grown

In addition to rice, the village farmers reported 24 other major crops, including numerous varieties of both Chinese and Western vegetables, that they planted frequently and in large quantities. In 1962, the most popular vegetable crop grown by village farmers was a type of Chinese watercress. Next, in descending order of popularity, came Western cabbage, melons of various types, and lotus root. Grown in smaller amounts were such vegetables as water chestnut, mustard greens, Chinese cabbage, spinach, leaf lettuce, taro, green beans, water spinach, tomatoes, sweet potatoes, and sugar cane.

These numerous varieties of vegetables were divided by the farmers into several types. One type, known as "water vegetables," consisted of vegetables like lotus root and watercress which could be grown on irrigated fields in place of rice for the duration of the rice-growing season. Another type, winter vegetables, included tomatoes, cabbage, Chinese cabbage, and lettuce, which could be grown on the paddy fields during the winter months after the second rice crop had been harvested. A third type of vegetables consisted of various beans and melons which could be grown during the hottest and wettest part of the summer in place of the first rice crop. Finally, there was a type called "highland vegetables," which included tomatoes, corn, cane, melons, beans, sweet potatoes, and turnips.

From the first to the seventh month of the Chinese lunar calendar, the weather in Hong Kong is rainy and hot, suitable for growing crops like lotus root and watercress which, unlike other vegetables that are difficult to grow during this period, thrive on heat and moisture. Vegetable production is low at this time, but since market prices are high, many farmers gamble and grow all kinds of vegetables in the hope that a few of the crops will survive. Most of the vegetables, particularly the European types, grow best in the cool, dry months of late fall and winter. However, since the supply is greatest at this time, the prices are often low.

It is clear that successful vegetable growing requires knowledge and skill. The farmer must know his crops, as well as the proper time and manner in which to grow them, and he must also be familiar with the proper fertilizer for each crop. In addition, he must be able to judge which crops will bring the best prices at each time of the year and then bring each crop on the market at the most favorable time. The peasant farmer must adopt the attitude of a businessman if he is to be successful growing and selling vegetables; it is no longer enough for him merely to follow the old traditional agricultural practices learned from his father.

AGRICULTURAL METHODS

Water, Fertilizer, and Location of Fields

Good vegetable land must be near a stream, pond, or well, so that the vegetables can be watered daily. In fact, most vegetables must be watered twice daily or else they will quickly burn under the hot tropical sun. A tremendous amount of labor is expended in carrying the water to the fields in converted gasoline or kerosene tins hung on the ends of a carrying pole. However, not every field with a permanent supply of water is suitable for vegetables. Good vegetable land must have soil that is more sandy and porous than that of paddy fields to ensure that the vegetable beds will drain properly during the heavy rains of the summer months. It must also be close to the roads or vegetable-collecting depots so that not too much time and labor are lost in carrying the vegetables to the pick-up stations. Another reason the fields must be near the roads is that the supply of night soil for use as fertilizer on vegetable gardens is transported to the New Territories and deposited at storage stations. Men must be hired to carry the matured fertilizer to the vegetable fields, and, of course, the closer the fields are to the road, the less labor is required for this purpose.

In view of these requirements, it is not surprising that the areas of most intensive vegetable growing in the New Territories closely follow the road network. Ping Shan is blessed with most of the requirements for successful vegetable growing: the area is next to the main New Territories road; it has its own vegetable-collecting depot; and there are highland fields and good sources of irrigation water in the vicinity. With all these natural advantages, it has been comparatively easy for the village farmers to switch from the traditional rice agriculture to growing vegetables for market.

Farming Technology

The basic farm implements used by Ping Shan farmers are local products that are rough and crude but still quite serviceable. These traditional agricultural tools are listed below.

The *traditional plow* is made of hard wood and has an iron plough-share. It is drawn by a wooden yoke which rests on the neck of a water buffalo or cow. The plows come in two sizes; the larger size is used with the water buffalo, and the smaller size is used with the cow. The plow is said to last about ten years. The *harrow* is an iron implement that looks like a large rake. It is also used with the wooden yoke attached to the shoulders of the buffalo or cow, and it smooths and levels rice land after the field has been plowed.

The *hoes* used in the village are similar to Western hoes, except that the blade is much heavier and longer. The hoe is used to break up the field in the small corners which the plow cannot reach, to cut weeds in the fields, to irrigate, and to cut weeds and grass on the field boundaries.

The *long knife* is used to cut weeds off the top of the field boundaries and to level the boundaries. The *rice-harvesting knife* has serrated saw-tooth edges and is used only to cut the rice stalks during the harvest.

The *rice basin* is used to hold the rice stalks after cutting. It is a large wooden tub which protects the rice from the water in the paddy fields and holds any rice that might fall from the sheaves before threshing. The *rice-threshing tub* is a round, wooden, barrel-like tub. Inside the tub is a ladder-like wooden apparatus that resembles a wooden washboard against which the rice straw, after being cut, is beaten to knock the kernels off the straw into the tub. The rice-threshing tub is partially covered with a bamboo *rice screen* that is wrapped three-quarters of the way around the top of the tub to prevent the grain from flying out. The *rice basket* is a large, closely woven bamboo basket used for carrying unhusked rice.

The *carrying pole,* of which there are numerous sizes and shapes, is the universal mode of carrying burdens in China, especially in agricultural work. The pole is balanced on the carrier's shoulders, and burdens of approximately equal weight are suspended from both ends of the pole.

The *wind cabinet* is the hand-operated winnowing machine that separates the grain from the chaff. It consists of a large wooden box, which stands on raised wooden legs. There are several holes in the sides of the box, and thus it acts as a wind tunnel. At one end is a large wooden crank fan operated by a handle, and at the top is a funnel into which the unhusked dried rice is poured. As the rice is poured into the machine, the handle is turned to operate the fan. The heavier grains, full of rice, fall out the first holes in the tunnel. Both grain and chaff are collected by placing bamboo baskets under the holes.

The *water machine* is a wooden, box-like frame about ten feet long, inside of which is a wooden water wheel. A hand-operated crank is located at one end of the long narrow box. One end of the frame is placed in water and the other end in the field into which water is to be pumped. The crank is then turned and draws water up through the box and out the other end. This is the old method of irrigating fields. A seat can be placed over one end of the machine so that the crank can be pedaled by foot.

The *unhusked rice sieve* is a loosely woven tray of bamboo strips which is used to sift the rice and separate it from the dirt or other foreign matter that may be mixed in with the rice on the drying floor. The *rice sieve*, like that used to sift unhusked rice, is a round bamboo tray-like sieve, which was once used to separate the husked rice from the husks after it had been ground and polished in the old household mortars. This is no longer used.

The *wooden fertilizer bucket* is used both as a household latrine (in some households) and as a receptacle for carrying fertilizer to the fields.

In addition to these agricultural implements, there is other equipment that is no longer in use, such as the old stone and bamboo rice-milling machines formerly owned by most households and the foot-operated mortar formerly used to polish rice.

During the past few years, there have been several innovations in the farming technology of the village. One of the most important has been the introduction of the gasoline-operated water pumps. There are only four of these new pumps in Hang Mei, but they are frequently borrowed by other village farmers. The motorized pumps, however, have not completely replaced the older treadmill water pumps, since the latter can still be used in muddy water that would clog the new pumps.

The four pumps in Hang Mei village have been in use for only six or seven years. One of the village farmers told the following story of the introduction of the power pumps:

Tang Shiu, one of the largest and most successful farmers in the village, bought his pump in 1960. That year was very dry and so there was not enough rain for the second rice crop. He had ordered an old-style water pump, but it was not delivered in time, so he bought one of the new pumps instead. Altogether, including the hoses, it cost him about $800. His fields were near the stream, so he thought the pump would be useful. He said that the old water wheel was too much trouble to use because it was too slow and required two people to operate it.

Tang Shiu lent his pump to two brothers, who were the second most successful farmers in the village. They tried out the pump and saw that it was more useful than their old water machine. Soon after that, the two brothers bought their own pumps.

Then Hong Sam saw Tang Shiu using his pump in the fields. Since Hong Sam also had a good water supply near his fields, he bought a pump. The other farmers of the village don't have pumps yet, either because they have no water supply or because they cannot afford to buy one.

It is probably no accident that Tang Shiu was the person who introduced pumps into the village. He is one of the most successful farmers, the acknowledged informal leader of the village farmers, and, most importantly, one of the few village farmers from the "Six Families" group. Therefore, the innovation was probably adopted, not merely for utilitarian reasons, but because the new pumps were prestige symbols.

The most useful mechanical aid to the village farmers is the bicycle. Bicycles are used for general transportation to the fields and to the nearby market town; they are also used to transport goods such as farm produce and pigs to market. No one in the village knows exactly when bicycles were introduced into Ping Shan, but everyone agrees that they have been used a long time. Almost every family in the village now has at least one bicycle. Sometimes an entire family rides on the bicycle; the farmer pedals and the wife sits on the back holding a child in each arm. One of the many astounding bicycle-riding feats of the villagers is to transport a live pig weighing several hundred pounds on the back of a bicycle.

In recent years, the government has built small concrete paths which lead from the main roads to the more remote villages. This has had the effect of increasing vegetable cultivation in those areas that are some distance from the roads because the farmers can now transport their vegetables by bicycle to the pick-up stations and to the market towns. Before these paths were constructed, it was necessary to transport the vegetables to the main road by means of carrying pole.

Although the bicycle was still widely used by village farmers in 1962, it was rapidly being replaced for some purposes by the buses, small taxis, and panel trucks that are becoming more common as the road network extends out from the town to the villages. Many village farmers now ride the bus instead of their bicycles to the market town, and some now transport their goods to and from the market town in the small trucks and taxis. Panel trucks will probably soon replace the bicycle as the main means of transportation from the village to the market town, but the bicycle will still be useful as a means of transportation to and from the fields.

Another important innovation in agricultural technology is the increasing use of chemical fertilizers by village farmers. Foreign chemical fertilizers had been used to a limited extent before the war, but since the war this has become much more common. At present the villagers use many kinds of chemical fertilizers imported from Japan, Germany, and the United States. The fertilizers are sold by the feed and farm-supply stores in the market town. The farmers appear to be shrewd judges of the advantages and disadvantages of each type of fertilizer weighed against its cost, and they usually try each brand as it comes on the market. Traditional Chinese fertilizers such as night soil, dried peanut cakes, animal manure, and human urine, are still used for some purposes, supplementing the chemical fertilizers.

The Hong Kong Government is currently carrying out a program of transporting night soil from the urban areas to the vegetable farmers in the New Territories. The outsider vegetable farmers make more use of the night soil than do the village farmers, who assert that it is too much trouble to carry the manure from the storage stations to their fields and too expensive to hire someone to do it for them. Outsider vegetable farmers in the vicinity also use some of the more exotic traditional Chinese fertilizers, such as duck feathers and fish bone, for special vegetable crops. The village farmers have a complex system of matching fertilizers with the appropriate crops and with certain stages in the growth of each crop. This system is exact and detailed but too complicated to outline here.

One older farmer of the village said that there had been a noticeable increase in rice production during his lifetime because of the use of chemical fertilizer on the paddy fields. He said that, "in the old days 1 d.c. of rice land would yield only 200 catties of rice per harvest, whereas now it is common to have a yield of 300 catties per harvest." He said that they get this larger yield per unit area even though the increased use of chemical fertilizers requires the farmers to space the rice seedlings farther apart. If the rice is planted too closely together, the crop will produce large amounts of straw but very little grain.

The village farmers did not have a high opinion of what they had heard about attempts of the Chinese Communist Government to increase rice production, asserting that the "close planting" program of the Communists would result in large crops of rice straw but very little grain. They were much amused by the stories of the close-planting experiments in the years of the "great leap forward." One story they told was about a field in which the Communists had placed a sign reading, "This field will produce ten thousand piculs of rice"; it turned out that although the field produced a very fine thick straw, it produced very little grain. Another story is about a closely planted field that caught fire in mid-summer owing to the intense heat produced by the growing rice; the cadres had to mobilize the peasants with fans to cool off the crop!

Although the village farmers are willing to experiment with new agricultural techniques and new farm technology, they are shrewd judges of such experiments and are not slow to reject innovations they do not consider practical. Two important innovations almost universally used by the village farmers are insecticides and insecticide sprayers. Before the war the farmers said they used a type of insecticide which they had to mix with water and apply to each plant individually. The use of modern insecticides since the war has greatly reduced the crop loss formerly caused by disease and pests. The newer insecticides were introduced by the farm-supply stores in the market town and their use was explained to the farmers. When the Ping Shan Cooperative was established by the government, it supplied each village, including Hang Mei, with an insecticide sprayer. According to one farmer, this led to quarrels in the village because everyone wanted to use the sprayer at the same time. To avoid this trouble and inconvenience, the farmers have gradually acquired their own sprayers with the help of an Agricultural Aid Association in the New Territories. The first farmer in the village to buy his own insecticide sprayer was Tang Shiu, the same person who introduced the water pump. At present, almost every farmer in the village owns an insecticide sprayer or has easy access to one. This has greatly increased the production of vegetable crops and has eliminated the need to flood the fields every few years to kill the pests and insects that accumulate after two or three years of vegetable cultivation. The flooding procedure limited the farmer's production, because it prevented him from planting his entire farm in vegetables (C. K. Yang, 1959b:29) ; with insecticides, however, he gets maximum use of his land, year after year.

Vegetable Gardening Technology of the Outsiders

The outsider vegetable farmers, who do not need all the traditional agricultural implements used by the *pen-ti* farmers, make use of the following tools: two or three *hoes* to dig up and shape the garden; a *hand harrow* to smooth and level the garden; *watering buckets* and *carrying poles* for watering; *wooden fertilizer buckets* to carry fertilizer; a cement *fertilizer maturing pond* (optional) ; a gasoline-powered *pump* for irrigation (optional) .

The outsider vegetable farmers do not plough their fields unless they are unusually large, and, if necessary, they can hire someone to do it for them. As a result, they do not own ploughs, harnesses, harrows, cows, or buffalo. The *pen-ti* farmers, however, frequently grow large fields of slower maturing vegetables, and thus many of them still use the traditional implements. However, as the switch to vegetable gardening proceeds, most of the traditional tools will probably disappear, and most cattle and buffalo will be sold.

Farm Animals

Draft animals used by the village farmers are of two kinds: the water buffalo, nine of which are owned by the villagers, and the small native cow of which the villagers own twenty-three. The cattle cannot perform as much work as the buffalo but are much easier to care for. Water buffalo are stronger and are used to plough saltwater fields (reclaimed from the sea) , whereas the cows are used to plough ordinary fields.

Of the 42 farmers surveyed in Ping Shan, 29 owned one or more head of cattle or buffalo, and 13 owned none. Of the 13 who owned none, 1 used his brother's cow, 3 took care of the cattle of others in return for the use of the animals, 1 borrowed a neighbor's cow, 5 did not need a cow because their gardens were small, and 3 had recently sold their buffalo because they have other jobs and now farm only a little land. There is no shortage of draft animals in Hang Mei; everyone who needs an animal either has his own or has easy access to the use of one. A few of the smaller farmers help other farmers to work their fields in exchange for the occasional use of an animal for ploughing. This practice seems to have been more prevalent in the past than at present, for now most farmers can afford to buy their own animals if they are needed.

Traditionally, cattle and buffalo were cared for by the younger girls and boys of the village. Almost all of the older men and women of farm background could remember tending cattle as youngsters; in the old days, it offered the boys and girls of the same or adjacent villages an opportunity to get away from the supervision of their elders and to engage in games and sweet-potato roasts. This practice is not as common today as it was in the past because all the young people are now in school and do not have time to care for cattle except in the late afternoon. There is a complete set of songs which vary in each locality and were traditionally sung by the boys while tending cattle; now, however, these are remembered only by the older farmers.

Irrigation

The water used for irrigation by Ping Shan farmers comes from the small streams that crisscross the plain and also from springs and wells. The use of irrigation water is not formally regulated, the principle being "first come, first served." Since all the farmers of one village usually farm adjacent fields, they have little difficulty in sharing irrigation water, and most disputes occur between farmers from different villages or lineages whose fields adjoin one another. Such quarrels, particularly in times of water scarcity, are not infrequent in the New Territories. Most of the older villagers remember a major dispute that occurred between the Ping Shan villages and the villages of the Ha Tsuen branch of the Tang clan, which are situated a few miles to the west. This dispute led to a major intervillage war that is said to have lasted for thirty years. There have also been quarrels over water between the villages of Ping Shan and Shan Ha, a village which lies on the other side of the Ping Shan farming territory.

Now that vegetable gardening is increasing in importance and a permanent water supply is so crucial, many of the vegetable farmers, and particularly those who own power pumps, are digging wells near their fields. Some vegetable gardeners have constructed cement ponds near their fields, in which they store their irrigation water. In fact, some farmers now have two cement ponds, one for the storage of water and the other for the maturing of fertilizer. A storage pond for fertilizer naturally eliminates the need to carry large quantities of wet fertilizer from the village. The practice is to put fertilizer, usually in the proportion of two dippers of human manure to one bucket of water, into the pond and let it stand one week before using. (The proportion of water to manure varies with the crop that is being fertilized.)

Some of the outsider vegetable gardeners and a few of the *pen-ti* farmers are using a method of vegetable-growing, which works only in fields with a permanent supply of water. Ditches, several feet deep, are cut across the fields, and the excavated dirt is used to build up rounded mounds between the ditches on which the vegetables are planted. The ditches are continually filled with water, and the farmers use a long-handled dipper to transfer the water to the mounds several times daily. This, of course, saves the labor required to carry water to the fields in bucket sprinklers. A miniature wooden boat carrying fertilizer (mixed in water) floats through the fields in the irrigation channels; the fertilizer is scooped from the boat onto the vegetable mounds. The digging of these ditches is extremely time-consuming and difficult, and most of the *pen-ti* farmers have not yet adopted this practice, which is suitable only for small fields and for particular kinds of vegetables.

The Ping Shan farmers are "progressive farmers" in that they take an essentially rational attitude towards innovations in farm technology and farm practices: they do not hesitate to adopt new methods that appear to be better than traditional ones. Their quick adoption of power pumps, chemical fertilizers, insecticides, and new techniques of vegetable cultivation is evidence of this rational attitude. One of the major reasons these innovations have been rapidly accepted is that the farmers, owing to improvements in their economic situation in the postwar years, now have the financial means to take advantage of them. The adoption of technical innovations, then, is tied closely to improvement in the farmer's financial situation, which is dependent upon available markets for his goods and improved marketing facilities. These factors, in turn, are intimately connected with the overall economic development of the colony, especially with the growth of the manufacturing sector in the urban areas, for with the growth of industry and commerce in the city and the gradual extension of these into the countryside, the farmer's economic position improves. Capitalist industrial development in Hong Kong's urban areas has thus set off a chain of events that has benefited the agricultural sector of the economy. Without industrial and commercial expansion in the cities and the overall economic development of the colony, innovations in farm technology would not have been economically feasible.

FARM MANAGEMENT

Farm Labor

Labor is the most important factor in agricultural production. This is especially true of vegetable gardening where only a small piece of land is needed and the value of the product is determined largely by the amount of labor expended on the land.

In Hang Mei, almost all the farm work is done by the farm family, and hired labor is not an important factor. Of the 36 farmers who supplied this type of information, only 12 hired labor during 1962, with the number of days of hired labor varying from 5 to 365. Excluding 2 full-time year-round laborers who were hired on 2 of the village farms, the average number of day units of labor hired per farm per year was 22.5.

One of the full-time hired laborers works for an outsider vegetable farmer who farms about 5.5 d.c. of watercress. This crop requires intensive labor as well as attention from a man experienced and skilled in its cultivation; it also brings the best price of any vegetable on the market. The farmer hired his laborer, a refugee who was a specialist in this crop, in 1962 and made enough profit to be able to pay him $200 per month plus meals and extras such as cigarettes and tea. The second full-time laborer on a year-round basis was hired in 1962 by Tang Naam, who manages the largest farm in the village and who was able to hire a refugee for the entire year at the low salary of $450 plus room and board. Because Tang Naam planted almost all of his land that year in one specialized vegetable crop, lotus root, and because the market price for this crop was low that year, he lost money hiring the laborer, in spite of such low wages, and did not plan to hire a full-time laborer the following year.

There are several reasons why the village farmers tend not to hire permanent farm laborers. The most important reason is that the general prosperity of the colony has driven farm wages up so high that village farmers cannot afford to hire full-time labor. A full-time laborer must usually be paid at least $200 per month, plus room and board. Laborers will not normally work for less than this because they can easily get other jobs in the market town or city. Another reason is that the farms are so small that the family is usually able to furnish the required labor. If necessary, short-term daily help can be hired for the plowing and threshing periods. Also, the farmers say that hiring labor to help in vegetable gardening is not profitable, because growing vegetables demands care and skill, and hired laborers do not generally take great pains in their work and it would be too much trouble for the farmer to supervise the laborers constantly. It is significant that both the permanent laborers hired in 1962 worked under the immediate supervision of an operating farmer.

Therefore, labor is usually hired for only a few days at a time, often during busy periods when the farmers need extra help. The following examples make this clear:

Case I. Tang Tsoi-paak farms 11 d.c., with 4 d.c. planted in rice plus winter vegetables, 2 d.c. in vegetables all year, and 5 d.c. planted in sugar cane. He and his wife, who spends most of her time with the household chores, furnish the only labor for the farm. In 1961, he hired 10 labor days to help him transplant and harvest his rice crop. He paid $7 per day without meals and $5 per day with meals. He usually hired women from the poorer families of the village.

Case II. Tang Iok-t'eng farms 3 d.c. of vegetables throughout the year. He and his wife furnish almost all the labor on the farm. This amount of land is the absolute maximum in vegetables that they can farm by themselves. They hired 10 labor days in 1962 to help them hoe (instead of plow) their fields between vegetable crops. They paid $5 plus meals and usually hired women from the poorer families of the village.

Case III. Lam Lik farms 3 d.c. of vegetables. He is the major source of labor for his farm, since his wife is usually kept busy with the household chores and tending their numerous children. In her spare time, she raises pigs. He hired 10 labor days in 1961 to help him weed his vegetables and to help cut and carry the vegetables to the pick-up station on the road. He paid $5 per day, without meals, to a woman of a poor village family.

Case IV. Lam Muk farms 10 d.c., with 7 d.c. devoted to two rice crops a year and 3 d.c. devoted entirely to vegetable gardening. He and his wife work full-time on their land, but at the busy periods of rice agriculture they need extra help to transplant and harvest their crop. In 1961 they hired 30 labor days; they paid $5.50 per day without meals and hired women from poorer village families.

Case V. Tang Shu farms 16 d.c., with 2 d.c. in rice, 5 d.c. in rice plus winter vegetables, and 9 d.c. in lotus root, melons and vegetables. The labor supplied by his family consists of himself, his wife, and his eldest daughter, with some help from the younger children. In 1961, he hired 72 labor days to transplant, harvest, and weed the rice. He usually hires women from the village and pays them $5.50 per day, plus meals.

From these representative examples, it is evident that most labor hired by village farmers is short-term to help in rice transplanting and harvesting and, to a lesser extent, to help at busy times in vegetable gardening. The average daily wage, in 1961, was about $7 per day plus meals for men, and $5 per day plus meals for women.

There are three main sources of farm labor for the farmers: refugee men, boat people from a nearby boat community, and women from the poorer families of the village. Occasionally, some of the poorer farmers of the village will hire out for a day or two, but this is not very common because vegetable cultivation, even on very small farms, keeps the farmers busy all year. Farm laborers are scarce in Ping Shan Hsiang as a whole. A recent census report [4] shows that only 149 out of 1,987 agricultural workers in Ping Shan Hsiang were employed as farm laborers.

No one in the village worked his farm entirely with hired labor. If a farmer rents land, as most do, and then hires labor to work it, the labor costs will eat up his profits; indeed, unless the market price for vegetables is unusually high, he will probably lose money. The best policy, according to the village farmers, is for a farmer to sublet rented land that he cannot farm himself to a tenant; in this way he can be assured of a fixed income, even if it is quite small.

This practice of subletting rented fields for a profit is a recent phe-

[4] Barnett, 1961:Vol. III, p. 61, Table 409.

nomenon, resulting from the rise in rents on land suitable for vegetable farming. The refugee farmers are willing to pay high rent, because in the New Territories land is quite scarce and much in demand.
The *pen-ti* farmers therefore rent land from their ancestral hall and
make money by subletting it at a higher rent to outsiders.

Men are the major source of labor on the family farms. Women, especially younger women with children, must spend most of their time
on household chores and in caring for the children. Young married
women with children are able to work full-time on the farm only if the
husband's mother or another female relative is living with the family;
the older woman can take care of the house, cook, and care for the
children, leaving her daughter-in-law free to work in the fields. If there
is no one to help the farmer's wife, she may work part time on the
farm, but she leaves for the fields in mid-morning, after finishing her
chores, and returns home from the fields early in the afternoon to prepare the evening meal. Most housewives are not able to participate
fully in farm work until one of their daughters becomes old enough to
care for the younger children and to help with household chores. This
is one reason why Chinese mothers prefer to have a daughter as a first
child.

There are only two joint farm families, consisting of two married
brothers with their wives and children, in the village, but they are
among the most prosperous and successful. In both families the men's
mothers are alive and take care of the household and the children, and
the wives are free to work full-time in the fields. The work team thus
consists of the two men and their wives; they are much more effective
as a team than if the two couples worked their land separately. The
joint farm family, even with its obvious economic advantages, is not
common in the village because jealousy and friction between the two
couples over such things as the work load, children, and finances,
almost always force the brothers to divide the family, especially after
the death of the grandmother.

Of the village farm families, 12 are nuclear families; 18 are stem
families (nuclear plus 1 of the husband's parents) ; 2 are joint families;
4 are headed by widows or widowers; and 6 are broken nuclear
families of diverse composition. Of the 18 stem families, 15 have the
husband's mother living with the family.

As I have mentioned previously, the children of the farm families
help much less now than they did in prewar days. Many of the
daughters in farm families help their parents on the farm only until
they marry, or until they go to work in the city as factory workers or
servants. Continuity between father and son on the family farm is also
disintegrating, since many of the younger men are moving into non-

agricultural occupations. The loss of the children's labor has under-
mined the farm family's function as an integral productive unit and
has placed more of the labor burden on the parents.

Women perform all the agricultural tasks that men do, even plow-
ing the fields when their husbands are abroad or at work in the city.
Younger children are given lighter tasks, such as tending the family
cow or buffalo. The following examples are typical of the daily routine
of the village farmers:

Case I. Tsoi Paak gets up in the morning at 6:20 A.M. From 6:30
until 7:00, he is at the village market in front of the ancestral hall
buying vegetables and meat for the morning meal. At 7:00, he returns
home and goes to work in his fields, which are nearby. He works
steadily in the fields until noon, at which time he returns home to eat
the morning meal prepared by his wife. At 12:30 P.M. he returns to the
fields and works there until 3:00. At that time he walks over to the
village teahouse, located about a quarter of a mile away on the main
road, where he has tea and Chinese pastry or buttered toast. He is
joined in the teahouse by some other farmers of the village, who take
a tea break at the same time every day. After tea, Tsoi Paak returns to
his fields where he works until dusk, which, in the summer months, is
about 8:00 P.M. He then goes home, takes a bath, and eats dinner.
Throughout the year his routine is almost the same except for a few
days off for the major Chinese holidays, such as Ch'ing Ming and New
Year.

Case II. Lam T'im, a poor farmer of the village, goes to work at 7:30
in the morning and works in the fields until noon, when he goes home
to eat. At 1:00 P.M., he returns to his fields and works until dark.

Case III. Tang Shu rises at 6:30 A.M. in the summer and at 8:00 in the
winter. He goes directly to his fields and works until 11:00 A.M., when
he returns home to eat his morning meal. He rests from 11:30 until
1:00 P.M., and then takes time for a tea break with his friends in the
local teahouse. After tea he returns to the fields and works until dusk.

On the average, the village farmers work ten hours a day during
most of the year. In the summer they work a little longer, and in the
winter they do not work quite so long. Their work day is broken up by
the midday meal and by a tea break in the afternoon. This agricultural work pattern is different from that of the prewar days. As one of
the older farmers related:

In the old days the whole family went to work in the fields. Even if
all of the family members did not work, they had to go there to eat because the noon meal was always carried to the fields to save time. The

meal was usually prepared and carried to the workers by the farmer's wife, his daughter, or his aged mother. This practice is still carried on by some of the poorer farm families of the village.

In the old days we also had a snack of sweet potato and rice congee at about three o'clock in the afternoon. Now many of the farmers can afford to go to the teahouse. Sometimes we buy soft drinks and take them to the fields to drink.

The added luxury of being able to take tea in the afternoon is much appreciated and enjoyed by the farmers, who always cite this as one example of their improved situation. The farmers gather informally at the teahouse and talk over the latest market information or catch up on the latest gossip. The life of the farm woman has also improved, although it is still by no means easy. Formerly, the women had to make and mend all the clothes for the family; now old clothes are thrown away and new ones are purchased from the market-town shops. In the old days, the woman had to carry water from the village wells; nowadays many farm households have running water. However, in spite of these improvements, most girls do not want to marry farmers because they know their lives will be difficult.

The improvements in the lives of the village farmers are, of course, the result of increased income, which allows a higher standard of living—better housing, better food, and a better education for their children. In addition to these larger benefits, the farmers also enjoy some of the small luxuries of life, such as expensive American cigarettes and transistor radios which they listen to while working in the fields.

Land Rent

The great majority of Ping Shan farmers rented all or at least part of their farm land, and thus land rent is a factor in the farm economy important enough to deserve detailed consideration. Of the 42 farmers surveyed, 35, or 83.3 per cent, farmed only rented land; 5, or 11.9 per cent of the sample, owned part of their farms and rented the rest; and only 2 farmers, or 4.8 per cent, owned all of their farms.

Although most farms were made up entirely of rented land, the whole farm was rarely rented from the same landlord. Usually small parcels of land, consisting of three or more fields, were rented for a lump sum. The fields in these parcels were of both good and bad quality because otherwise, according to the village farmers, no one would rent the poorer fields. Usually, then, each farm was composed of several parcels of land rented from different landlords and located in different areas around the village.

Of the 62 land parcels rented by the farmers in the sample, 19 were

Ping Ha Road

Hang Mei village

Central ancestral halls of Ping Shan

A village lane

Village farmers: old and new style of d

The interior of a village store

A village woman   A village broom-maker

The interior of a home of a wealthy villager

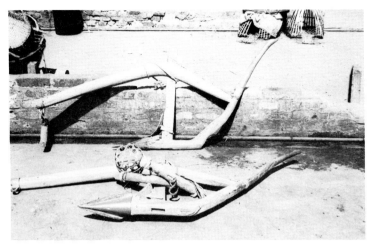

A traditional plow

A harrow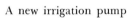

A "wind machine"

A new irrigation pump

Watering cans

rented from private owners, 42 from ancestral estates in Hang Mei, and 1 from a Hang Tau ancestral hall. Ninety-one d.c. of land were rented from private landlords, while 189 d.c. were rented from ancestral estates. It must not be construed from this that most farmers in the village rented land from the ancestral hall to which they belonged, for they did not. Most large ancestral estates in the village belonged to wealthy lineage segments like the Six Families, which contained few farmers. On the other hand, most farmers in the village were from relatively poor lineage segments that owned only small ancestral estates. Thus, most farmers in the village and in the two adjoining villages represented in the sample rented land from the large Hang Mei ancestral estates in which they had no share. Only 8 parcels, containing 45 d.c. of land, were rented from ancestral estates in which the farmers had a share. Twenty parcels, comprising 61 d.c. of land, were rented from ancestral estates in which the farmers had no share, although the ancestral estates and the farmers were of the same village. Thirteen parcels, containing 61 d.c. of land, were rented from ancestral estates in Hang Mei by farmers from the two adjoining villages of Tong Fong and San Tsuen. And one parcel of land of 10 d.c. was rented from a Hang Mei ancestral hall by an outsider vegetable farmer. Although the farmers of the village rented most of their land from ancestral halls in the village, they formed only a small percentage of the tenants of the large ancestral estates of Hang Mei, most of whom were from other villages and lineages in the surrounding countryside.

Most of the *pen-ti* farmers have rented the same fields for years or even generations, and the amount of rent they pay continues to be based on the old agricultural system of two rice crops a year (and no vegetable crops), in spite of the fact that most of the village land is now devoted to vegetable growing, which produces a much more valuable crop per unit than does rice agriculture. The amount of rent per field is actually figured in "rent piculs" [5] of rice. Those farmers who continue to grow rice may use a portion of their crop to pay their rent, whereas those who now grow only vegetables usually pay the cash equivalent at the prevailing market price of the rent piculs due on their land. If land is rented to new tenants (especially outsiders) for vegetable growing, the traditional rent is often considerably increased.

[5] A picul is a unit of weight equivalent to 133 lbs. One picul = 100 catties; and 1 cattie = 1.33 lbs. A "rent picul" is slightly heavier than an ordinary picul, and is equivalent to 177 lbs. An ordinary picul is the standard unit of weight used to measure everything except the rice that the tenant pays his landlord as rent. It is not clear how this heavier rent picul originated, but it has been an established practice for the villagers to pay their land rent in "rent piculs" for as long as they can remember. The rent picul may have been created by the Tangs and other powerful landlords in the New Territories to exploit the weaker lineages of the area, but this is only speculation.

The new tenants usually pay their rent in cash, and, at present, the rent charged by village landlords on vegetable fields rented to out-siders varies from a minimum of $100 to a maximum of $400 per d.c. per year, depending upon the quality of the field.

The yield of rice land in the Ping Shan region varies greatly from field to field depending upon the fertility of the soil, the presence or absence of water for irrigation, the amount of fertilizer applied, and the amount of labor expended. I did not make a systematic investiga-tion of rice yields in Ping Shan, but I did obtain a number of esti-mates on yields from a few experienced farmers in the village. Their estimates were fairly consistent as to the average rice yields produced on the different qualities of paddy land. The general consensus was that the poorest rice land produced about 2.1 piculs per d.c. per harvest, or about 4.2 piculs of unhusked rice per year. Estimates as to the yield of medium grade, or average fields, ranged from 2 to 3 piculs per d.c. per harvest, or from 4 to 6 piculs per year. For the best rice fields, estimates of yields ranged from 6 to 10 piculs per d.c. per year, with 4 piculs per harvest and 8 piculs per year the most common estimates. Averaging all qualities of land together, the farmers esti-mated that most land in the area produced a yield of 3 piculs per d.c. per harvest and 6 piculs per year.

Figures given in the annual report of the Hong Kong Department of Agriculture and Forestry for 1958–59,[6] a normal year, indicated that the average yield on rice land in the colony was approximately 2.7 piculs per d.c. per harvest, or 5.4 piculs per d.c. per year. In its report for the year 1960–61, a year in which there was not sufficient spring rain to allow the planting of the first rice crop on most land in the colony, the same department presented figures giving the average rice yield as 1.9 piculs per harvest, or 3.8 piculs per d.c. per year.[7] The figures given for a normal year are slightly lower than the average yield estimated for Ping Shan, perhaps corroborating the claim of local farmers that Ping Shan fields are better than the average fields of the colony.

For the village of Nanching, C. K. Yang (1959 b: 127) reports that the average yield per *mow* per harvest varied from 2 to 4.5 piculs per harvest and from 4 to 9 piculs per *mow* per year. The most common figure in Nanching was 3.5 piculs per *mow* per harvest, or 7 piculs per *mow* per year. These are roughly the same estimates as those given for Ping Shan. Both estimates are higher than the figures obtained from the Department of Agriculture of Hong Kong.

Information on rents paid on Ping Shan farms was available for 36 of the 42 farms surveyed, comprising approximately 285 d.c. of land.

[6] Director of Agriculture and Forestry, 1960:Appendix 3, p. 72.
[7] Director of Agriculture and Forestry, 1961:Appendix 3, p. 47.

The total amount of rent paid by the farmers on this land was 536 piculs of unhusked rice, or 403 rent piculs of unhusked rice. These figures give an average rent of 1.9 ordinary piculs, or 1.4 rent piculs, of unhusked rice per d.c. per year. The distribution of the amount of rent paid per d.c. by the village farmers is shown in Table 14. As this table indicates, there was a great variation in the amount of rent paid per d.c. per year, although the majority of the farmers paid between 1.1 and 2.0 rent piculs. This variation, however, is due not so much to differences in crop yield as to other factors, such as the fertility of the field, the availability of water, and the distance of the field from the village.

TABLE 14

DISTRIBUTION OF RENTS PAID ON PING SHAN FARMS IN 1962

Average Rent per D.C. per Year (in rent piculs)	Number of Farms
Less than 1.0	2
1.0–1.5	18
1.6–2.0	10
2.1–2.5	3
2.6–3.0	1
3.1–3.5	1
3.6–4.0	1
Total	36 [a]

[a] The rent paid on 6 farms in the survey is not known. Based on the above figures for 36 farms, the average rent paid per d.c. per year is 1.4 rent piculs, or 1.9 standard piculs.

Strangely enough, paddy fields still have a higher average rent in the Ping Shan sample than highland fields, which are now mainly used for growing vegetables. Whereas the average rent on all fields in the sample was 1.4 rent piculs per d.c. per year, the average rent on paddy fields is approximately 2 rent piculs per d.c. per year, or an average of about 45 per cent of the rice produced on the field. This is because the highland fields were traditionally less valuable than the paddy fields and commanded a lower rent. Even though most of the highland fields are now planted in vegetables; the rents charged on them has not kept pace with their increased value.

In no case does the rent paid on a field exceed 50 per cent of the crop produced, and the figure is that high only in abnormal years when there is a dispute between landlord and tenant over the total crop yield. In bad years, when adverse weather conditions limit rice production, tenants request a reduction in rent. The tenant usually invites the landlord to inspect the field to verify that rice production is below normal. Ordinarily the landlord then grants the tenant's request; if, however, he does not, both landlord and tenant are present at harvesttime, and the crop is divided equally between them. In those years when the spring rains do not come and the farmer is unable to plant the first rice crop, it is customary for the landlord to charge 60 per cent of the original rent (the rent is not cut in half, since it is widely assumed that, in the absence of a first crop, the second crop will be better than usual).

Several villagers reported that in the days before the British assumed control of the New Territories the landlords demanded even higher rents in abnormal years. In crop divisions, for example, they were said to have taken 60 per cent, leaving only 40 per cent for the farmer. And, in the years when there was no first rice crop, they were said to have charged 70 per cent of the usual rent, instead of the 60 per cent they now charge. The village farmers said that the landlords had reduced these rent requirements because they were afraid that the tenants would complain to the government and that trouble would ensue. This may or may not be true, but if it is, it is one example of the way in which the British government has restricted the social, political, and economic domination of the weak lineages by the wealthy, landowning lineages in the New Territories.

There is one further example of the growing independence of tenant farmers. Before the war, it was common practice in Ping Shan for a tenant who rented a large amount of land to present a duck, in addition to the rent, to the landlord or to the elder who administered the ancestral lands. This custom is no longer widely practiced; with a few exceptions, tenants are now refusing to give this extra symbolic tribute.

The Economics of Rice Farming

Given the figures above for the average yield of rice land and the average rents paid on rice fields, it is possible to present a rough estimate of the economics of rice farming based on the cultivation of one d.c. of average rice land for one year (see Table 15). On the basis of this analysis, Ping Shan farmers can make approximately $107 on one d.c. of rice per year. It should be noted that credit was given for the sale of rice straw (used as fuel) at the current market price, even though most farmers use the fuel themselves and do not sell it on the market. Also, the cost of the farmer's labor is not figured in the analysis. The average amount of labor required to produce two crops a year on one d.c. of land in Ping Shan is, according to village farmers, about

13 labor days. If this labor is figured at $6 per day, the current wage scale, the value of labor would be $78. If the cost of labor is subtracted from the net profit, the adjusted net profit amounts to only $29 on one d.c. of rice for one year.

TABLE 15

THE ECONOMICS OF RICE FARMING

Expenses:	
Seed (seven catties per crop)	$ 10
Fertilizer	40
Depreciation of farm tools	1
Rent (2.7 piculs of unhusked rice)	99
Total	$150
Income:	
Rice (6 piculs @ $37 per picul)	$222
Rice Straw (3.5 piculs per crop, 7 piculs per year	
@ $5 per picul)	35
Gross income	257
Minus expenses	150
Net profit	$107

It is clear then that the farmer can make very little money by growing rice on rented land. If he owns his own land, his total profit, not counting labor costs, is approximately $206. However, since most village farmers do not own their own land, the net profit of $107 is the amount actually made from one d.c. of rice per year by the overwhelming majority of the farmers.

Economics of Vegetable Growing

It is much more difficult to present a representative picture of the expenses and profits involved in vegetable growing than in rice agriculture. There is a bewildering array of vegetable crops, all of which have different market prices that fluctuate not only from year to year but from month to month. The vegetable farmers themselves do not keep any systematic records of their expenses and profits, and they have difficulty even remembering how much they made from a given crop in the previous year. When asked to give an estimate of the average profit made on one d.c. of vegetable land a year, most farmers flatly refused, saying that there were simply too many variables involved. In fact, the village farmers said that it was impossible to construct a reasonably accurate picture of the average profits made in vegetables.

Nevertheless, with these difficulties in mind, I have made an attempt to present an ordered picture of the economics of vegetable growing, since this is the major source of income for the village farmers. It must be noted that the following analysis consists of nothing more than the best guesses possible under the circumstances.

According to a number of detailed estimates by village farmers, the average weight of one crop of vegetables produced on one d.c. of vegetable land was 32 piculs. Further, in the annual reports of the Hong Kong Department of Agriculture, the average wholesale market price for all vegetables sold through the Vegetable Marketing Organization was $21 per picul in 1959–60, and $25 per picul in 1960–61.[8] The year 1960–61 was a fairly good year for vegetable farmers because the weather was ideal and market prices were high. Therefore, in this analysis a conservative figure of $20 per picul will be used as the average market price paid for vegetables in the colony. If the average yield is about 32 piculs and the average market price is $20 per picul, then the income from one d.c. of land planted in one vegetable crop is about $640; if farmed intensively, with five crops a year, one d.c. then yields a total gross income of $3,200 annually. Using these estimates, I think Table 16 gives a good approximation of the current situation.

TABLE 16

THE ECONOMICS OF VEGETABLE GROWING

Expenses:	
Seeds (average of $5 per crop, 5 crops per year)	$ 25
Fertilizer @ $40 per crop	200
Rent (2 rent piculs per year)	100
Insecticide	80
Marketing commission (17 per cent of total sales)	544
Total expenses	$ 949
Income: [a]	
Vegetables ($640 per crop, 5 crops per year)	$3,200
Minus expenses	949
Net profit	$2,251

[a] This is an optional estimate of profits on 1 d.c. of vegetable land where the land is worked at maximum intensity.

Among the variables involved in estimating the amount of profits obtainable from vegetable gardening are the amount of labor applied to the land and the market sense of the farmer. A skilled and hard-working farmer can make as much money on 2 d.c. of land as a less

[8] Director of Agriculture and Forestry, 1960:Appendix 4; Director of Agriculture and Forestry, 1960:Appendix 4, p. 48.

energetic farmer with no market sense makes farming twice this amount. He does this first by increasing the intensity of his labor application, thus offsetting the greater amount of land available to other farmers; and, second, by planting 4 to 8 crops a year of fast-maturing vegetables that bring high market prices. This in general is the farming pattern of the outsiders, who often make more on a few d.c. of land than the *pen-ti* farmers make on 10 or 15 d.c., since the farmers with more land have to grow slow-maturing vegetables that require less labor and which also have a lower market price. (As we have seen, most farmers cannot afford to hire additional labor because of its high cost.)

Since the average-sized farm in the village is 7 d.c., it is clear that most of the farmers do not farm small enough farms to allow the maximum profit per d.c. in vegetable gardening. Consequently, most farmers do not average as much profit on their vegetable fields as is estimated above. The income of *pen-ti* farmers is probably closer to $1,000 or $1,500 per d.c. of vegetable land, or about half the profit per d.c. that the refugees make on their fields.

According to estimates given by several farmers, the maximum amount of land that an average family of five (a man, his wife, and three children) can farm without hired labor is 3 or 4 d.c. of vegetable gardens, 8 to 10 d.c. of rice plus winter vegetables, or 12 d.c. of rice. If a farmer plants an entire farm of 12 d.c. in rice, his total net income for the year, after rent is deducted, will be 12 times $107, or about $1,284. Another farmer, planting 8 d.c. in rice and 3 d.c. in winter vegetables, will make $856 from his rice crop and $1,500 from the winter vegetables (figured at $500 per winter vegetable crop per d.c.), a total income of about $2,356 for the year. On the other hand, if a third man farms 3 d.c. intensively in vegetables, as most outsiders do, he can have an income of $6,753 per year (three times $2,251). Clearly, the rapid shift to smaller farm size and intensive vegetable gardening makes good economic sense.

The following examples of the actual income made by growing various crops on village farms confirm, in general, the accuracy of the estimates given above.

Case I. Tank Tak in one year made $2,180 profit growing vegetables on one d.c. of land. He said that the average income from intensive, year-round vegetable farming was about $1,500 per d.c. per year. He also estimated that one can make about $690 in one year growing two crops of rice plus winter vegetables, if the land is owned by the farmer.

Case II. An outsider vegetable farmer near the village made, according to him, over $2,000 profit per d.c. on 3 d.c. of land in one year. He also said that he made $1,000 one year growing watercress on one d.c.

Case III. Tang Neng said that in 1961, a good year, if you grew vegetables the entire year you could make at least $1,000 per d.c., and could possibly make as much as $2,000 per d.c., if you were lucky.

Case IV. Tank Sam said that the average refugee farms about 2 d.c. of land and makes about $1,800 profit per d.c. per year.

Case V. Tang Paak said, "We farm vegetables now. Even if the average market price is as low as ten dollars per picul, as it has been this year (1962), we can make a good living. When the prices are higher and we are lucky to hit the market at just the right time, we can make a lot of money."

Farm Income

The farmers were by far the most friendly and cooperative group in the village, and thus I was able to question them directly on their income, a subject I was not able to discuss with any other group. Of the 42 farmers surveyed, only 7 refused to disclose information on their income. The results of the survey confirm that the economic position of village farmers has improved greatly since the war. They are no longer the poorest group in the village; on the whole, they are as well off as any other segment of the village population.

The distribution of farm income in Ping Shan is presented in Table 17. In the survey, the farmers were asked to give their incomes for 1961 and 1962; the income figures in the table represent an average for those two years.

Farm incomes in 1961 and 1962 ranged from $300 per year to as much as $9,600. The largest income group (8 farmers) earned between $2,501 and $3,000 a year, or from $200 to $250 a month. Slightly more than half of the farmers (51 per cent) had an income of $3,500 or less per year, or less than $300 per month.

The average income for 1961, a very good year for vegetable growing, was $4,621 per farm. In 1962, a bad year because of unfavorable weather conditions, the average income per farm was only $3,941, a drop of about 15 per cent. The combined mean income per farm for the two years was $4,281, or about $357 per month per farm (this would be the equivalent of US $764 per year, or US $64 per month).

It should be noted that these figures represent income from the sale of farm produce only, and do not include income obtained from other sources, such as land and house rent, shares from the ancestral estates, or income from other members of the family engaged in nonagricultural occupations. This supplementary income assumes large propor-

TABLE 17

DISTRIBUTION OF FARM INCOME IN PING SHAN

Yearly Income (in HK$)	Number of Farm Families [a]
300–1,000	2
1,001–1,500	1
1,501–2,000	1
2,001–2,500	1
2,501–3,000	8
3,001–3,500	5
3,501–4,000	3
4,001–4,500	1
4,501–5,000	4
5,001–5,500	1
5,501–6,000	0
6,001–6,500	1
6,501–7,000	3
7,001–7,500	1
7,501–8,000	0
8,001–8,500	2
8,501–9,000	0
9,001–9,500	1
Total	35

[a] The income for each of the 35 families in this table represents an average of the income reported for the years 1961 and 1962. The average income per family per year was $4,281. This varied from $4,621 in 1961 to $3,941 in 1962.

tions in a few of the farm families, so that the standard of living for some is higher than that suggested by these figures alone.

FARMING AS AN OCCUPATION

In spite of the increasing prosperity of the village farmers, many would rather work at another job if they had the opportunity. The reasons for this can ultimately be found in basic Chinese social values. In the first place, farming, with its back-breaking labor from dawn to dusk throughout the year, has always been considered a low-status occupation in Chinese society, in spite of the somewhat hypocritical traditional Confucian theory that farmers held the second highest position in the social hierarchy, above the artisans and the merchants and just below the scholar-literati group. Farmers are looked down upon by the city people and the upper-class Chinese as superstitious, conservative, and uneducated country bumpkins, and they frequently encounter this attitude now that they have more direct contact with urban Chinese. The village farmers are even looked down upon by the outsiders resident in the village, many of whom are urban Chinese originally from Canton or Hong Kong.

The young people of the village, many of whom are well educated and have had contact with urban Chinese and Western standards, have adopted this attitude of disdain and are increasingly reluctant to take up such a low-status occupation. They desire both wealth and social mobility, and these can be realized only in the nonagricultural sector of the Hong Kong economy. In the postwar years, this sector has been able to furnish jobs for the rural population. These jobs are more popular than farming because they are higher status occupations. Moreover, the work is not as physically demanding, and the income, although it may be less than a successful farmer earns, is regular and dependable. It now appears that only a depression in the Hong Kong economy, with an accompanying increase in unemployment, will prevent the young villagers from seeking work in the towns and cities. They will farm only from necessity, not by choice.

The movement of villagers out of agriculture into nonagricultural occupations is one of two significant trends in the agricultural sector of the village economy. Many of the farmers in the village said that they did not expect their sons to follow in their footsteps, and many members of farm families have already moved into nonagricultural occupations. Of the 42 farm families surveyed, 14 had members of the family engaged full time in nonagricultural employment, most of whom were the sons of farmers, although in a few instances the head of the family worked outside the village, leaving the women and children to farm.

There is simply not enough agricultural land available in the New Territories to provide full employment for all of the village population (this statement would hold true for China in general), and the only effective way to provide full employment for the villagers is to create new jobs outside agriculture. At the moment, such jobs are being provided, and if economic development continues at its present rate, the trend away from agricultural into nonagricultural occupations will undoubtedly continue. Even at present, only 23 per cent of the village workers are employed in agriculture. A decrease in the percentage of the work force employed in agriculture is a general trend in every society once its economy moves into what Rostow (1960:9) has called "the take-off stage" of economic growth.

The second significant trend in the agricultural sector of the village economy is the change in agriculture from the old subsistence-oriented two-crop rice economy to a reliance on vegetable growing. This in turn has brought about not only the increasing involvement of the villagers in the wider economic system outside the village, but also a basic change in their orientation. They are no longer "peasants"; now they are more properly described as "farmers" and are more akin to businessmen than to old-style peasants. It is no longer possible for them to "hold the market at arm's length."

THE FARMERS AND THE COOPERATIVE

Ping Shan at present has a local vegetable-marketing cooperative established by the government after the war when the Vegetable Marketing Organization was created. The Ping Shan cooperative is located about a quarter-mile from the village in a handsome new building built with government funds. Most of the Ping Shan farmers sell their vegetables at the cooperative, which is now run by them under the supervision of the government.

It is interesting to note not only how this semicollectivist, government-sponsored organization has fitted into the lives of the village farmers but also the attitudes that the villagers have taken towards it. This question is of special interest because it might offer some hint as to the attitude of the peasantry on mainland China towards the collectivization of agriculture that has taken place since the Communist revolution.

The village farmers have not accepted the cooperative with unmixed enthusiasm. Of the 35 farmers in the sample who offered information on the cooperative, 18 were members, whereas 17 were not. The reason most often given for joining the organization is that it was supposed to make low-interest funds available for the farmers to borrow. However, only once since the cooperative was established in 1955 have funds been available, and the farmers were permitted to borrow only $200 each. Some members of the cooperative joined simply because they felt it was a good organization.

The nonmember farmers advance many reasons for not joining the cooperative, one being that they do not need to borrow money (assuming that loan funds were available), and they do not see any benefit that they personally could derive from membership in the organization. Another reason often given for not joining is that the cooperative, along with the compulsory Vegetable Marketing Organization, was forced upon the farmers by the Hong Kong government and deprived them of the freedom to sell their vegetables as they see fit. This attitude is apparent in the following quotations from village farmers who are not members of the cooperative:

He doesn't belong to the cooperative because he can make more money selling his vegetables elsewhere. He has the freedom to sell his vegetables to anyone he pleases.

I don't belong to the cooperative because I don't need to borrow money and there is no freedom in the cooperative. If you are a member, you must sell your vegetables to the cooperative and you have no freedom to sell them elsewhere.

Tang Kok doesn't belong to the cooperative. He doesn't need to borrow money and since it is a lot of trouble, he doesn't join. He sells his vegetables there anyway.

Fung Hong belongs to the cooperative because he hopes the cooperative will eventually have money to borrow for use as capital.

Many of the farmers are suspicious of the government's motives in establishing both the cooperatives and the Vegetable Marketing Organization. They believe that the government set up these organizations in order to make money from the farmers. This is confirmed for some farmers by the fact that the government deducts about 17 per cent of the farmer's selling price. Many farmers think the government keeps this money as profit; in reality, however, the money is used to pay the operating costs of the cooperative. The suspicious attitude of some village farmers towards the government is evident in the following statements:

They sent notices to the villages. Then they sent out trucks to collect the vegetables. The Hong Kong Government did this because they saw that they could make money. That's the way the Hong Kong Government is.

The government forced the farmers to sell vegetables to the Government Market in Kowloon. All the farmers suffered a great loss from this. Now when we sell our vegetables, for each dollar of the market price we get only eighty-three cents. I don't know what happens to the other seventeen cents. The farmers say that the government makes a lot of money from this.

We don't have to sell our rice through the Government Marketing Organization because the owners of the rice mills had connections with the government, while the vegetable farmers did not.

There are other reasons why half of the village farmers are not members. Some farmers did not join because they do not grow many vegetables. Another reason is that one of the villagers operates his own wholesale business, and many of the farmers sell their vegetables to him, either out of opposition to the government or because they are bound to him by personal ties. Moreover, the private wholesaler sometimes gives a better price than the government. Other farmers who raise certain kinds of produce such as taro, sugar cane, sweet potatoes, lotus root, and peanuts, do not belong to the cooperative since it handles only green vegetables. Consequently, these farmers usually sell their crops directly to merchants in Yuen Long.

The major reason why half the farmers have not joined the cooperative is simply because they can have the benefits of the organization without becoming members. The government requires that all vegetables be sold through the organization, or through licensed brokers, but does not require that all farmers be members of the cooperative. Consequently, nonmembers can sell their vegetables through the marketing organization and receive the same benefits as the members. If the government allowed only cooperative members to sell vegetables through the organization, it is almost certain that most of the farmers would have to join. Until the government makes such a regulation, however, a large number of the village farmers probably will not join.

The farmers, both members and nonmembers, approach the cooperative and the Marketing Organization with a hard-headed and practical question: "What is in it for me?" Those farmers who are members of the cooperative realize the economic benefits of the marketing system, but they are still afraid that they are being exploited by the government in ways that they cannot quite put their finger on. Moreover, many members are not too happy with the way the organization is run. The following quotations are representative of the more common criticisms:

The Ping Shan cooperative does not have money available for the farmers to borrow.

The farmers say that the government does not take proper care of their vegetables and lets them spoil and wilt so that they do not bring a good price on the market.

Last year the cooperative was badly managed. When you cut vegetables in the fields you must have enough baskets to carry your vegetables to the weighing station. Those people who grow only a few vegetables use up more than their share of the baskets so that we large vegetable farmers do not have enough.

In spite of all these criticisms, in 1962 the cooperative and the Vegetable Marketing Organization were established parts of the village farm economy and were accepted or at least tolerated by most of the village farmers. By objective standards, the Vegetable Marketing

Organization and, to a lesser extent, the cooperative have been a complete success and of great benefit to the village farmers. They have, in large part, been responsible for the rapid and easy change from the old system of rice agriculture, which kept the farmers impoverished, to the new system of vegetable gardening, which has allowed them to prosper. They have also solved the marketing problem by permitting the farmers to obtain a greater part of the market value of their crops in direct income. It as been estimated that in the traditional marketing procedures in rural China, before the Communist revolution, the commissions and profits accruing to the middlemen accounted for more than one-half the marketing cost, leaving little profit for the farmers (Ong, 1955:5). This problem had been largely solved in the New Territories mainly through the efforts of the Hong Kong government.

IV
The Ownership and Management of Property

The economic development of Hong Kong, in addition to affecting the occupational structure and the agricultural sector of the Hang Mei village economy, is also affecting the villagers' traditional system of property ownership and management. Basically, the pressure of economic forces has brought about changes in land tenure, and these in turn have brought about a weakening of the lineage system and crucial changes in the structure of interpersonal relations in the economic sphere. Whereas dealings in property ownership and management were formerly based upon personal ties, they are increasingly being based upon impersonal contractual relations.

THE OWNERSHIP OF PROPERTY

Land Ownership

There are two major types of land ownership in Ping Shan: (1) collective landholdings, owned by corporate groups; and (2) private landholdings, owned by a single individual or jointly by a group of brothers.

Collective landholdings in Hang Mei village are of three types: association land, temple land, and land owned in common by kinship groups. Association land is represented in the village by the 0.57 acres owned by Ping Shan Kung So, a political association headed by Ping Shan and composed of numerous villages in the western part of the New Territories. Temple land is represented by the several d.c. of land held in the name of the Hang Mei Village Temple. The income from this land is used to pay for a caretaker and for the materials used for worship in the temple. Like association land, temple land is of negligible importance in the village; most of the collective land is owned by kinship groups—by the lineage or lineage segments.

Altogether, the people of the village own 455.5 acres of land, comprising about 3,900 fields. Few villages in the New Territories own as much land as Hang Mei. Of the Ping Shan villagers, Hang Tau villagers own 86 acres of land; San Tsuen villagers own 7.7 acres; Hung Uk villagers own 5 acres; Tong Fong villagers own 2 acres; Sheung Cheung Wai villagers own 22 acres; Kiu Tau Wai villagers own 10 acres; and Fui Sha Wai villagers own 86 acres, about the same as Hang Tau.

The distribution of Hang Mei land ownership is shown in Table 18. Of the 455.5 acres of land owned by Hang Mei villagers, only 31.8 acres, or 7 per cent of the land, are privately owned, whereas 423.7 acres, or 93 per cent of the land, are owned collectively. Of the 31.8 acres of privately owned land, 4 acres are owned by more than one person—usually by pairs of brothers—and 27.8 acres are owned by single family heads. Only 41 families, or 24 per cent of the families of Hang Mei, own private land; the remaining 131 families own no private land at all.

TABLE 18

HANG MEI LAND OWNERSHIP DIVIDED INTO COMMON LANDS
AND PRIVATELY OWNED LAND

Type of Ownership	Percentage of Village Land	Acres
Common land	93	423.7
Private land	7	31.8
Totals	100	455.5

The distribution of private land ownership in the village is shown in Table 19. Of the families who own private land, 19, or slightly less than half of the 41 landowning families, own less than one-half acre; 9 families own from 0.6 acres to 1.5 acres; and 8 families own from 1.6 acres to 4.0 acres. None of the Ping Shan landowning families could be called "landlords," since the largest private estate consists of only 3.9 acres. There are landlords in the New Territories who own vast quantities of land, but none are to be found in Hang Mei or in any other of the Ping Shan villages.

The value of these small private landholdings, however, should not be underestimated because, at present, well-located land in the New Territories is extremely valuable. It is possible, as some villagers have recently done, to sell two small fields and have enough money to build a new village house worth from $7,000 to $10,000. Also, it is still a matter of social prestige in the village to have "your own number," which is the way the villagers usually speak of land ownership, referring to the number for each landholding on the rent rolls in the Yuen Long District Land Office. Most of the private landowners in the village are members of the Six Families subbranch of the lineage. Since very few members of this subbranch are engaged in agriculture, most of this private land is rented to farmers in Hang Mei and in other villages near the land.

TABLE 19

DISTRIBUTION OF PRIVATE LAND OWNERSHIP IN
HANG MEI VILLAGE [a] (1962)

Size of Private Holdings (in acres)	Number of Holdings
0.0–0.5	19
0.6–1.0	6
1.1–1.5	3
1.6–2.0	2
2.1–2.5	3
2.6–3.0	2
3.1–3.5	0
3.6–4.0	1
Total	36

[a] The number of holdings, 36, is less than the number of landholding families, 41, because, as previously indicated, some holdings are owned jointly by brothers.

The 423.7 acres of collectively owned land belong to 30 different ancestral landholding estates in Hang Mei village. This land, however, is not equally distributed among these estates, as is shown clearly in Table 20. Eleven of the collective holdings of ancestral land, or 37 per cent, are very small, less than 1 acre in size. Fifteen of the holdings, or 50 per cent, are from 1.1 to 15.0 acres. There are 2 medium-size holdings consisting of between 20.1 and 40.0 acres. And there are 2 extremely large ancestral estates, one of which belongs to the Six Families and consists of 178.4 acres, and the other of which is owned by Wai Shan Hall and consists of 119.4 acres. As these figures indicate, a large portion of the collectively owned land, as well as a large percentage of the privately owned land, belongs to the Six Families, giving this group preponderant economic and political power in Hang Mei and in the other villages of Ping Shan.

TABLE 20

DISTRIBUTION OF COLLECTIVELY OWNED ANCESTRAL
LAND IN HANG MEI (1962)

Size of Collective Holdings (in acres)	Number of Holdings
0.1–1.0	11
1.1–5.0	9
5.1–10.0	5
10.1–15.0	1
15.1–20.0	0
20.1–30.0	1
30.1–40.0	1
over 40	2
Total	30

House Ownership

Most of the *pen-ti* villagers own their houses and their house sites, and many have one or more additional houses that they rent out. Altogether, in 1962 there were 119 families in the village that owned houses. Seventy-three of these families owned only 1 house; 27 owned 2 houses; 12 owned 3 houses; 1 family owned 5 houses; 4 families owned 6 houses; and 2 families owned 7 houses.

Nowadays, even the Ha Fu members of the village own both their houses and their house sites. This has not always been the case, for although the Ha Fu always owned their houses, the Tangs retained ownership of the Ha Fu house sites, which they rented to the Ha Fu for $0.50 per year, to cover the tax on the land, and 20 catties of unhusked rice per year. However, since 1930, all of the Ha Fu families have managed to purchase their house sites. Those who bought early paid $25; those who bought later paid $40; and some of the Ha Fu eventually had to pay as much as $100. Now that the Ha Fu own their house sites, they are no longer hesitant to rebuild or repair their houses, and in the last several years many of them have built new houses. Some of the more prosperous Ha Fu families now have surplus houses which they rent to the outsider families.

Of the outsiders living in the village, only one, a curio dealer in Kowloon, has built his own house. He does not, however, own his house site but has leased it for a period of twenty years. All of the other outsiders live in surplus houses owned by village families which they rent on a monthly basis. Naturally these surplus houses have become extremely valuable property, and the demand for housing continues to increase as more and more outsiders move into the village from the urban areas.

Not all surplus houses are rented to outsiders (some are occupied by the sons and second wives of the owners), but those families with houses to rent are receiving a substantial supplement to their incomes. For example, if a family which owns three extra houses can rent each for $70 or $80 per month, its supplemental income would amount to the average monthly wages of an unskilled worker in the colony. Moreover, rents are rapidly increasing in the village. When I moved into the village in the fall of 1961, I paid $100 per month for a new house. This rent was considered very high by the villagers, but when I left in February 1963, my house was rented for $120 per month—even before I had moved out! A small house, next door to mine, was built in the early part of 1962 and was immediately rented to outsiders (one family to each floor) for $120 per month. Overall, in 1962 rents in Hang Mei ranged from $15 and $20 per month for small sheds in the back of the village that once were used by farmers to store straw and keep cattle, to as much as $150 per month for the newly built, "modern-style" houses which have electricity and running water. The average rent for the entire village was $40 per month, but most of the houses that rented for this amount were older and smaller and had been rented to the same tenants for long periods of time. As in the case of land, village landlords are reluctant to raise the rent of tenants who have occupied their houses for several years. Were this not the case, rents would undoubtedly have risen even faster than they have.

The villagers have been quick to seize upon this new source of income, and now everyone in the village with available capital is building houses to rent out. Some of the villagers are even selling their privately owned land to obtain capital. Since Hang Mei is close to the main road and has good bus service, it is an ideal place of residence for outsider families moving into the New Territories, and they are moving into the village as fast as houses are made available for them to rent. Naturally houses are being built as quickly as possible. During the eighteen months that I lived in Hang Mei, eight new houses were built, three of them in the last two months of 1962. Of the eight houses, five were built specifically for renting to outsiders.

The building and renting of houses has become a prime topic of conversation for the villagers. They often discuss such matters as the proper design and height of a house; how to build a house to get maximum income from minimum construction costs; the amount of rental to be derived from each square foot of house space; new government regulations on the building of village houses; and how to get around the government building inspector. The village storekeeper, who prides himself on his business acumen, now carries a steel tape measure in his pocket at all times so that he can measure village houses and house lots. Just before I left the village, he and his brother sold $10,000 worth of land to raise money to build an apartment house on the main road of the village.

The prospects for making money from house rent look even brighter for the immediate future. Eight new factories are under construction near the village, and it is likely that the men who come to work in them will need living space. If this trend continues, the old landowning families of the village will change from landlords living on land rent to landlords living on the rent from houses and apartment buildings!

Land Values and Land Transactions

The Ping Shan people claim to have owned much more land in pre-British times than they do at present. They maintain that many of their tenants fraudulently claimed ownership of their land when the British carried out a land survey soon after they took over the New Territories. According to a report by the then Deputy Land Officer, Bruce Shepard (1900:266–269), when the British first occupied the New Territories, the large and powerful landlord lineages like Ping Shan claimed great areas of land which they had never occupied but which they had leased in perpetuity to others, who undertook the cultivation of the land. These tenants paid a sum of money to the dominant lineages under the impression that this money was a land tax that was forwarded to the government. The landlord lineages, however, regarded this money as rent. Consequently, the Tangs considered these lands to be their own, even though they had no title to the land. The tenants, taking advantage of the confusion during the period of the land survey, claimed the land for themselves. The British generally upheld the claims of the tenants, who were after all in possession of the land, so that the land was registered in the tenants' names. The tenant farmers soon ceased to pay rent to the Tangs, and the land became their property. According to the people of Ping Shan, they lost great quantities of land at this time, and even to this day the villagers can point out large sections of the Yuen Long Valley which they consider to belong to Ping Shan.

In addition to this initial loss of land and rental income at the turn of the century, some private land has been sold by the villagers in the past fifty years. Although there is no information available as to the exact amount of this land, it appears that there are about eleven families from the Six Families group who once had private holdings of land but now own little or none. Some families of the village, tempted by the steadily rising land prices, have sold odd pieces of land in the past few decades, and this trend is continuing as the villagers try to raise money to build houses and to obtain capital for other business ventures. More highland fields have been sold than paddy fields, since government zoning regulations will not permit houses or other structures to be built on paddy land. The effect of these regulations has been to reverse the relative values of highland and rice land, with the prices for highland fields now surpassing those for paddy fields. A paddy field that was worth about $200 per d.c. before the war is now worth from $1,500 to $2,000, whereas a highland field that was formerly worth $100 to $200 per d.c. is now worth $7,000 or more, depending upon its location.

Land is so valuable and so much in demand that it is hard for the villagers to resist the temptation to sell. The men of the village, especially those who own private lands or who have shares in the large ancestral estates, talk incessantly about land deals, and many are engaged, either on a full- or part-time basis, in a land brokerage business. The new economic conditions and the increased land values have changed the traditional regulations governing land sales. Formerly, it was a lineage regulation that land must be offered for sale to members of the lineage before it could be sold to outsiders. However, after the war, outsiders offered more money for land than most villagers could afford. The original landowners were unable to resist the higher prices, and thus the regulation requiring them to sell to a fellow kinsman was overriden.

At present, the villagers still have vast wealth vested in their common landholdings, although there is some indication that they will begin to sell these as well. Some of this land has already been requisitioned by the government for the building of roads and other public works, and in 1961 and 1962 some of the ancestral land had already been sold to private buyers. The ancestral land would probably be sold much more rapidly if it were not so difficult to get all the members of the kin group to agree to the sale. Each member of the kin group is so afraid that other members of the group are secretly making more money from the sale than he is (often a not unfounded suspicion) that he is reluctant to approve the transaction. Nonetheless, it appears that the villagers, using no more foresight in handling their common landholdings than they have in handling their private lands, will not be able to resist the temptation to sell their ancestral lands at the increasingly higher prices that are being offered. If this happens, it will complete the process of land sales that began before the war, and the villagers will ultimately lose much of their heritage.

THE MANAGEMENT OF ANCESTRAL ESTATES

Each ancestral estate of considerable size in the village has a regular system for managing its property. The management system, with some slight variations, is similar in all the kin corporations of the village.

Elders and Trustees

Theoretically, the persons with the most responsibility for managing the ancestral lands within each group are the *chia-chang*, the elders of the group. These are the most senior members of the group in genealogical terms; that is, they are the oldest men in the oldest generation. They are not necessarily the oldest members of the group but, in fact, they are usually elderly men. Since each corporate lineage segment in the village is divided into two or more major branches descended from the sons of the founder of the ancestral estate, each *fang*, as these high level segments within the group are called, has an elder —the most senior member of that branch. He is called the *chia-chang* of that particular *fang*. Since each corporate kin group has two or more *fang*, it will also have two or more *chia-chang*. For example, Wai Shan Hall is composed of three major branches, or *fang*, at the highest level, which are descended from the three sons of the Wai Shan ancestor; Wai Shan Hall, therefore, has three *chia-chang*—one to represent each *fang*. Likewise, the Six Families group have six *chia-chang* because the group is divided internally into six *fang*, descended from the six sons of the ancestor of the group.

Among the *chia-chang* of any particular group, one will be more senior than the others: he will either be of a higher generation than the other *chia-chang* or, if they are all the same generation, he will be the eldest. This most senior elder is called the *ta chia-chang*, the "great elder" of the group, and he has the most power in dealing with ancestral affairs. For example, Yat T'ai Hall is divided into three *fang*. Each *fang* has one *chia-chang* to represent its interests in the wider kin group. The *chia-chang* of one of the *fang* is more senior than the other two *chia-chang*, and therefore he is the *ta chia-chang* of Yat T'ai Hall.

In addition to the *chia-chang*, there are also one or more trustees for each ancestral estate in the village. Unlike the *chia-chang* system, the trustee system is not a traditional institution. It was established in the early part of this century by the Hong Kong government to insure that several reputable members of the kin group would be legally responsible for the ancestral lands. The names of the trustees are registered on the Crown Rent Rolls as the legal owners of the ancestral lands. The trustees are not chosen according to kinship seniority as are the *chia-chang*, but are appointed by the members of each group and are usually among the most prominent and wealthy men of the group. Usually, one or two trustees are appointed by each *fang*, so that in a kin group consisting of three *fang* there will probably be six trustees. Trustees are appointed for life, on good behavior, and after one trustee has died another is chosen by his *fang*; not infrequently, a son is chosen to fill the position left vacant by his father's death.

By establishing the system of trustees, the Hong Kong government naturally limited the authority of the *chia-chang*, forcing them to share their authority with the trustees. As the registered legal owners of the ancestral lands, the trustees were able to control all buying and selling of this property, since they had to sign all of the official papers involved in land transactions. Since there has been so much conflict over the proposed selling of ancestral land in recent years, the government has gone even further and now requires all such transactions to be approved in writing by all male members of the group over sixteen years of age. The buyers of kin-group land also demand that these transactions be approved in writing by all male members of the group because they fear that in the absence of such approval their title to the land might be contested by members of the group who will claim that they had never relinquished their rights to the land. The traditional, almost exclusive right of the *chia-chang* to rent ancestral lands to tenants has also been severely limited because the members of the group, fearing that the elders may gain personal advantages in the form of bribes, no longer trust them to make decisions in these important matters. Decisions involving the renting or leasing of land to new tenants are now made by all adult male members of the group at a special meeting.

The *chia-chang*, however, still have some authority over the ancestral estates. The *ta chia-chang* has the responsibility of announcing and chairing all meetings of the group called to make decisions concerning the management or disposition of the ancestral lands. He is also responsible for posting government notices that have to do with the property of the group and for calling them to the attention of members of the group. The *chia-chang* still must sign all lease agreements concerning the ancestral lands before the contract is valid, and they have the power to renew the leases of existing tenants.

The *chia-chang* of the larger ancestral estates in the village have many opportunities to make semilegal "black money" (bribes or "tips"). For example, when tenants come to the *chia-chang* to get their lease renewed, they usually are required to give the elders a token sum. The traditional sum paid to the *chia-chang* had been $10, but this has increased in recent years. The elders receive even greater sums of money from people who wish to lease land from the estate for the first time.

In recent years, the elders have also received black money from groups within the village who wish to use the ancestral lands in real estate transactions for their own private gain. One group in particular has been quite successful in the past few years in bribing the elders to support their efforts to purchase sections of the ancestral land. Upon receiving the bribes, the elders agree not to oppose the sale of the land and also agree to use their influence in persuading the younger men of the village not to oppose the sale. Many of the younger men of the village, particularly those who are better educated, have lost all respect for these corrupt elders who knuckle under to the powerful men of the village and use their position for their own personal benefit. The *chia-chang* have, of course, always been open to the influence of the wealthy and powerful men of the village, who could bribe or browbeat them into submission. This was true even in traditional times when the gentry, those men who had passed at least the lowest imperial examination, played a dominant role in the management of the ancestral properties of their kin groups, in spite of the fact that this was supposed to be the sole responsibility of the *chia-chang*. The last surviving gentry member of Hang Mei village, who died in 1920, was said to have been the manager of all important ancestral land estates in the village. With the passing of the old gentry in the village, a new gentry has arisen; composed of wealthy and politically powerful men, as well as some gangster elements, this new gentry probably dominates the *chia-chang* even more than the old gentry did.

As has been mentioned above, in the past few years there has been an increasing tendency for power over the common lands to be vested in the entire adult male membership of the group, and not with the elders or the trustees alone. In reality, however, the "democratization" of common-land management has not yet proceeded very far, since most of the poorer and weaker members of the lineage pay little attention to the management of the ancestral estates, and the younger men still usually follow the dictates of their fathers. In effect, then, the management of the ancestral estates is still in the hands of the *chia-chang*, who in turn are often pawns of the powerful men of the village.

The Manager

In addition to the *chia-chang* and the trustees, each kin group also has a manager who keeps the account books, collects the rents, and distributes the income from the group's ancestral estate. The tenure of office for the manager of the ancestral lands varies from one group to another within the village. In some groups the manager serves for only one year at a time, whereas in other groups, one manager may serve throughout his lifetime. Life tenure, however, is not common in the village and is usually found only in the smaller ancestral estates that do not have sizable property holdings. Most "kin-corporations," if they may be called by that term, stipulate that the managership is to be rotated every year among the different subbranches, or *fang*, that make up the group.

For example, in the Six Families group, each of the families, or *fang*, has the right to appoint the manager of the Chap Ng Tsoh property for one year at a time. In the first year, the first *fang* has the right to appoint the manager; the next year, the second *fang* has this right, and so on. According to the villagers, this system insures that no one branch of the group will misuse the income from the ancestral lands for its own benefit. It is also supposed to prevent any one manager from stealing or otherwise misusing the income of the estate.

It is probably no accident that the Six Families and Wai Shan Hall use the revolving manager system, whereas Yat T'ai Hall and some of the other smaller ancestral estates of the village appoint permanent managers. Since Yat T'ai Hall has such a small amount of property, no one is afraid that the manager will misuse the common funds. On the other hand, the Six Families have so much property and money that special regulations are necessary to ensure that no one succumbs to the temptation to misuse funds at the expense of the group. When large amounts of money and property are at stake, none of the villagers trust their lineage brothers, and each *fang* within the lineage segment is suspicious of the others.

The selection of managers for the ancestral estates is more complicated than might appear from the discussion above, because each *fang* of the kin group is in turn divided into several subbranches at a lower level of segmentation. Theoretically, the right to act as manager for the *fang* each time its turn comes around is supposed to rotate among the subbranches within each *fang*. This arrangement, however, is much too complicated, and usually the manager who will represent the *fang* is selected by more informal methods. Some groups draw lots to see who will have the privilege of acting as manager for a particular *fang* during its tenure of management. In other groups, a person who is educated and who knows how to keep accounts may be allowed to serve as manager. Many men of the village, especially the illiterate farmers, do not like to manage the books and are willing to let a better educated "brother" do this for them.

Even if the less educated and the poorer members of the kin group should desire to manage the ancestral properties, they seldom have a chance to do so. Most groups prefer to have a wealthy man serve as manager on the assumption that a wealthy man will be less likely to steal from the rent receipts. Moreover, a wealthy man usually has property in the village in the form of land and houses, so if such a person should abscond with the rent receipts, the group can confiscate his property and his share of income from the ancestral estate to make up for the money he has stolen. Each *fang* of a kin group is responsible as a group to the other *fangs* for the rental funds gathered in the year when it has the responsibility for managing the common property. If a manager from one *fang* steals or misuses the common funds, all the members of his *fang* must make up the loss. Given this rule, each *fang* tries to ensure that the manager appointed to represent it is not only trustworthy but knows how to manage the books.

The stealing and misuse of funds by managers of the ancestral estates is not infrequent in the village. One man, who served as manager one year, ran away with thousands of dollars in rent receipts and has never been heard from. In the neighboring village of Hang Tau, a manager took several thousand dollars of funds belonging to the estate of one of the ancestral halls. Since he was unable to repay this money, all his property and houses were confiscated by his kin group and, as further punishment, he and his son were deprived of their share of the sacrificial pork from the ancestral sacrifices. In 1961, a member of the village, who was managing the Wai Shan Hall property, spent $2,000 that belonged to the ancestral hall and left only an IOU in the account books. His misuse of the funds was apparently kept secret from the rest of the village except for a few elders. One day, an elder of the group who was not on good terms with the culprit disclosed the secret to a young man from a branch of the Six Families that was at that time feuding with the culprit's branch over the disposal of some of the ancestral property. The young man immediately went to the police station and had the culprit arrested. The culprit's younger brother had to replace the funds before the police would release his brother. This case came to my attention when I heard the culprit threatening to beat the elder who disclosed the secret.

Some of the villagers maintain there is no way that a manager can swindle money from the ancestral estate's rent receipts because he has to present the account books for inspection every New Year at a meeting held in the ancestral hall. These books contain a list of all the property owned by the group, together with the amount of rent due on each field and the name of the tenant who leases the field. Attached to the books are the deeds for the property owned by the group and the leases or rental agreements made with each tenant. Every year, the total income and the total expenses are entered into the book, along with a record of how the surplus income of the group was distributed to the members. Theoretically, every male member of the kin group over sixteen years of age has the right to inspect the account books if he wishes to do so. As a further check, the *chia-chang* must sign the book to certify that it is in order. Finally the new manager checks the book before it is handed over to him for the current year, since he does not wish to be held responsible for the errors of the previous manager.

Actually, in traditional times as at present, usually only a handful of men of the group know about the financial affairs of the ancestral estate. It would be quite possible for this small group of elders to appropriate some of the funds for their own use. Some such complicity between the elders and the manager is indicated in the case cited above where the manager for the previous year had left an IOU for $2,000 in the account books. A case did occur in a neighboring lineage where, according to the account given me by a government official, a group of elders systematically swindled funds from the common property of their group. Aside from these cases, however, there is no indication that the swindling of common funds occurred in any of the Ping Shan kin groups. Moreover, if such activities did occur, they would be kept secret from the rest of the village and would be very difficult to detect unless one had access to the account books.

Theoretically the manager receives no remuneration for managing the estate of his kin group, but there are opportunities for able and intelligent men to make some money from their position. The principal way that a manager can profit from his position is to loan out the cash receipts at interest during the year and hope that the loans are repaid in time for him to be able to account for the money at the end of the year. This is a risky venture, but some managers try it. The manager can also use the cash rent receipts as interest-free capital for short-term business ventures during the year. However, most managers do not attempt these practices for fear they will not be able to produce the money at the end of the year. If a manager cannot balance his accounts at year's end, he is completely disgraced before his entire kin group.

A safer way for the manager to make some profit arises from the fact that for every picul of rice (133 catties) he collects from tenants, he is held accountable for only 130 catties per picul. This rule is to allow for spoilage and shrinkage, but if a manager is lucky, he can make some money on the three catties for which he is not held in account.

Chi-hsiu and Chia-fen Land

The ancestral lands are divided into two major categories: the *chi-hsiu* land, and the *chia-fen* land. Land in the *chi-hsiu* category is owned in common by all members of the kin group, and every male member of the group has an equal share in this part of the estate. The rental income from *chi-hsiu* land is used for several purposes: to pay the land tax on the ancestral estate; to pay for the religious sacrifices and ceremonies of the group; to repair the boundaries of the fields in case of flood; and for various welfare activities, such as helping pay the funeral expenses for deceased members of the group. The income left over after paying for taxes and the ancestral sacrifices is divided equally among the male members of the group. The proceeds from the sale of *chi-hsiu* land are also divided in this way, with every male getting an equal share.

During the time of the Ch'ing Dynasty, part of the income from the *chi-hsiu* section of the ancestral lands was used to give a stipend to members of the group who had passed the imperial examinations and achieved gentry status. Every gentry member of the group had a fixed income of so many piculs of ancestral rice per year. This custom was discontinued soon after the overthrow of the Ch'ing Dynasty and the establishment of the Republic in 1911. The change occurred, according to some of the older villagers, when one of the members of the Six Families group, who had received an M.D. degree from a Peking University, returned to the village and claimed his stipend from the common lands on the assumption that his modern university degree was equivalent to the old gentry degree. The other *fang* of the Six Families group objected to this on the grounds that the new degree was not equivalent to the traditional degree. After much argument, they finally refused to give a stipend to the modern university graduate. After this incident, Hang Mei no longer gave stipends from the ancestral lands to the educated men of the village. Moreover, the village does not give grants-in-aid or fellowships to the able students of the village as do some other lineages in the New Territories, such as Kam Tin. In Kam Tin, even primary school students receive a small monthly stipend from the ancestral estate, and other lineages of the New Territories still give prizes to graduates of middle schools and universities.

In contrast to the *chi-hsiu* lands, the *chia-fen* section of the ancestral estate is owned by branches and families and not by individual members of the group. The smaller estates of the village do not have sizable *chia-fen* portions in their ancestral estates, but in the larger ancestral estates, such as those of the Six Families and Wai Shan Hall, the great majority of lands are in this category. The income from the *chia-fen* section of the ancestral land is divided among the members of the group as private income, but each male member does not get an equal share of the income. The income is divided according to the principle of ownership, with the share paid to each branch or family determined by the lines of lineage segmentation. For example, if the founder of an ancestral estate had two sons, the income from the *chia-fen* portion of the estate would be divided into two equal parts, with the two sons getting equal shares. If one of these two sons gave birth to six sons, then his share of the *chia-fen* land income (one-half) would be divided after his death into six equal shares, each of which would consist of one-twelfth of the original estate. If the other son of the founder had only one son, then he would get is father's entire share, or one-half of the original estate. Thus, the members of the third generation of the kin group would share unequally in the income derived from the *chia-fen* land.

This method of division can be seen more clearly in Figure 2. The numbers beside the individuals in the genealogy indicate the portion they receive of the total income from the *chia-fen* section of the estate. This same principle of division is followed when dividing the income from the sale of any piece of land from the *chia-fen* sector.

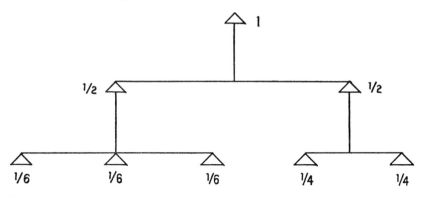

FIGURE 2

Since most of the ancestral lands of large estates are in the *chia-fen* it is immediately apparent that the income and benefits from any ancestral estate are not shared equally by all members of the group. The subbranch of the group having most members will receive a smaller portion of income per capita than those branches having fewer members. This principle of unequal distribution of income from the *chia-fen* lands applies to segments of the group not only at the highest level, but also at the lower levels of segmentation within each subgroup.

Most of the conflicts that arise in village kin groups stem from the fact that the principles of ownership and income distribution are different for the *chi-hsiu* and the *chia-fen* lands. Moreover, as the value of the ancestral land and the income from this land increases, the conflicts become more intense and more numerous. As the following examples of recent conflicts illustrate, it is a general rule that the larger the sum of money at stake, the more conflict among the subgroups that form a kin corporation.

Case I. Wai Shan Hall, at the highest level, is divided into three *fang*. One of these *fang* is again subdivided into two subbranches. Until recently, one of the subbranches was represented by only one old lady, whereas the other subbranch contained a large number of people. These two subbranches according to custom share equally in the income from their *fang*'s portion of Wai Shan Hall's *chia-fen* land. The income of the *fang* is approximately 200 rent piculs of rice per year and this income is divided, according to custom, into two equal shares of 100 rent piculs each. One share rightfully goes to the old lady, while the other share has to be divided among the many members of the other subbranch.

During the Japanese occupation, when times were bad and many people had barely enough to eat, the other subbranch refused to allow the widow to receive her full share of the income. They expropriated all but a little of the rice to divide among themselves. After the war, the widow took her case to the courts and the dispute was decided in her favor—on the condition that she adopt a son as legal heir to her husband. The other subbranch spent a great deal of money in the litigation, which, as is common in cases concerning the villagers of the New Territories, was decided, not according to British law, but according to traditional Chinese custom. The widow did adopt a son and he, at present, is supposedly receiving his full rightful share of the income from the ancestral lands, but I have heard rumors to the effect that the other subbranch was still taking most of the rice and giving him only 20 rent piculs per year.

Case II. The wealthy Six Families group, as the name implies, is divided, at the highest level, into six *fang*. The total membership of the group is approximately three hundred, but this population is not divided equally among the six *fang*. Some *fang* consist of from fifty to one hundred persons, whereas other *fang* are much smaller. The smallest *fang* is the sixth, which contains only three male adults. This *fang* is divided into two subbranches, with one man constituting one subbranch and two men making up the other subbranch. Since the sixth *fang* receives one-sixth of the entire rental income from the *chia-fen* lands of the Six Families vast ancestral lands, and since this income is divided equally between the two subbranches of this *fang*, one man receives one-twelfth of the entire income of the Six Families group. This is in contrast to some of the other *fang*, which must divide the same income among as many as fifty people.

The man who receives one-twelfth of the total income from the ancestral estate has been trying over the past decade to get a court ruling that would divide the lands of the ancestral estate among the various *fang* and then further subdivide the land until every individual member of the group would have his share of the estate as his own private property. It is not difficult to see that if the suggestion of this man were followed, and if the lands were divided along genealogical lines according to the customary rule, he would become an extremely wealthy man overnight. This plan is opposed by those *fang* having many members but is supported by two of the other *fang*, which also have few members. So far, however, efforts to divide the land have been unsuccessful because the populous *fang* have the numerical strength and are thus able to vote down any proposals to divide the land. The *fang* with many members have, however, offered to compromise with those that want the land divided. They will agree to the division of the land if half of the land is divided according to the system whereby every male gets an equal share, with the other half divided according to genealogical lines. The other group has refused to compromise, so the situation, in 1962, remained a standoff.

These examples illustrate the type of conflict that exists within some of the larger ancestral estates. Although the same type of conflict was probably not unknown in traditional times, it has become so intense in recent years that it threatens the very existence of the kin groups. The conflicts within kin groups can, of course, be largely attributed to the increasing value of land on the one hand, and the weakening of traditional values on the other. As a result of these trends, the villagers are more concerned with furthering their individual economic interests than they are with maintaining the collective interest of the group as a whole.

Contradictory as it may seem, however, the intensified conflict between kin group segments has, at least for the moment, served to maintain the integrity of the groups. At present, most kinship groups are held together only because they own common property. As I have mentioned previously, the sale of such property must be approved by every adult male in the kin group. Because various *fang* within a single kin group are often in conflict, it is difficult to get all of the male members of the group to agree to the sale of ancestral property, and thus the property (as well as the kin group) is maintained intact. In the absence of such intense conflict, it seems likely that much of the ancestral property would soon be sold, and the kin group, deprived of its economic base, would cease to exist as an economic and social unit.

Income Distribution

The system for collecting and distributing the income from the *chia-fen* land is extremely complicated. The income from these lands is not, as might be expected, collected together in one lump sum every year and then distributed to the members of the group. To ensure that each constituent branch of the kin group receives an equal and fair income from the common lands, the *chia-fen* land is divided up into as many portions as there are subgroups in the lineage segment that owns the estate. In the Six Families group there are six *fang*, so the *chia-fen* land owned by the group has been divided into six permanent sections, which theoretically yield approximately the same amount of rental income each year. Each *fang* of the group collects the rent from only one of the six land sections each year, but it never collects the rent from the same section two years in a row, since the sections of the *chia-fen* land are rotated from *fang* to *fang* every year. For example, the Six Families group contains six *fang*—1, 2, 3, 4, 5, 6—and, therefore, the *chia-fen* land owned by the group is divided into six portions— A, B, C, D, E, F. The first year, *fang* 1 receives the rent from land portion B, and so on, until, in the seventh year, it again receives the rent from land section A. According to the villagers, this is one method of ensuring that each subgroup will get a fair rental income from the ancestral estate.

The sections of land into which the *chia-fen* land is divided were approximately equal in traditional days when the rental income from the land was fixed, but in recent years rents on some of the fields have increased, so that some sections yield more income than others. Since the ideal is for each *fang* to have approximately the same income each year, an attempt has been made to reestablish the equality (in terms of rental income) of the various sections of the *chia-fen* land. Because the rising rents have occurred mainly on land rented out for cash for the purpose of erecting buildings, growing vegetables, or establishing chicken or pig farms, a common method used by the villagers to maintain the balance of the system is to take this land out of the *chia-fen* portion of the ancestral estate and place it in the *chi-hsiu* part where the increased income can be distributed equally to every male member of the village. A paddy field is then taken from the *chi-hsiu* section to replace the field removed from the *chia-fen* sector. This ensures the equal value of rents yielded by each section of the *chia-fen* land and ensures that each branch of the kin group will have an approximately equal income each year, no matter from which *chia-fen* land section they receive the rent. This patchwork method is certainly no permanent solution to the problem; even at present, the *chia-fen* land sections are somewhat unequal, and they undoubtedly will be thrown further out of balance in the future.

As I have mentioned previously, most of the thirty ancestral estates in the village are quite small and consist mainly of *chi-hsiu* lands. Generally these smaller estates have just enough income to pay taxes and ceremonial expenses, with little or no surplus funds to divide among their members. Consequently, most of the smaller estates are managed more informally than the larger ones. One popular method of management allows each branch of a kinship group to receive all the rent from the entire estate for one year in turn. In that year, the branch that receives the rent is responsible for paying the ritual expenses of the entire group. To make sure that no subgroup attempts to cheat the rest of the group by skimping on the ritual material and the sacrificial pork, the quality of the material that must be furnished every year is fixed. If the branch that receives the rent in a particular year has any income left over after it has paid the land tax and the ritual expenses, it is divided among its members. However, if the harvest is bad one year and not enough rental income is received to cover expenses, then the branch whose turn it is to pay these expenses must make up the deficit from its own pockets.

Private Benefit from the Ancestral Estate

In addition to receiving income from the ancestral lands, there are other ways that members of a group can benefit from their ancestral estates. A common method is to rent land from one's own kin group at a very cheap price and to use this land for agricultural or business purposes. Another method is to rent land cheaply from one's ancestral estate and sublet this land to tenants for a higher rent, pocketing the difference. Several villagers, estimated that approximately one-third of the Six Families' ancestral estate was rented to members of the group who used the land for their private benefit, but this is mere speculation.

One much discussed case of this type concerns Tang San, a member of the Six Families, who rented a large piece of Chap Ng Tsoh land located on the New Territories' main road. In the last few years this land has become extremely valuable because of its good location. Tang San rented this land for $30 per year many years ago when rent was much cheaper. In 1961 he built a new restaurant on this property and is now receiving a sizable income from this business, although he still pays only $30 a year in rent. Other members of the group have grumbled about this low rent because they feel that Tang San is getting the sole benefit of land that belongs to the Six Families as a whole. There has been some talk in the village about raising the rent on the property, but no action has been taken and most likely nothing will be done, since any attempt to raise the rent would only cause conflict within the group. Furthermore, Tang San might demand that the rent be raised on all other land leased to members of the Six Families.

Most members of Hang Mei kin groups, especially the poorer ones, are not able to exploit common lands for their own benefit. Most of the benefits derived from the village ancestral lands are enjoyed by only a small group of powerful men—political leaders, racketeers, and real estate operators—who have connections with low-ranking employees in the District Land Office and with business interests in Kowloon. From these outside contacts this small group of men is able to find out which property held by the ancestral estates of the village is in demand for business purposes. By shady means, such as bribing the elders and other members of the group, they are able to gain control of ancestral property and sell it, at a profit, to the interested outsiders. Such underhanded dealings are kept secret from the other villagers if possible, but even if some of the villagers are aware that a particular group is seeking to use common property for its own private benefit, most of them are afraid to challenge the authority of such powerful men.

I observed one particularly flagrant example of the use of common land for the benefit of private groups within the village in 1962, when a real estate company, formed by the dominant clique of the village and headed by the local political leader, bribed and bullied the members of Wai Shan Hall into selling a substantial amount of ancestral land to their company. The company first enlisted the support of the *chia-chang* and the trustees of Wai Shan Hall by promising them substantial bribes. In return, the elders and trustees agreed to convince the other members of the kin group to sell the land. Various sums of money were then paid to each member of the kin group in return for their signatures on the bill of sale. Those who protested loudest and longest were given more money to still their protests, but most members agreed to the sale for the paltry sum of $20. After the land had been sold to the company, it was then resold, according to previous arrangement, to a city merchant for a substantial sum of money. The village real estate company is said to have made thousands of dollars in this land transaction, and one of the elders was able to buy a gold wristwatch worth $1,200 with his share of the profit from the land sale. It is probable that powerful men have always been able to control the village in such a fashion, but it is only recently that economic conditions have allowed such great profits to be made.

Some of the wealthier members of the village, including the real estate group mentioned above, can also benefit from the ancestral lands in a more legal and aboveboard way through the village custom of calling for bids when there is a dispute over the renting or selling of the ancestral lands. If a member of the group objects to the renting or selling of land either to a member of the group or to an outsider on the grounds that the price is too low, he will usually be challenged to buy or rent the land at the same price. This method is often used by wealthier members of the group to still criticism when they attempt to buy or rent common land; the poorer villagers cannot afford to object to the disposition of the common property because they would not be able to accept the challenge to buy or rent the land themselves at the same price.

One way that poorer members of the group can derive personal economic advantage from the ancestral estate is to bid for the privilege of furnishing the sacrificial pork and other worshipping materials for the ancestral sacrifices. About ten days before the worshipping ceremonies at the ancestor's grave, the manager of the estate will call for bids from members of the group. If a member is successful in his bid, he may be able to make as much as $50. Of course, he has to go to the trouble of buying the pigs, butchering them, cutting them up, and carrying all the worshipping materials to the grave site.

The Management of Common Land—An Antiquated System

The foregoing discussion of the management of the ancestral lands suggests that it is an anachronistic and inefficient system, which does not supply the kin groups with nearly as much income as it should. I made estimates of the potential income of several of the larger ancestral estates of the village, based on the amount of land owned and the average rental that should be received on this land if it were rented only to growers of rice. This is a conservative estimate because, in fact, much of the land is rented to pig and chicken farmers and to vegetable growers, who pay much higher rent than do rice farmers. The actual income of these estates, as reported by knowledgeable villagers, was only about one-half the estimated potential income.

Perhaps the most important reason why the income from the ancestral lands is so low is that the management sytem of these lands is based on older and more traditional economic conditions and has not adapted to the conditions of the postwar years. In the old days, when land values were stable and determined solely by the amount of rice rent a piece of land would yield each year, the ancestral estates required little supervision. The ancestral fields were rented out to the same tenants for generations, and rents were fixed at traditional rates. The landlord groups simply collected their rent piculs of rice once a year. Nowadays, however, the value of the land is increasing rapidly, and much of the land has been converted from rice agriculture to the much more productive vegetable gardening. To ensure that the maximum income can be obtained from each piece of ancestral land, close supervision and careful management are needed.

Unfortunately, however, the management of the ancestral land is still left largely in the hands of the traditional-minded elders who lack the business acumen necessary to manage the estates properly. The elders are usually more interested in the small amounts of "black money" they can exact from tenants than they are in making sure that the group as a whole receives maximum income. There is also a general lack of interest in the management of the common lands on the part of the group members themselves; since the land belongs to everyone, no one pays much attention to its management. Some of the villagers do not even know where most of their kin group's lands are situated!

As a result of this lax system of management, many tenants who rent land from Hang Mei ancestral estates for a few piculs of unhusked rice a year are making substantial profits by subletting their fields to outsider vegetable farmers who are willing to pay much higher rent for the land. Also, many tenant farmers who farm Hang Mei land are now increasing their profits by growing vegetables, yet they continue to pay the traditional rents. The change from rice agriculture to vegetable gardening thus benefits the tenant farmers but not the landlord. This is one reason why the relative economic position of landlord and tenant has almost been reversed in recent years. As one thoroughly disgusted elder from the Six Families group told me, "In the old days, the tenants used to borrow enough money from the landlords to pay for their seed rice. Nowadays, the landlords are going to the farmer to ask for an advance on the yearly rent."

This situation is recognized by some of the villagers. As part owners of the ancestral land, which in the case of the Six Families is worth at least several million dollars, many villagers cannot understand why they are not receiving more than the few paltry piculs of unhusked rice a year. Some of the better educated and more progressive villagers have advanced suggestions as to how the ancestral property could be put to better use. One suggestion, widely discussed in the village, is that the rent receipts from the ancestral lands should be used to purchase income-producing property in the market town, such as apartment houses or shops. Some have even suggested that part of the ancestral property should be sold to raise capital for these investments. The income from town property could be used to increase the personal income of the village families or for welfare purposes, such as furnishing scholarships for the abler students of the village.

These suggestions, however, have met with little or no success. The conservative *chia-chang*, afraid that their authority will be further limited and that their income from managing the estates will be eliminated, oppose all such efforts. These suggestions are also opposed by those powerful groups within the village who are successfully using the ancestral land for their own benefit. The most important reason why such reforms are not adopted is that they depend on the cooperation of the kin group members to promote the general welfare of the group as a whole. But, as I have noted above, the individuals and subbranches within corporate kin groups are so suspicious of each other and so fearful that other members of the group will somehow reap advantages from new arrangements that cooperation and hence innovation are not possible.

This antiquated system of common land management continued to be used in the village in 1962, and there appeared to be very little chance that it would change. Unlike the farmers who have adapted to changing agricultural conditions and the other villagers who have adapted to changing occupational patterns, the system of managing the common lands has simply not been able to adapt to changing economic conditions. There are thus differential rates of effectiveness in the adaptation of the traditional economic structure of the village to economic development; collective interests have adapted much more slowly and much less successfully than have the individual members of the village.

LAND TENURE

Traditionally, the rights to leased land in the New Territories have been divided into two parts: (1) the right to farm the land, which was granted in perpetuity to the tenant; and (2) the right to collect rent on the land, which was reserved by the landlord. Bruce Shepard (1900:266–269), a Deputy Land Officer at the time of the British take-over, described the traditional system of land tenure as follows:

The relation between landlord and tenant is often a complicated one, chiefly owing to the system of perpetual lease. Under such lease the landlords have practically renounced all rights to the exercise of ownership and are contented to do nothing further than to receive rent. They can sell this right of receiving rent, but the land is

otherwise under the absolute control of the cultivators who often sell
their perpetual leases.

The landlord is called the owner of the "Ti Kwat [*ti-ku*]," which
may be termed the right of receiving rent. The tenant is said to possess
the "T'o P'i [*t'u-p'i*]," or the right of cultivation.

The existence of such a system of divided rights to the land is confirmed by the villagers of Hang Mei, although they do not use the
above terms. The villagers say that in traditional times land was conceived of as consisting of two parts: (1) the *mien*, or face of the
land, which "almost" belonged to the tenant farmers; and (2) the
ti, or subsurface of the land, which was owned by the landlord and gave
him the right to collect rent. These terms differ from those used above
by the government writer, but the meaning is almost the same.

This system of tenure was associated with the widely understood
traditional rule in the village that a landlord or a kin group could not
arbitrarily recall land from one of their tenants and rent it to someone
else. Land could only be recalled if the landlord himself or a member of
the kin group which owned the land wished to farm it, but even under
these circumstances it was often difficult to recall land. If a member of
a landlord group wished to recall a piece of ancestral land from a
tenant to farm himself, he would first have to consult the elder of his
ancestral hall who was in charge of renting the land. This elder would
probably tell his kinsman to discuss it with the tenant to see if the tenant was willing to return the land. If the tenant would not agree to
give up his land, the member of the landlord group could probably
not regain it, even though he theoretically had the right to do so.

Land was difficult to take away from a tenant farmer because, for
one reason among others, he and his lineage had effective ways of protecting their rights to the land, including the use of force. Thus, even
if the landlord and his lineage had sufficient force to throw the tenant
off the land, this was not usually done because they knew that the tenant and his lineage might well retaliate with force. And, even if the
tenant did not resort to force, he had other effective ways of protecting
his claim to the land, some of which are evident in the following story
told by a villager.

Once a member of a Hang Mei ancestral hall took some land back
from a Seak Po villager (Seak Po is a village near Hang Mei) and
rented it to a family from Hang Mei.

However, the only good water supply for the field was a pond in
front of Seak Po village, and the Seak Po villagers refused to allow the
Hang Mei farmer to draw water from the pond. Time and time again
the usurper's irrigation ditches would be destroyed during the night

and even part of his crop mysteriously disappeared from the field. Finally, the Hang Mei farmer realized that he could not possibly farm the field so he returned it to the landlord, who in turn, rented it back to the original tenant from Seak Po.

Therefore, in fact as well as in theory, there was a permanent tenancy system in the New Territories in traditional times. As long as the tenant paid his rent, he had a perpetual right to farm the land. Moreover, this right did not cease with the death of the tenant farmer; it was inherited by his sons. It was possible for the tenant farmer to sublet the right to farm his leased land to another farmer. This was not uncommon in traditional days, and consequently many of the record books of the ancestral estates were often hopelessly outdated. The man entered in the books as the renter of the land was quite often deceased, and the actual cultivator of the soil might have been his descendent or someone who had subleased the land from the original tenant.

Under this traditional system of tenure, the landlords usually paid little attention to their land and were content merely to continue collecting the rent. Land sales consisted of selling the right to receive rent from the land, rather than selling the land itself; the villagers spoke of purchasing so many rent piculs, rather than of buying so many d.c. of land. In keeping with this system of tenure, it was a common practice when a landlord died for his sons to keep his estate intact and to divide between them only the rental rice. In this way, the sons avoided the quarrels that invariably arose when an attempt was made to divide the land itself. Moreover, if the inheritance consisted only of one or two fields, it was much better to divide the income from the land than to fragment the fields.

Just as the tenant farmer had the privilege of subletting his right to farm the land, the landlord had the privilege of mortgaging the right to receive rent. The landlord borrowed a lump sum of money; the lender in return was given, as interest, the landlord's right to receive rent or the landlord's share of rent from his ancestral estate until the loan was repaid. This mortgaging system is still in operation in the village. One young man from the Six Families originally had the right to collect a large share of rent rice from his ancestral estate. However, he now receives no rent because his father mortgaged his share to the village storekeeper, who is also a member of the Six Families and who collects a sizable amount of rent from the ancestral land each year as interest for loans that he has made to his kinsmen. The young man can regain his right to collect his share of rent only by repaying the original loan.

For several reasons, the divided tenure system was well suited to the traditional, prewar agricultural situation in which economic conditions remained stable. First, land was used primarily for rice cultivation and rented out for 40 to 50 per cent of the rice it produced each year. Because there was no change in farming technology for generations, the productivity of the land did not increase, and rents, long fixed at the maximum amounts based on rice cultivation, also remained stable. Second, before the war, land was not so scarce and a situation in which tenants continually were led to bid against one another was unknown. Under these circumstances, there was really no good reason for the landlord to change tenants.

In the postwar economic situation, however, this system of land tenure is anachronistic. Land has become scarce and more valuable, and, owing to certain technological innovations, the productivity of the land has greatly increased. The landlord, aware of the increased value of his property, now wishes to receive higher rents, or he wishes to sell his land for industrial, commercial, or other purposes to buyers from the city. The landlords have gradually adopted the modern Western concept of land ownership, which works on the assumption that a person either "owns" certain property or he does not. The tenant farmers, pressured by the landlords to give up land that they and their families have farmed for generations, usually assert their traditional rights and flatly refuse to get off the land unless they are compensated by the landlord. This contradiction between the traditional and modern systems of land ownership and tenure has been the cause of endless conflict and litigation between the landlords and their tenants.

In most cases the tenant's traditional rights have been upheld by the government and even the landlords themselves recognize to a certain extent that the tenant has rights in the land. Usually, the tenant tries to demand as much money as possible to compensate for giving up the land, and sometimes he gets a larger share of the purchase price for the land than does the landlord! Often the tenant demands so much money that the landlord ultimately decides that he cannot afford to sell the land. Two examples will serve to illustrate the difficulties involved in selling land.

Case I. Yat T'ai Hall (a Hang Mei ancestral Hall) owned a piece of land near Sha Kong village which the government requisitioned for the purpose of building a road. The tenant farmer was an old villager from Sha Kong whose family had farmed the land for generations.

In the final settlement, Yat T'ai Hall received thirty cents per square foot for the land from the government. The government paid the tenant farmer eighteen cents per square foot for his rights in the land and an additional fifteen cents per square foot to pay for the crops that he was growing on the field. In this case the tenant received more money from the land sale than Yat T'ai Hall, the theoretical owner of the land!

Case II. The Six Families wished to sell a large piece of property located on the main New Territories road, about three miles from the village, to a buyer from Hong Kong. This buyer offered the Six Families HK $2.50 per square foot. The group of tenant farmers who were farming the land then demanded fifty cents per square foot to compensate for their rights.

The Six Families considered this demand to be so high that they finally decided simply not to sell the land. It was said that the Six Families did not attempt to force the tenants off the land because they knew the government would support the claims of their tenants.

The landlords are also experiencing difficulties in trying to recall land from a traditional tenant in order to rent it to another tenant (usually a refugee vegetable farmer) who is willing to pay more rent. To date, the private landowners have been more successful than the collective landlords in obtaining higher rents, primarily because they supervise their property more carefully. Nonetheless, some of the collective landlords are beginning to demand higher rents, although they usually affect a compromise with the original tenant that allows him to retain possession of the land. Usually, if an elder gets a higher bid to rent a certain piece of land, he will inform the tenant of the new offer and make an arrangement whereby, in return for a little "black money," the original tenant can pay one-half of the increased rent bid by the outsider and still get his lease renewed.

The villagers say that in traditional times it was not nearly so common as it is at present for a written contract to exist between landlord and tenant. In the last few years, however, the economic temptations for the landlords to raise rents and take back land from traditional tenants has become so great that the tenants, in spite of the fact that the government has been upholding their traditional rights, are rapidly realizing the importance of having some legal document to protect their interests. Because land is scarce and rents are high, a tenant farmer faces economic disaster if he loses his land. It is not, however, only the tenants who are demanding written contracts; it is also in the landlord's interest to have written contracts with his tenants for a stipulated period. This in turn makes it easier for the landlord to evict the tenant from the property if he wishes to sell it or change tenants.

Like many other sectors of the village economy and society, the system of land tenure is in a state of flux, with a strong trend away from

traditionalistic relations and towards more specific and defined contractual relations. The reason for this change is that the old system,
depending as it did upon traditional values and customs, is unable to
meet the demands of the new economy, which stresses individual self-
interest in the market as the dominant type of economic action and
which rests upon functionally specific impersonal relations epitomized
by the written contract. By its very nature, the new economy weakened
traditional values and customs, and because these are no longer capable of regulating the relations between people and land, they must
give way to a new system. At present, the old system is rapidly
breaking down; new institutions are developing to take the place of
the old, but it will be some time before they are established well
enough to serve as a reliable guide.

V

The Penetration of the Market

The penetration of urban industrial and commercial influences into the rural areas of the New Territories in the last two decades has reduced the self-sufficiency of the village economy. The villagers are being increasingly caught up in a network of commercial relations that extends outward from the village, not only to the market town and the urban area of the colony, but also to the world market. Economic development has brought increased purchasing power and prosperity to the villagers and has enabled them to take advantage of new goods and services. The demand for these new goods and services has been created through the villagers' contact with the outside world. The villagers now buy fans made in Japan, watches from Switzerland, and water pumps from the United States. No longer is the economy of the village subsistence-oriented; nowadays almost everything the villagers use, from food to fertilizer, is purchased in the market. No longer are the villagers able to hold the market at arm's length, for it has become an integral and indispensable part of their lives.

THE VILLAGE MARKET

In the New Territories there are many markets of various sizes and kinds. The largest and most important are the market towns with their permanent shops, teahouses, handicraft establishments, and stores. There are also specialized markets, such as the fish markets located in the coastal fishing villages. In addition to these larger markets, almost every sizable cluster of villages, such as the eight villages of Ping Shan, has its own village market.

The village market of Ping Shan has been in existence for as long as any of the villagers can remember. Forty or fifty years ago, according to some of the older villagers, it was much smaller and was located, not on the school basketball court as it is at present, but several hundred yards away, behind the Ping Shan pagoda. In those days fewer people attended the market, and there were fewer items for sale—only pork, salt, dried fish, and vegetables. Before the British came to the New Territories, the village market was held twice daily—once in the early morning and once in the early afternoon—to provide fresh meat and vegetables for the morning and evening meals. Almost all the fresh food requirements of the villagers were furnished by the village market; few villagers walked along the paddy fields to the then very small market of Yuen Long.

The Ping Shan market has undergone considerable development and change since those days. It is now much larger, since it serves not only the villagers of Ping Shan but also many outsiders from the vegetable farms and the pig and chicken farms in the surrounding countryside. It is also attended by all the school children of Ping Shan, who stop to have snacks of congee or bean soup before school starts at 8:00 A.M. in the central ancestral hall, immediately behind the market. Nowadays, the market is held only once each day— from 7:00 to 9:00 A.M. in the morning—since most of the villagers now go to Yuen Long, the market town, to buy the evening *sung* (all Chinese food which is eaten with rice is called *sung,* or "something to go with rice") . The village market would be even larger than it is if it were not for the fact that many of the people from the Ping Shan village of Fui Sha Wai, which is located close to the main road, prefer to ride the bus to Yuen Long instead of crossing the fields to come to Hang Mei. Yuen Long now overshadows the village market in importance, even for the purchase of daily necessities, because it is only five minutes away by bus.

Ping Shan market has not only grown in size since the war, there has also been an increase in the variety of goods offered for sale. On an average market day, I noted the following articles and foods:

fresh pork and beef (3 butcher stalls)
books, stationery, and toys (1 stand)
freshly baked sweet rolls (1 seller)
Western-style bread (from Kowloon) (1 seller)
fish loaf (1 seller)
noodles (1 seller)
variety goods, such as mothballs, combs, thread, and toothpaste (1
    stand)
various kinds of fresh fish (4 sellers)
dried fish (3 sellers)
worshipping paraphernalia, such as firecrackers, candles, incense
    sticks, ritual papers, and paper money (1 stand)
Chinese-style pastries (1 seller)

sugar cane (1 seller)

fruit—American oranges, apples, and bananas (1 seller)

eggs (3 sellers)

various kinds of fresh vegetables (25 sellers)

noodles and eggs (1 seller)

dried beans and herbs (1 seller)

dried Chinese sausage (1 seller)

appliances, such as radios, electric fans, and irons (from Kowloon) (1 seller)

cooked or prepared foods for the villagers' morning snacks, such as rice congee, sweet bean soup, and noodles (6 sellers)

cloth (1 seller)

Altogether, there were fifty-nine peddlers and hawkers selling in the village market. They were aligned in parallel rows on the dirt basketball court with their wares set in front of them on small stands or baskets. Very few sellers in the village market were from the Ping Shan villages. Most were people from the surrounding vegetable farms; a few were from Kowloon and Yuen Long; and some were from Lau Fau Shan, a fishing village on the coast of Deep Bay, several miles away. The butchers and congee sellers were outsiders living in the village.

The Ping Shan market begins every morning just before 7:00 A.M., and soon after that there are one or two hundred people in the marketplace. By 7:30, the number of people increases to four hundred. After taking a morning snack, they mill around in the market making their purchases. The number increases gradually until, at the high point of the market, as many as five hundred people are sometimes present. The market begins to thin out shortly after 8:00 A.M., when the children start to school and the villagers return home with their purchases.

A few of the villagers exchange pleasantries and gossip with their friends from the other Ping Shan villages, but there is actually very little conversation among the villagers in the market aside from the inevitable haggling. Most of the villagers go about their business quickly, making their purchases and returning home. One difference between the present market and the market held forty or fifty years ago is that nowadays women are present in some numbers. In traditional times, women were not allowed to come to the market because it was considered improper for them to mix with the men.

The most striking feature of the present market was the presence of a man from Kowloon who had German and Japanese appliances displayed on the top of his car parked next to the marketplace. Some of the transistor radios were turned on loudly to demonstrate their quality. An even more incongruous sight was the hawker selling chicken wings, piece by piece, from frozen food packages imported from Australia and the United States. This was the same type of frozen chicken that American housewives buy in supermarkets, which gives some indication of how closely the village is tied to wider networks of commerce and exchange.

VILLAGE STORES

The penetration of the market into the village is better demonstrated by the village stores than by the village market. Altogether, in 1962, there were 19 shops, stores, and permanent hawker stands in the villages of Hang Mei, Hang Tau, and Tong Fong. They consisted of 5 grocery and general stores; 3 rice and feed stores; 2 pharmacies; 2 small teahouses; 3 congee stands (also selling bean soup and the like) ; 1 beer and soft drink store; 1 paper and school supplies store; and 2 permanent candy and cookie stands. Most of these village businesses were extremely small operations, requiring little capital investment and yielding little profit. The most substantial businesses were the grocery stores, the rice and feed stores, and the pharmacies.

According to a few of the older villagers, there have always been one or two general stores in the village. In the past, these stores usually didn't last long, and the owners were rapidly succeeded by other villagers who wanted to try their hand at storekeeping. All of the present businesses in the village have opened since the war, and the number of shops and stores has gradually increased to keep pace with the growing population of the villages and the surrounding countryside. One new pharmaceutical store opened in the village in late 1962, and several new permanent hawker stands were established at about the same time. Most of the businesses in the village are run by outsiders from Kowloon or other parts of the colony.

One grocery and general store, located on the road that runs between Hang Mei and Tong Fong, is owned and operated by two brothers from the Six Families group. The goods sold in their store were as follows:

soft drinks (Coca Cola, Pepsi Cola, and other locally made soft
    drinks)
beer (local and Danish)
cigarettes (popular English and American brands, plus some locally
    made Hong Kong cigarettes)
bar soap

detergent (an American brand)
soya bean sauce
cookies (English-style "biscuits" made locally)
candies (English)
cooking oil (locally made peanut oil)
white sugar (made in Hong Kong)
dried beans
worshipping paraphernalia
toothpicks
starch (an English product)
writing paper and pencils
matches (made in Hong Kong and Macao)
mosquito coils (burned to keep away mosquitoes)
tea
kerosene
salt
canned goods (a wide variety, including sardines from Japan and
   the U. S., Del Monte pork and beans, pineapple, corned beef,
   cereal oats, and canned abalone)
Swiss evaporated milk (for babies)
toilet tissue

The Tang brothers' grocery store is small and business is very slow,
consisting mostly of candy and cookies sold to the village children, and
cigarettes sold to the men. As do all the other store proprietors in the
village, they buy their goods from retail houses in Yuen Long, which,
in turn, get their goods from larger wholesale houses in the cities.
According to the Tang brothers' estimate, their average daily volume
of sales was only about $25 (about US$4.50), with a profit of $5 per
day.

Another of the village stores is a combination grocery and tea shop
owned and operated by Uncle Moou, as he is called by all the
villagers, a refugee from Jong Shan County on the mainland near
Macao. Originally from a rich peasant family, he escaped to Hong
Kong in 1949 and for several years worked in the city as a waiter and
then as an operator of a stand selling noodles. In 1953, he gathered
together his meager savings and opened a noodle stand in the village.
A few years later, he opened his combination tea shop and grocery
store in which he serves coffee and toast, soft drinks, and beer, and
stocks a complete line of groceries. In addition to those items stocked
by the Tang brothers, Uncle Moou also stocks such commodities as
fresh and salted eggs, salted ducks' eggs, bean noodles, soft bean curd,

Chinese medicinal herbs, mushrooms, peanuts, flour, potatoes, brushes, wooden slippers, and a large variety of canned meats. To further supplement his income, he rents out his shop to mahjong players in the evening. His average volume of business ranges from $30 dollars a day during the winter months to $60 dollars a day during the summer months, when he sells more soft drinks. He claims that he makes an average overall profit of about 15 per cent on his gross sales volume.

In the past few years, three rice and feed stores have opened in the village. They sell rice to most of the villagers and animal feed to the chicken and pig farmers in the vicinity. Before the war, rice was not sold in the village on a large scale because most of the villagers either grew their own rice or bought it in Yuen Long. Nowadays, the rice stores in the village do a lucrative business because all of the villagers, including the farmers, purchase their rice from the stores. Since Yuen Long rice is of especially good quality, its retail price is about $0.70 per cattie. Rice imported from South East Asia (most of the rice consumed in the colony is imported from this area), which is of poorer quality, sells for about $0.50 to $0.60 per cattie. Therefore, all the villagers, even the farmers, sell all their rice in the market town and buy the cheaper imported rice for their own consumption. The rice stores in the village are all owned by Chaochou people who came originally from northern Kwangtung and Fukien provinces, and who now control the retail rice business in the colony.

Wo Hing, who owns the oldest and largest rice and feed store in the village, has by far the largest volume of business. The other two stores opened in 1960 and as yet their business is not as well established. Wo Hing hires two full-time workers from the village to help unload the rice trucks, tend the store, and deliver rice and feed to the customers. According to his own estimate, Wo Hing has an average sales volume of about $60,000 per month and makes a gross profit of about 6 per cent of his gross sales—about $3,600 per month. Wo Hing is by far the most successful merchant in the village.

The most successful Chinese herb shop in the village is owned by an outsider from Hong Kong. He carries a complete line of Chinese herbal medicines and fills prescriptions given by the several Chinese doctors of the village. In addition to the traditional herbs, he also carries a few Western patent medicines such as cough syrup, aspirin, and laxatives. He employs one old Chinese refugee doctor as a resident physician for his shop. His shop averages about fifty customers a day and sells about $3,000 of medicine a month. He reportedly makes a 50 per cent profit on his gross sales volume. The average prescription cost for each patient is about $2 (or US$.36).

In the last few months of 1962, a new modern pharmacy was opened in the village by a large Hong Kong company. This store carries a more complete line of herbs than the other medicine shop in the village, as well as a large stock of Western patent medicines and toilet articles. During its first few months of operation, this store did not do much business because most of the villagers preferred to patronize the older shop.

The village store proprietors claim that business is not as good as it should be because the villagers prefer to shop in Yuen Long where there is a larger variety of goods for sale and the prices are slightly cheaper. Moreover, the villagers enjoy taking the bus to the market town where they meet friends and take in the sights. The general pattern of buying is for purchases of under $3 to be made in the village and larger purchases to be made in Yuen Long.

In general, the villagers have not been very successful in managing village businesses, and most of the shops are now owned and operated by outsiders. This is because the villagers are inefficient and lazy in their business practices, whereas the outsiders are efficient and eager to please their customers. Another reason is that business relations between villagers are incompatible with their kinship obligations. The major reason, however, seems to be that the villagers are so jealous of another villager's rise in wealth and prestige that they purposely do not patronize his store. When faced with the choice between allowing fellow villagers to make a profit from their trade or letting outsiders make the profit, they invariably choose the outsiders. Several of the villagers explicitly gave this explanation for the predominance of outsider businessmen.

In addition to the village stores, there is also a village barber shop, with four chairs, operated by two refugees who have moved out from Hong Kong. Haircuts are cheaper here than in the fancier shops of Yuen Long, which attempt to emulate the still fancier Shanghai barber shops in Hong Kong. Most of the villagers get their haircuts in the village, but the wealthier ones still prefer to go to Yuen Long because it is beneath their dignity to get a haircut in the village shop.

In addition to the barbers that operate the village shop, there are also itinerant barbers who come through the village periodically. Most of their business consists of cutting the children's hair. Other itinerant craftsmen and hawkers also come through the village from time to time, selling everything from ice cream to dried fish and repairing everything from knives to bamboo mats. Among these itinerants are blind musicians and storytellers who will sing a traditional folk ballad or tell a folktale for a few cups of rice.

THE MARKET TOWN

The market town of Yuen Long, located about two miles east of Ping Shan, has traditionally been the commercial center for the villages of the Yuen Long Valley. In traditional days, Yuen Long was a small market center with only a small resident population. Since the war, the town has rapidly grown in size and has begun to play an increasingly important role in the social and economic lives of its tributary villages.

Before the war, a market was held in Yuen Long on the 3, 6, and 9 days of the month, at which time all the villagers from the surrounding area would come to town to sell their farm products and to purchase needed food staples or other articles. Pigs, chickens, ducks, dogs, cats, and fish were sold in the market together with the farmers' surplus rice. In traditional times, as at present, there was much social activity in the teahouses and gambling places of the market town. Many villagers probably came to the market more for social and recreational activity than for economic reasons.

Since 1914, the market town has been controlled largely by the Hop Yick Company, a corporation owned jointly by many villagers in the Yuen Long Valley. Most produce sold in the market has to be weighed or measured on scales belonging to the company, and shops and stands have to be rented from the company. Although there has been continuing economic expansion in Yuen Long since 1898, the town really began to develop only after 1949, when refugee immigration into the valley assumed considerable proportions. In 1962, Yuen Long was a growing town with a permanent population of about 33,000 (including the surrounding villages that are gradually being incorporated into the town).

The core of the town's economy is the two large fresh food markets, which consist of hundreds of vegetable and meat stalls. It is here that Yuen Long dealers market most of the produce from the surrounding agricultural region.

In 1962, however, Yuen Long also contained several hundred shops, as well as many service establishments and places of entertainment. Many of the shops are small handicraft establishments which manufacture everything from baskets and wooden buckets to iron window frames for village houses. Most of these handicraft shops are family enterprises, with the shop serving both as a place of business and as a dwelling place. Contrary to what might be expected, the rise of industry and commerce has not led to the destruction of traditional handicraft industries; indeed, the number of small handicraft shops in Yuen Long is actually increasing.

There are also several modern stores in Yuen Long. Some of these sell electric appliances such as refrigerators, fans, radios, irons, electric heaters, and air conditioners. Most of these appliances are made in Japan or West Germany, but a few are American products. Yuen Long also boasts several large Western-style drug stores (as well as many traditional Chinese herb shops), Western-style clothing and tailoring establishments, and Western-style grocery stores. Moreover, a few years ago, a Ford dealer, supposedly from San Francisco, established an agency in Yuen Long.

The service facilities in Yuen Long now include both Western-style doctors and practitioners of traditional Chinese medicine. There is a government-operated clinic and hospital, although several doctors have private clinics. The service facilities also include several dry cleaning establishments which cater to the increasing number of men and boys who now wear Western suits.

The entertainment facilities consist of three motion picture theaters, gambling places, and many restaurants and teahouses. The theaters show both Western and Chinese films; the Chinese movies are either made in Hong Kong or imported from the mainland, but all Chinese in the colony agree that the mainland films are much superior to the local productions. The theaters charge a modest admission and are packed every night, as are the restaurants and teahouses. Several restaurants cater to young adults and teen-agers, who spend more time in the market town than the older villagers do. These restaurants serve Western-style food and have jukeboxes with all the latest American rock-and-roll records.

Whereas many of the goods and services of modern urban life were formerly found only in Kowloon or Victoria, almost all of them are now available in Yuen Long. Owing to the economic development in the Colony, and particularly in the New Territories, many of the villagers are now able to take advantage of these goods and services, and it is not surprising that they are spending more and more time in town. Many Ping Shan villagers have jobs in Yuen Long, and some of the children attend school there. Other villagers go to the market town almost daily to shop or attend the movies, and almost all important social occasions, such as marriages, birthdays, and the like, are cele-brated in Yuen Long restaurants. When the villagers are ill, they usually go to medical clinics in the market town (as well as to Chinese doctors and spirit mediums). Whereas most village women before the war gave birth to their children at home with the aid of a midwife, many of them now go to the Western-style hospital located just outside the market town. It seems clear that the market town is becoming increasingly important to the villagers and is rapidly replacing the village as the focal point of their lives.

Some of the businesses of the market town are owned by people from the villages in the surrounding countryside, but most of the large shops are owned by outsiders who are not native to the New Territories, many of them Chaochou or Sey-iap people. According to their own testimony, Ping Shan people have tried again and again to establish businesses in Yuen Long, but they have invariably failed. At present, Hop Yick Company owns half of the market town and thus has the dominant voice in the affairs of the town. In recent years, however, Hong Kong firms have opened branches in Yuen Long, and if this trend continues, it seems likely that the economy of the villages, the town, and the city will become even more closely connected than they are at present.

The development and expansion of Yuen Long during the past few years has been remarkable. During the time I was resident in Ping Shan, several large buildings were being constructed in the town, and at the end of 1962 a four-lane highway was being built from the town to the branch road that leads to Ping Shan. As the market town expands, a "ribbon development" of shops and stores is extending along the main road from Yuen Long to the Ping Shan villages. It is quite likely that as Yuen Long changes from a town into a small city, Ping Shan may change from a cluster of villages into a small town; in fact, similar developments have already occurred in Kam Tin and other areas of the New Territories. In any case, there is every indication that the market town will continue to play an increasingly important and influential role in the lives of the villagers.

VI

Family Finances and the Rising Standard of Living

In the foregoing chapters I have traced the gross patterns of change in the village economy brought about by the participation of the village in the economic development of the colony. I have repeatedly talked about the "increased prosperity" of the villagers as a result of their participation in this process. This chapter will be devoted to a detailed analysis of the effects of these economic forces on the standard of living of the villagers.

FAMILY INCOME IN THE VILLAGE

The sources of family income in the village have been mentioned in the course of our previous discussion. The major sources of income in the village, in order of importance, are: (1) business ventures; (2) salaries; (3) ancestral estates; (4) agricultural income; (5) sale of land; (6) land and house rent; and (7) pig raising. In addition, small sums of money are remitted to village families from members who have gone abroad to Europe and the United States, although the income from overseas Chinese is not important in Hang Mei because only a few of the villagers have gone abroad and little money is sent back to the village. In certain other villages of the New Territories, such as San Tin, where many of the men of the village have gone to England to work in Chinese restaurants, this income is much more important.

The problem of estimating the incomes of village families is a difficult one, since, except for the farmers, it was impossible to get direct information on family incomes from the villagers themselves. I felt that to ask such questions of village families would arouse so much suspicion that it might endanger my position in the village and make it impossible to carry out further research. It would also have been extremely bad manners because incomes are strictly family matters and are closely guarded secrets. Even many of the village women do not know how much money their husbands make, except in cases where they work for a regular salary.

This problem, however, was not insurmountable, for it was possible to get information by indirect means. In a house-to-house survey of the village, information was obtained as to the occupations of members of the family, the number of houses they owned, the amount of land they owned, the number of pigs they raised, and the amount of income they received from ancestral land. Given this basic information on the source of income for each family, it was then possible to estimate their approximate yearly income.

A great aid in this attempt to estimate family incomes was the fact that fellow villagers know about how much income is available to other people in the village; they know how much land and houses the other families have, the income they derive from this property, and how much the men make from their jobs. Since any one villager would have detailed information for only those groups to which he was most closely related, I obtained estimates on family incomes from several informants who were members of each of the major segments of the village population. Informants who had detailed and intimate knowledge of the economic circumstances of their own close kinsmen were asked to estimate the income for each family in detail—how much they made from their job, from farming, from house rent, from raising pigs, and so on. These estimates were then checked with my own calculations, which were based on the known average salary for each occupation in the colony, the average profit per pig, and an approximate knowledge of what each family received from the ancestral estates.

As a further check, the income figures were compared with estimates of family incomes given by the principal of the village primary school, who had taught in the village for fifteen years and was intimately acquainted with the economic circumstances of the village families. The figures were also checked by Mr. Chen, my assistant, who had lived in Hong Kong most of his life and had a clear idea of how much families could earn in various occupational positions and in various business enterprises. The family income figures presented here are then the result of this complicated procedure of indirect assessment. They are reasonable approximations and should be taken as such.

Distribution of Family Income

The distribution of family income among the groups of the village is presented in Table 21. The 172 families of the village were estimated to have a total income of $1,198,038 per year. This gives an average income of $6,965 per family per year (or about US$1,244). There was, however, great variation in average income among the different segments of the village population.

The 50 families of the Six Families (Lok Ka) group had a total income of $518,000, with an average income of $10,360 per family per year. If the income of the richest member of this group (he is also the richest man in the village and earns $129,000) is excluded, the average income of the Six Families group would be $7,780 per family, with the modal income group falling in the $4,000–5,000 a year bracket.

TABLE 21

DISTRIBUTION OF FAMILY INCOMES AMONG DIFFERENT SEGMENTS
OF THE VILLAGE POPULATION

	Total Number of Families	Total Income	Mean Family Income	Modal Income
Lok Ka families	50	$518,000	$10,360 ($7,780) [a]	$4–5,000
Wai Shan Hall families	22	$184,590	$8,390 ($6,663)	$4–5,000
Yat T'ai and other Hang Mei families	33	$148,708	$4,506	$3–4,000
Outsider families	48	$233,550	$4,866	$3–4,000
Ha Fu families	19	$113,190	$5,957	$3–4,000
Totals	172	$1,198,038		

[a] Figures in parenthesis represent the mean family income less the income of the richest man.

The 22 families of the Wai Shan Hall branch of the lineage (excluding the Six Families) had a total income of $184,590, or a mean income of $8,390 per family per year, the modal group being in the $4,000–5,000 range. If the income of the wealthiest member of this group (who earns $38,000 per year) is excluded, then the average income per family per year would be $6,663.

The members of Yat T'ai Hall and the other small branches of the lineage, which include 33 families, had a total income of $148,708 per year with an average income per family per year of $4,506. The modal income of this group falls in the $3,000–4,000 per year bracket.

The 19 Ha Fu families had a total income of $113,190. The average income is $5,957 per family per year, with the modal income bracket again in the $3,000–4,000 range.

The 48 outsider families had a total income of $233,550. This gives an average income per family of $4,866, with the modal income in the $3,000–4,000 range.

The comparative income levels of village groups presented above correspond closely to the opinion of the villagers as to the relative prosperity of the various sections of the village population. One interesting finding is that both the Ha Fu families and the outsider families have a higher average income than the poorer Tang families of the village, although the average incomes of these two groups fall far below those of the richer segments of the village population—the Six Families and the Wai Shan Hall groups. The outsiders have better paying jobs than most of the villagers, but they do not have income from land and house rents, nor do they raise pigs to supplement their income, as do the majority of the villagers.

The distribution of family incomes in the village population is shown in Table 22. It should be noted that these family income figures are based on *total* family income, and that many families have more than one wage earner. For the entire village, the modal income bracket is 3,000–4,000 per year (this is equivalent to US$536–714), or $250–333 per family per month.

Of the 172 families in the village, 4 (2.3 per cent) have incomes of less than $1,000. One hundred sixteen (67.5 per cent) have incomes of $1,001–6,000 per year, with the incomes within this range forming an almost perfect normal-distribution curve. Forty-one families (23.8 per cent) have incomes of $6,001–15,000; these families might be called the "middle income group." The "upper income group" of the village includes 11 families (6.4 per cent) with incomes that range from $15,001 to $129,780 per year. However, only 2 of these 11 families make over $38,000 per year: one makes $38,200 (US$6,820); and the other makes $129,780 (US$23,175).

For workers in the colony, the average salaries are $240-400 per month for skilled labor; $220–300 for semiskilled labor; and $100–250 for unskilled labor. The average monthly income for all male workers (women's salaries are lower than men's) in the colony appears to be from $250 to $300 a month, or from $3,000 to $3,600 per year. The average family income of the village, $6,965, is almost twice the income of the average worker in the colony. This is because the village families receive income from their ancestral estates, they own property

TABLE 22

DISTRIBUTION OF FAMILY INCOMES IN HANG MEI VILLAGE

Yearly Income ($ HK)	Number of Families	Percentage of Families
0–1,000	4	2.3
1,001–2,000	10	5.8
2,001–3,000	25	14.5
3,001–4,000	37	21.5
4,001–5,000	30	17.4
5,001–6,000	14	8.1
6,001–7,000	8	4.7
7,001–8,000	8	4.7
8,001–9,000	9	5.2
9,001–10,000	4	2.3
10,001–11,000	5	2.9
11,001–12,000	5	2.9
12,001–13,000	2	1.2
13,001–14,000	0	0.0
14,001–15,000	0	0.0
15,001–16,000	1	0.6
16,001–17,000	2	1.2
17,001–18,000	1	0.6
18,001–19,000	2	1.2
19,001 and over	5	2.9
Totals	172	100.0

from which they receive rent, and they raise pigs and engage in other supplementary income-producing activities.

When the total income of the village families, $1,198,038, is broken down into its various sources, an overall income pattern of great diversity emerges (see Table 23). This pattern not only contrasts with the urban pattern, where most income is derived from salaries, but also with that of the traditional peasant village, where most income would be derived from agriculture and land rent. An analysis of the structure of the overall income of a peasant village, such as the one given here, would seem to be a useful measure of the degree to which peasant village economies are involved with the external market: the greater the percentage of the income derived from salaries and business, the greater the extent to which economic development has affected the village. The fact that one-third of the total income of the Hang Mei villagers is derived from participation in salaried positions and that another one-third is derived from business activities (both regular and "miscellaneous") is further evidence that they are signifi-

cantly involved in the developing industrial and commercial economy
of the colony.

Half of the villagers' income from business comes from regular business enterprises and half from irregular or miscellaneous business
practices. The "miscellaneous" category includes all income from the
land brokerage business; this is because although not all income from
land brokerage activities is irregular, it is impossible in most cases to
tell what part is legitimate and what portion is not. This category also
includes money paid to the village elders who manage the ancestral
estates, money paid to members of kin groups to persuade them to sell
common lands, and gambling income. The estimate given for this type
of income is probably the least reliable of all the income figures because it is exceedingly difficult to discover how much money comes
from these sources. For obvious reasons, the amount of income derived
from these "under the table" activities is among the most closely
guarded secrets in the village.

TABLE 23

SOURCES OF VILLAGE INCOME

Source of Income	Absolute Income	Per Cent of total
Salaries	$399,900	33
"Miscellaneous" (business)	223,390	19
Business income	195,540	16
Common land income	115,380	10
Agricultural income	89,160	7
Land sales	52,556	4
House rent	45,800	4
Pig raising	42,640	4
Land rent (private)	31,968	3
Money from abroad	1,704	0
Totals	$1,198,038	100

The fact that this irregular income is sizable indicates that "adven-
turist" and economically "irrational" practices still persist in the village. Such practices are certainly not congruent with a fully developed
bureaucratic capitalist system where most of the population is engaged
in regular salaried occupations. Moreover, the income derived from
these practices is a parasitical type of income that does not create new
wealth. The importance of this type of income to the general village
population should not be overemphasized, however, because over half
of the income from these irregular sources is concentrated in the hands
of a few.

The remaining one-third of the villagers' income is about equally divided between land rent, house rent, ancestral estate income, and income from agriculture, pig raising, and land sales. Income from these sources are the "extras" that make the villagers' incomes larger than those of the outsiders or the average working man of the colony. A large part of the extra income has been available to the villagers only in the last two decades and is a direct result of economic development of the New Territories.

Other villages of the New Territories would probably present an income pattern different from that of Hang Mei because most other villages would not have so much income from house rent, land rent, the ancestral estates, and business activities. The income of the smaller villages of the New Territories would probably be about equally divided between agriculture, wage earnings, pig raising, and small business earnings. An income pattern similar to that of Hang Mei would probably be found only in the larger landlord villages that wield political power, for in the New Territories, at present, political power is easily translated into wealth.

The case of Tang Mah is a good example of how political power can be used to obtain additional income, most of which falls into the "miscellaneous" category.

Tang Mah is a member of the most powerful branch of the Six Families. For the past nine years he has been Chairman (*hsiang chang*) of the Ping Shan Hsiang Rural Committee. This position gives him both prestige and influence, and he has used his position not only to build up a powerful political machine in the New Territories but also to develop a land brokerage business with a few other men from Hang Mei. Because Tang Mah has connections throughout the New Territories and, more importantly, with business interests in the urban areas of the colony, he is able to handle real estate transactions between the local village population and outside interests. Basically, he arranges for outside interests to buy village property and then protects the outside interests against the villagers' arbitrary demands for money or against their objections to companies that wish to build near the village. It is difficult to estimate how much he receives from these transactions, but a conservative estimate would be $100,000, and an extremely reliable source said that he earned that much alone from one transaction in 1962.

Tang Mah, in addition to being Chairman of the Ping Shan Hsiang Rural Committee, is also Chairman of the Board of Directors of the Hop Yick Company. This position pays him a salary of $6,600 per year, and he earns an additional $6,000 from people who wish to lease shops in Yuen Long or to renew their leases. Moreover, he is also a partner in a travel service that charters planes to fly men from the

New Territories to London to work in Chinese restaurants; it is esti-mated that he makes about $1,800 from this business. Finally, he is often asked to use his influence with government officials in matters which concern villagers in his area, and in return for this service he often receives sizable gifts. In 1962, Tang Mah's total income from all sources was approximately $129,780.

Per Capita Income

As I have mentioned, in 1962, the sample population of some 984 persons had an overall income of $1,198,038. This means that the average per capita income of the villagers that year was $1,218 (US$218). If the extremely large income of the wealthiest man in the village ($129,780) is eliminated to make the figures more representa-tive, then the per capita income of the villagers would be $1,086 (US$194) per year, or an average of $91 (US$16) per month.

THE EXPENDITURE PATTERNS OF VILLAGE FAMILIES

In an attempt to determine the expenditure patterns of village families, I questioned 14 families on their budgets. The questionnaire that I used in this survey was an adaptation of one used by Edward F. Szczepanik (1956) in a survey of the patterns of expenditure among urban industrial workers of Hong Kong. I made an effort to include in the survey families from all of the economic and social sectors of the village, and thus the sample consisted of 3 outsider families, 3 Ha Fu families, 1 Yat T'ai Hall family, 3 Wai Shan Hall families, and 4 families from the Six Families group. The budgetary information that I obtained is intended to give a general picture of the expenditure patterns of the villagers and to show the range of variation within the village population.

The results of the budget survey are given in Table 24. On almost every item of expenditure there is wide variation among village families, reflecting the heterogeneity of income, occupation, family size, and consumption habits. The percentage of total expenditures on food varies from a high of 69 per cent in one Wai Shan Hall family, to a low of 31 per cent in one of the wealthier families of the Six Families group. There is a slight tendency for the families with higher incomes to spend a smaller percentage of their incomes on food. The overall average expenditure for food is about 55 per cent.

Expenditure for clothing ranges from a low of 1 per cent in one Six Families family, to a high of 6 per cent, with much variation between these extremes. The average amount spent on clothing in the village

TABLE 24

YEARLY EXPENDITURE PATTERNS OF FOURTEEN VILLAGE FAMILIES,
EXPRESSED IN PERCENTAGE OF TOTAL EXPENDITURE [a]

Items	Family Number [b]														Average
	1	2	3	4	5	6	7	8	9	10	11	12	13	14	
Food	31	34	64	54	61	58	63	57	69	65	52	67	47	53	55
Rent	0	0	0	0	0	0	0	3	0	0	0	0	13	4	1
Clothing	3	5	5	6	4	3	5	6	5	5	1	2	6	4	4
Fuel	2	2	2	3	0	7	7	6	3	1	1	1	2	4	3
Electricity	1	0	2	1	2	1	1	0	0	2	1	2	1	2	1
Cleaning	2	1	1	1	1	1	0	1	1	1	0	0	1	1	1
Education	35	33	11	6	13	0	3	4	1	0	4	2	6	1	9
Tobacco	0	0	0	10	0	3	3	6	7	15	4	4	2	0	4
Medical expense	5	0	0	3	1	1	0	1	1	0	17	2	3	3	3
Fares	1	7	1	1	1	2	2	3	0	2	1	0	6	9	3
Household	5	1	0	0	3	0	1	1	3	1	1	0	1	0	1
Haircuts	0	0	2	1	2	0	0	2	0	1	0	2	2	1	1
Newspapers	1	0	2	1	0	1	0	1	3	1	0	0	1	2	1
Shoe repair	0	0	0	0	0	0	0	0	0	0	0	0	0	0	0
Social expense	5	7	1	4	1	5	0	1	2	5	7	7	2	6	4
Religion	9	4	3	5	9	13	10	3	3	1	9	1	7	6	6
Amusement	0	4	5	4	4	5	2	7	0	0	1	8	0	4	3
Totals	100	98	99	100	102	100	97	102	98	100	99	98	100	100	100

[a] All figures have been rounded to the nearest whole per cent.

[b] Families 1, 2, 3, and 11 are from the Six Families group; Wai Shan Hall is represented by families 6, 7, and 9; family 5 is from Yat T'ai Hall; the Ha Fu families are 4, 10, and 12; and the Outsider families are 8, 13, and 14.

was 4 per cent, compared to 5.4 per cent spent by the industrial workers in Hong Kong (see Table 25). The difference, while not large, can probably be explained by the fact that most urban families, who are more conscious than the villagers of outward appearance and first impressions, wear Western-style clothes and shoes which are more expensive than the traditional clothing that many of the villagers continue to wear. However, in 1962, an increasing number of villagers were adopting Western attire, and if this trend continues, the amount spent on clothes in the village will probably increase.

The expenditure for fuel in the village averages 3 per cent, in comparison to 4.6 per cent spent by the urban workers. The lower expenditure in the village is probably due to the fact that most villagers burn rice straw, sawdust from lumber yards, or grass and

TABLE 25

BUDGETS OF VILLAGERS COMPARED WITH THE BUDGETS OF
HONG KONG INDUSTRIAL WORKERS IN 1955

Budget Items	Percentage of Total Budget	
	Villagers 1962	Workers 1955
Food	55	53.8
Rent	1	9.6
Clothing (including shoes)	4	5.4
Fuel	3	4.6
Electricity	1	0.8
Cleaning	1	1.8
Education	9	3.5
Tobacco	4	4.9
Medical expense	3	1.8
Fares	3	2.5
Household equipment	1	1.0
Hairdressing	1	1.9
Newspapers and stationery	1	1.0
Shoe repair	0	0.2
Miscellaneous		7.3
a. Amusement and social		
expenses	4	
b. Religion	6	
c. Pocket money	3	
Totals	100	100.1

Source (of the information on expenditure patterns of urban workers in 1955): Edward F. Szcepanik, *The Cost of Living in Hong Kong* (Hong Kong University Press, 1956).

twigs carried from the hillsides by the women, whereas almost all of the urban workers use kerosene stoves.

Of the 14 families in the sample, 11 have electric lights; the others burn kerosene lanterns. The average expenditure for electricity by village families is only 1 per cent, which is about the same as the 0.8 per cent given in the urban survey.

The percentage spent for "cleaning" (soap, laundry, dry cleaning) averages 1 per cent among village families, compared to 1.8 per cent in the urban areas (see Table 25). This undoubtedly reflects the fact that the urban population wears more Western-style clothes and white shirts than do the villagers, for only Western-style clothing is dry cleaned and sent to the laundry. Many village women wash their clothes at the village well and use very little soap, which cuts down on cleaning expenditures.

The families in the sample spent, on the average, 9 per cent of their total expenditures on education, compared to 3.5 per cent spent by the urban workers in 1955. The village average is inflated because the sample includes the 2 families (from the Six Families group) who have the highest expenditure on education in the village—35 per cent and 33 per cent. But, even if allowance is made for these 2 families, it still appears that the villagers spend a higher percentage than the urban industrial workers on education.

The villagers are very much aware of the importance of education in the new society, and thus most of them are willing to sacrifice to give their children the best education possible. Almost all of the village children attend the primary school in the village, which costs about $2.50 per month. It is also becoming common for village children to go on to middle school (equivalent to American high school education), although in some of the poorer families only the boys attend middle school. Middle school is much more expensive than primary school, averaging about $50 per month; and, if a child is sent to a middle school in the city, it is even more expensive since room and board must also be paid. A college or university education is usually out of the question for all but the children of the wealthiest village families. No village family can afford to send their children to Hong Kong University, which is extremely expensive, but some go to Taiwan universities, aided by fellowships from the Chinese Nationalist Government, and one boy from the village left in 1962 to attend an Australian university.

Most of the village men now smoke manufactured cigarettes, although a few of the older men continue to roll their own, using the native Chinese tobacco. American, English, and cheaper Hong Kong cigarettes made from American tobacco are all smoked by villagers, with American brands being the most popular. Lucky Strike cigarettes are sold in great quantities at New Year's time when they are used as a "lucky gift" in place of the traditional "lucky money" wrapped in red paper envelopes. Phillip Morris has never caught on in Hong Kong because the transliteration of the name, in Cantonese, is *"moo lei ci,"* or "unlucky"! The popularity of smoking among the villagers is reflected in the average 4 per cent spent by village families for tobacco. The urban workers spend more on tobacco, an average of 4.9 per cent, probably because more city women smoke than village women. It is quite common to see village farmers smoking American cigarettes that cost US$0.19 a pack in Hong Kong. The fact that the villagers can afford this comparatively expensive habit is a good indication of their increased prosperity and higher standard of living, since the money spent for one package of American cigarettes is enough to buy a daily supply of rice for the average village family.

Expenditures for medical care average 3 per cent among the families surveyed, which is slightly higher than the 1.8 per cent spent by urban workers in 1955 (see Table 25). Medical costs for the villagers are comparatively cheap because they have access to the inexpensive medical care offered by the government clinic and hospital in Yuen Long. One visit to the government clinic costs only $1, and there are also several inexpensive private clinics in the market town. If a village family has high medical expenses, this is usually due to tuberculosis, which is quite common in the colony. High medical expenditures are reflected in the budget of one family from the Six Families group, which spends 17 per cent of its entire expenditures on medical care (see Table 24).

Average expenditure for bus and taxi fares by the villagers was 3 per cent, almost the same as the 2.5 per cent in the urban sample. This is a good indication of the frequency with which the villagers ride buses and taxis. Some of the middle school and college students of the village ride the bus to school in Yuen Long or Kowloon, and a few of the villagers employed in the city commute back and forth by bus or taxi. By far the largest part of the money spent on fares, however, is spent on transportation between the village and the market town.

Household expenses for furniture, appliances, dishes, and the like average about 1 per cent of family expenditures. Before the war, expenditure for these items was probably even less because the traditional peasant furniture and household equipment were extremely durable. In the last few years, however, the villagers have begun to purchase Western-style furniture, as well as appliances and radios.

Expenditures for newspapers and stationery average 1 per cent, which is almost the same as the 1.0 per cent reported for urban industrial workers in the colony (see Table 25). Literacy is comparatively high among the villagers, particularly among the men and the young people. Although very few books are purchased for other than school purposes, at least 35 of the villagers subscribe regularly to daily Chinese newspapers published in the colony.

The "miscellaneous" category in the village survey (see Table 25) included amusement and social expenses, religious expenses, and pocket money. The religious expenses include expenditures for festivals, as well as money spent for worshipping in the home, in temples, and at the family ancestral graves. The average expenditure among village families for these items was 4 per cent for amusement and social expenses, 6 per cent for religious expenses, and 3 per cent for pocket money, adding up to a total average expenditure of 13 per cent; the total average figure reported for urban workers was only 7.3 per cent (see Table 25). The village figure is high for several reasons. First, most villagers have more than enough income to meet their basic living expenses, and they thus can afford more entertainment. Another reason is that kinship relationships and the observance of traditional festivals are more important in the village than they are in the city; the villagers spend large sums of money celebrating the traditional festivals and they must frequently buy gifts for their relatives and kinsmen.

In summary, the major difference between the patterns of expenditure of the villagers, as compared to those of the urban workers, is that the villagers spend less money on such items as rent, clothing, and fuel. The savings made by the villagers on these categories are used for heavier expenditures on such items as food, education, religious expenses, as well as social expenses and amusement.

Average Family Budgets

The average total expenditure by the village families in the survey was $5,559, or $463 per month. If, based on this figure, the average percentage spent on each budgetary item is converted into monetary terms, then the figures shown in Table 26 are obtained. These figures represent what the average village family spends on each budgetary item per year.

TABLE 26

AVERAGE EXPENDITURES OF FOURTEEN VILLAGE FAMILIES IN 1962

Budget Items	Average Per Cent	Per Year (in HK$)
Food	55	3,056
Rent	1	56
Clothing	4	222
Fuel	3	167
Electricity	1	56
Cleaning	1	56
Education	9	500
Tobacco	4	222
Medical expense	3	167
Fares	3	167
Household equipment	1	56
Haircuts	1	56
Newspapers and stationery	1	56
Social expense	4	222
Religion	6	333
Amusement and pocket money	3	167
Totals	100	5,559

TABLE 27

EXPENDITURES REQUIRED TO MAINTAIN A COMFORTABLE STANDARD
OF LIVING BY A VILLAGE FAMILY OF FIVE [a]

Budget Items	Per Month (in HK$)	Per Year (in HK$)
Food	262	3,144
Rent [b]		
Clothing	15	180
Fuel	12	144
Electricity	7	84
Cleaning	3	36
Education	59	708
Tobacco	30	360
Fares	12	144
Medical expense	10	120
Household equipment [c]		
Hairdressing	2	24
Newspapers and stationery [c]		
Amusement	61	732
Religion and social expense	42	504
Totals	515	6,180

[a] I asked several villagers to estimate expenditures for the above items, and the figures in this table represent an average of their estimates.

[b] The villagers do not pay rent.

[c] There were no estimates for these items.

In addition to the budgetary survey that I conducted among the 14 village families, I asked several other villagers to estimate how much a village family of 5 (2 adults, 2 primary school children, and 1 middle school child would have to spend each month to maintain a comfortable level of living (see Table 27). The average estimate of the villagers themselves is slightly higher than the average monthly expenditure of the 14 families for which detailed budgets were available: $515 as compared to $463, a difference of $52 per month.

The estimated and actual expenditures on each individual item are substantially the same, with the exception of those for clothing, education, tobacco, and the miscellaneous items of pocket money, religious expenses, and amusement and social expenses. The discrepancy between the estimated expenditure for "clothing" and the actual average expenditure of the 14 families might be explained by the fact that the villagers tended to base their estimates of money needed for clothing solely on the amount spent for clothes at New Year (according to traditional Chinese custom, all village families buy a complete set of new clothes for every member of the family) and did not take into account the money spent on miscellaneous clothing purchases throughout the rest of the year.

The expenses estimated for education were based on the assumption that an "average family" contained two primary school students and one middle school student; this estimated expense came to $708 a year (see Table 27). However, the actual survey results of 14 families (see Table 26) showed an average of only $500 spent per year on education. This discrepancy is explained by the fact that there are simply not as many children in middle school as we had assumed in our conception of the "average family."

The greatest discrepancy between the estimated expenditure and the actual expenditure was in the items (called "miscellaneous" in Table 24) of pocket money, religious expenses, and amusement and social expenses. In the survey results, the average expenditure for these items was $555 for the combined categories of "religion" and "social expenses," and $167 for "amusement and pocket money" (see Table 26). In the estimates given by villagers, however, it was suggested that the villagers would have to spend about $500 per year to meet their religious and social expenses, and that pocket money and amusements would require $732 per year. The estimated expenditure required for religious and social expenses was quite close to the amount actually spent by the 14 families in the budget survey, but the estimated $732 needed for amusements was much higher than the $167 average amount actually spent. The discrepancy between these two figures might be due to the fact that the villagers in my survey were embarrassed and reluctant to disclose the actual amount they spent on gambling, and for obvious reasons I did not press them on this issue.

It is difficult to estimate how much money the villagers actually do spend on gambling, but it must be a substantial sum; several villagers estimated that many families (perhaps most of them) lose at least $45 a month gambling. The men, whenever they have money, gamble in the market town and elsewhere. Many of the villagers gamble every evening in several village houses which are turned into informal gambling halls. Some of the village women who have leisure time gamble almost continually, day and night. A large number of women, headed by the village spirit medium, have formed a village women's gambling association whose rules state that each member must gamble every day or pay a small fine. The women usually gamble for smaller stakes than the men because they do not have as much money, but the total amount gambled per year by the women is sizable.

Many of the villagers also participate in a lottery carried on by Yuen

Long gambling houses, and many buy tickets in the periodic government lottery which is associated with the horse races sponsored by the
Royal Hong Kong Jockey Club. There is also some betting on soccer
matches. It is not inaccurate to say that the majority of the villagers,
both men and women, gamble whenever they have the money and the
opportunity to do so, and that gambling is truly the most popular
pastime of the villagers.

Since the villagers estimate that a comfortable living requires an expenditure of about $515 a month, or $6,180 a year, the question arises
as to how many of the villagers have an income that would enable
them to live at this standard. It is immediately apparent (see Table
22) that over 60 per cent of the village family incomes are less than
that required. Of the various groups in the village, the Six Families
(with an average income of $10,360) and the Wai Shan Hall families
(with $8,390) stand easily above the mark (see Table 21) ; but the Ha
Fu families (with an average income of $5,957), the Yat T'ai Hall
families (with $4,506), and the outsider families (with $4,866) fall
below it. The average annual income of all the families in the village,
$6,965, is more than enough to meet the required expenditure, but
since there is so much variation in village incomes (modal income is
only $3,000–4,000 per year), most village families have less than a
"comfortable" standard of living.

Actually, even fewer families than the above figures suggest maintain this desired standard of living. This is because the village income
figures presented above (see Table 22) include the earnings of unmarried sons and daughters and family heads who work and stay in Kowloon most of the time. In many cases a large part of the earnings of
these people is not available to meet family expenses. Some of the unmarried sons and daughters do not contribute any of their wages to
their parents, and among those who do, the amount contributed varies
from person to person. A large proportion of the income of family
heads working in the city is spent for food and lodging, and in many
instances the remainder is "wasted" in gambling halls, teahouses, and
dance halls. Thus, a great portion of the money earned in the city
never returns to the village, and the income figures for many families
do not represent the actual amount available for the basic budgetary
items being considered here. As a result, in many cases the level of living of village families is lower than their income suggests.

If a family does not have the $500 monthly income that is needed to
attain a comfortable standard of living, they must spend less on one or
more of the budgetary items. As a general rule, the poor village families usually spend less on food, clothing, and cigarettes—especially
food. A family with more income eats more food of a better quality,
including fresh fish, pork, and chicken; a family with less income eats

pork or chicken only occasionally and buys small fish instead of the larger, more expensive fish. The villagers say that the first indication of increased income in a village family is an increase in the quantity and quality of the food they purchase in the village market. Education is also sensitive to income. If a family is poor, they will send only their sons to middle school. This is the continuation of the traditional attitude that a girl is not a permanent member of the family since she must eventually marry out. The villagers still say that girls are "goods on which one loses," and where a choice must be made between educating a son or a daughter, the son always receives the better education.

LEVELS OF LIVING OF THREE VILLAGE FAMILIES

A description of the levels of living of three representative village families will give some idea of the wide range of living levels that existed in the village in 1962. Family A represents the highest level of living; family B the middle; and family C the lowest.

Family A is that of the local political leader, the wealthiest man in the village. This family lives in a new Western-style house, built in 1962, which is by far the finest and most expensive house in the village. The house contains four bedrooms: one for the family head, one for his wife, and two for their eight children. In addition, the house has a living room, a kitchen, a bathroom, and rooms for the two servants employed by the family.

The modern bathroom, with a tub and a flush toilet, is the first one of its type in the village. Large electric ceiling fans are located throughout the house (several other village families have air conditioners). The kitchen is a compromise between traditional and modern styles: it contains a traditional wood-burning stove for the concave Chinese frying pans, but in addition has an electric range. The kitchen also has a modern Japanese refrigerator, similar to those found in the kitchens of several other of the well-to-do families of the village. The furniture is all new and of the semi-Western style that is common in the urban areas. There is a large German radio costing $700 in the living room. The house has running water, electricity, and a private telephone—the first in the village. It also has an enclosed porch running around the second floor of the building.

Family B is a farm family that owns 10 d.c. of land in addition to several houses. Most families in the village have a level of living that is similar to that of Family B. The head of the family does not farm very diligently because he has sufficient income for his family without having to work very hard. His house is of the traditional type but, like most of the houses owned by the Tang villagers, it is large and well built. The house has two bedrooms, one main hall, and an enclosed patio, as well as two other sizable rooms—one used for the kitchen and the other for storage. The wife of Farmer B works in a small food processing factory near Yuen Long whenever she can get work. His aged mother, now too old to work, does little besides putter around the house. The teen-age son of the family is enrolled in a private middle school in Yuen Long and wants to be a policeman when he graduates. The thirteen-year-old daughter is in the sixth grade of the village primary school.

Family B's house is equipped with electricity and running water, and they also own a Japanese-made transistor radio, an electric fan, and a new iron of German make. In the main bedroom, shared by Farmer B, his wife, and the two children (his mother has the other bedroom to herself), there is one bed made of wooden planks covered with a woven mat and supported at either end by wooden saw-horses, one cheap modern-style bed, and an enclosed bed of traditional style. The furniture is all of very cheap quality, except for a Western-style writing desk and a dining table inlaid with stone. As in almost every other house in the village, there is a large Japanese pendulum clock hanging on the wall of the main hall. The main hall is usually cluttered with odd farm implements, baskets, and papers. This hall serves as the dining room as well as the general living room of the house. The family has no toilet except for a large ceramic pot.

Family C is a Ha Fu farm family which is among the poorest families of the village. They live in a small dilapidated house at the rear of the village, which is only about one-half the size of Family B's and is built of sun-dried mud bricks. The house has only two rooms: one large combination living, dining, and cooking room; and one small bedroom at the rear. The only beds are long wooden planks thrown across saw-horses and covered with mats of woven rice straw. All five members of the family sleep on two of these large platform-like beds. The house has no electricity and no piped water supply; kerosene lamps are used for light and water is carried from the nearby village well. The family owns no radio or other modern appliances. Their furniture, which was made locally, is very old, rough, and cheap. Fertilizer buckets serve as the household toilet and the waste is carried to the fields and used as fertilizer. The mud-brick walls of the house are in a sad state of repair, making the house almost totally worthless.

Food

Family A spends at least $15 a day for *sung* to go with their rice. This, however, is only for the wife and children, since the head of the family usually eats in restaurants in Yuen Long or Kowloon. The family eats only the best food and they have fresh fish, meat, and vegetables every day. On festival days the family has large quantities of chicken, duck, pork, and other delicacies. All eight children of the family have money to buy food and sweets during the day at the village stores. In addition to the two regular meals, almost every night after the head returns home from his business activity, his wife serves the Chinese equivalent of a "midnight snack," which consists of choice foods for the head, his friends, hangers-on, and the elders of the Six Families group, who are invited to the house to discuss village affairs. In the morning the family eats rice congee and bread, and drinks Ovaltine.

Family B spends about $4 a day for *sung*. The morning and evening meals are about the same and vary little throughout the year, except on festival days. These meals usually consist of: one dish of salted fish; one dish of good fresh fish; one dish of fresh vegetables; and one dish of either pork, eggs, or soup (two or three times a week).

Every morning the middle school-age son gets thirty cents to buy a morning snack at school and the daughter gets ten cents to buy a bowl of rice congee at the village market before starting school. The head's aged mother and his wife always eat a breakfast snack at the village market in the morning. The head drinks coffee or tea and eats Chinese pastries every morning at the teahouse near the village; in the afternoon he has another snack at the teahouse or in Yuen Long. On festival days the family usually spends $10 for pork and chicken.

Family C, consisting of the head, his wife, and their two small daughters, have only one dollar a day to buy *sung* for the two meals. When they have no money they do not buy *sung* at all and eat only rice congee flavored with soy sauce. They buy the cheaper salted fish and the small sardine-sized fish of the poorest quality. Since they eat vegetables from their own fields, they seldom buy any in the village market. The head of the family, unlike most village farmers, never goes to tea, and he smokes the cheap native Chinese tobacco. Sometimes the children have money to buy snacks at the market before going to school, but usually they do not. The family eats pork or chicken only on the major festival days.

Clothing

The head of Family A wears excellent quality Western-style suits every day of the year. He has about six different suits, tailored in Kowloon, which cost as much as $150 each. He has several pairs of Western-style leather shoes worth over $40 a pair. His wife, when at home or in the village, wears expensive women's slacks. When she goes to the market town or to the city, she wears expensive Chinese dresses of modern Hong Kong style. The children of the family all wear good quality Western-style clothes. The clothes for the smaller children are made by the mother on her sewing machine, while the clothing for the older children is purchased in Yuen Long shops.

The head of Family B, when he works in the fields, wears good quality Western-style khaki shorts and a T-shirt, together with a panama hat to protect him against the sun. When not at work in the fields, he wears good quality traditional Chinese clothes and leather shoes of Western style that cost $18 a pair. His wife wears the better quality traditional Chinese women's clothes of which she has many outfits. She usually wears Japanese-made rubber sandals. The school uniform of the son consists of slacks, a white shirt with tie, and a sport coat. He has two Western-style suits made in Yuen Long, Western-style shoes, and several pairs of slacks. His clothing is of medium quality and price. The daughter of the family has both Western and traditional Chinese clothes of medium quality.

The clothing of Family C is much cheaper and of poorer quality than that of the other two families. The head wears the cheapest traditional Chinese-style clothing which costs only $12 per suit. He wears traditional Chinese-style cloth shoes that cost $2.80 a pair. The clothes he wears in the village are usually torn or patched, but when he goes to Yuen Long he usually wears clothes of a similar cheap quality that are in good condition. His wife wears cheap traditional Chinese-style women's clothes and usually goes barefoot. The children wear ragged and patched clothes of Chinese type with a few odd pieces of Western clothes mixed in. They usually wear rubber or plastic Japanese-made sandals and do not wear leather shoes.

Entertainment

The head of Family A goes to Kowloon almost every day and usually does not return home until late evening. He spends much of his time discussing business in the restaurants of Yuen Long and Kowloon, and sees American films several times a week in the Kowloon theatres. He attends all the soccer games played by the Yuen Long soccer team and sometimes passes out free tickets to the Village Representatives of Ping Shan Hsiang. He is always accompanied by three or four members of the village (his close business and political associates) and pays almost all of their entertainment expenses. His wife spends most of the day gambling with village women. She goes to Yuen Long for tea and a movie about two or three times a week. The children go to the show at least three times a week accompanied by one of the family's servants. The children have a wide assortment of toys to play with.

The head of Family B goes to the movies in Yuen Long several times a month and has tea twice daily. His wife goes to the movies in Yuen Long with several village women only once or twice a month, but she gambles regularly every evening. The son and daughter go to the movies several times a week.

Family C has almost no entertainment and no leisure time except on major holidays. The family never goes to a teahouse or a restaurant and seldom does the head or his wife gamble. The children must help their parents in the fields and have little time to play; they have no toys.

Services

Family A owns a new, expensive British automobile which is driven by the head's younger brother whom he employs as a chauffeur. The head of the family has a private office in Yuen Long where he employs several assistants as well as a secretary. When a family member is ill they always consult private doctors and never go to the government clinic in Yuen Long. When the head's wife gives birth, she always has a private room in the Yuen Long hospital. The head of Family A has his hair cut in Kowloon barber shops and would never get a haircut in the lower-class shops of Yuen Long. His wife has a new style permanent wave and gets her hair set in a Yuen Long beauty shop every week. Except for sewing, she has nothing to do at home but bear children and care for her husband. All the work in the family, including child care, is performed by the servants.

Family B has only a bicycle, used by the head and his son, but nowadays when they go to Yuen Long they usually ride the bus. The head and his son have their hair cut in the village barber shop. His wife still has her hair in the traditional married women's style and has never had a permanent wave. Family B has none of the services that Family A enjoys.

Family C has no bicycle. The head gets his hair cut in the village shop. Like Family B, when a member of the family is ill, they go to the government clinic or consult a Chinese doctor and seldom if ever see a private doctor.

These examples illustrate the great variation in levels of living among village families. Family A is an extreme case, because no other family in the village enjoys nearly so high a level of life. Family C represents the other extreme, for few families of the village are so poor. Most families in the village have about the same level of living as Family B.

No family in the village is in danger of starving. If one is poor, it is always possible to find work as a construction worker at $6 a day. The situation is much better in this respect than it was before the war, when temporary work was more difficult to find. Relief for some of the poorest village families is available from American missionary groups in Yuen Long, but few families require this aid. Some of the widows of the village receive aid from the Yuen Long District Office. All village families who are willing and able to work can now attain at least a minimum standard of living.

FAMILY FINANCE: SAVING AND BORROWING MONEY

The amount of money that village families save and the amount of debt they incur are such secret family matters that it was not possible to secure information on these questions, even from indirect sources. Some informants said that every family tried to save a small portion of its income—at least 10 per cent—but this may or may not be true.

The traditional economic attitude of the villagers seems to have been one of thrifty provision for the major ceremonial events in life, such as marriage, house building, and death. Money was hard to come by in the prewar days, and the villagers were extremely careful to conserve what little they had against emergencies and old age. Anyone acquainted with overseas Chinese will testify to this deeply ingrained habit of thrift.

However, since the war and particularly in the last decade, there seems to have been a basic and drastic change in the villagers' attitude towards saving. Now every segment of the village population is comparatively prosperous, and the villagers have opportunities to make money faster and easier than they ever could in the past. With this increased wealth has come an even greater increase in expectations and demands, and most villagers are no longer content with a low level of living. The villagers wish to possess all of the new prestigious items of urban Westernized culture, and thus their demands outstrip their rising incomes. Because their incomes fall short of their expectations, the villagers claim that they are still poor, even though their incomes are much greater than they were in the past. It is possible that the villagers feel even poorer now than they did before, because poverty—the difference between expected standards of living and actual levels of living—is culturally determined, and the gap between present expectations and actuality may be even greater now than it was in the past.

It would appear that one-third of the village families, since they have more than enough income to maintain a comfortable level of living by present village standards, would be able to save money. From general observation, however, it seems that most villagers spend all they earn, and that very few families actually save much money.

One of the main uses for surplus funds is education, which is considered to be one of the main responsibilities of village parents, and most of them try to fulfill it as best they can. There is also a practical aspect to this, because an investment in the children's education (particularly in that of the sons) is an investment in social security. If a family can produce a successful son, they can look forward to his support in their old age. The prime example of this in the village is the case of Tang Tsuen, who by working hard on his farm managed to send his son to a Taiwan university. His son returned to Hong Kong after graduation and obtained a high salaried position in the government water works department. When his son got this job, the farmer immediately retired and now spends his days wandering around the village and visiting the market town tea shops. This is an ideal pattern that all village families strive for—the father educates his son, and the son supports his parents in their old age. This also explains why village families are reluctant to educate their daughters, for if a daughter is successful, the entire benefit of her education will go to her husband's family upon her marriage, whereas a son will always stay at home. Obligations to the younger generation have a practical turn in the eyes of the villagers.

Before the war, when money was scarce and economic opportunities were few, there was apparently more borrowing than there is at present. The farmers, especially, needed to borrow money for living costs between the two rice harvests, and it was a common pattern for the tenant farmers to borrow from their landlords. Nowadays the farmers almost never need to borrow money, since they have a continuous income throughout the year from their vegetable crops and pigs. In fact, it is more common for landlords to request advances on the rent than for village farmers to borrow from the landlords.

Although the situation is not very clear, there seem to have been two ways of borrowing money in traditional times. The first method was one of outright mortgage, and there were at least two mortgaging systems. Under the first system, a sum of money would be borrowed, land would be offered as security, and a formal contract would be drawn up (with a witness) which fixed the date for repaying the principal and interest. If the loan was not repaid by this date, the lender could take possession of the land. However, the moneylender could not take the land without obligations to the borrower, because the amount loaned was always smaller than the value of the land put up as security. Consequently, the moneylender would have to pay a sum of money to the borrower to make up the difference, or part of the difference, between the amount of the defaulted loan and the value of the land.

The other system of land mortgaging in Ping Shan was known as the *ting*, or "deposit" system. This system was used to pawn not only land but also the right to receive rent from the ancestral estate (see above, p. 119). Money was borrowed from a moneylender, who was given the right to receive the rent from the land or to use the land in lieu of interest payments. It is not clear from available information whether this was a perpetual mortgage lease whereby the borrower could resume his ownership rights upon repaying the principal, or whether, after a certain period of time, the ownership of the land would pass to the lender. In the case of mortgaging the right to receive the share of the common land income, the right was only temporary, and the borrower could redeem his right to collect his share at any time by repaying the principal of the original loan.

Another common method of borrowing money in traditional times was by forming a "money loan association." These associations were usually formed by a man who expected some major expense in the near future, such as a wedding or a new house. He would contact a number of his kinsmen, relatives, or friends, and persuade them to join the association. All members joined on the basis of their personal relationship to the head, and the members frequently did not know each other. No one but an honest and reputable person was able to form an association, because otherwise no one would trust him. The methods of operating these societies have been described adequately elsewhere (Gamble, 1954:260–271) and need not be repeated here.

There was a variant of the money loan associations in Ping Shan called the "rice loan association." The only differences from the money loan associations were that rice was loaned instead of cash, and, since the meetings could be held only twice a year, after each rice harvest, the associations tended to be of longer duration than the money loan associations.

These traditional loan associations filled part of the need for low interest credit in traditional times and provided an alternative to the moneylender. They allowed a family not only to borrow money or rice without having to mortgage their property but also to avoid the shame that was traditionally connected with having to borrow.

Now that the villagers are more prosperous, there seems to be less need for the associations, and the villagers claimed that very few associations have been started in the village since the war. The villagers said that people nowadays were more reluctant to join associations because they could no longer trust others to fulfill their obligations. This may be true, because the only money loan association formed in the village during 1961–1962 of which I knew ended in default and caused much ill feeling between several of the villagers who had been members.

In Ping Shan, as in most peasant societies, interest rates were very high, averaging 30 to 36 per cent a year. If the lender and the borrower were on good terms, the interest rate might be lower, and if relations were especially close between the two parties, there might not be a formal agreement on interest, the borrower simply presenting a few ducks or other gifts to the lender when he repaid the loan.

Some villagers said that, before the war, if money was borrowed from a person within the village no contract was necessary, since repayment would be assured by the social disgrace and gossip that would result in case of a failure to pay a debt. Moreover, a person who was known not to have repaid a loan would never be able to borrow again. Nowadays, however, even close kinsmen sometimes have contracts drawn up that are witnessed by a third party. This might indicate a breakdown of solidarity and trust among kinsmen and fellow villagers, but the historical data is too poor to warrant this inference.

Opinion differs as to whether it was more common for villagers to borrow from friends, relatives, or lineal kinsmen. Some said that one would first tend to ask one's friends for a loan to avoid gossip and embarrassment in the village. Others said that for smaller sums of money it was customary to borrow from village kinsmen, and for larger amounts they usually borrowed from the wife's family. Some villagers held that it was better to borrow from relatives and friends than from village kinsmen because disputes over debts were incompatible with the feelings of mutual solidarity and brotherliness that were ideally supposed to prevail among the men of the lineage.

In 1962, there were four known moneylenders in the village. One old widow had $300 capital which she loaned out in small sums, usually to other women of the village. She is much feared by other villagers because if a person does not repay the loan on time, she sits on their doorstep until the debt is paid, declaring their perfidy in a loud voice for all the village to hear. Needless to say, she usually collects her money.

Another moneylender of the village was Tang Kin, who reputedly had $10,000 obtained from a piece of land that he sold. He uses this sum as capital for his moneylending operations. He charges 36 per cent interest per year, and it is said that he regularly makes $3,600 a year in profit.

The third village moneylender is Tang Na, one of the village storekeepers. He loans money to his kinsmen in the Six Families group and takes their shares of the ancestral land rent as collateral for the loan. He reputedly loans $200 for the right to collect one picul of unhusked rice per year (worth about $40). It is said that he insists upon a written contract, even when loaning money to his close kinsmen.

The fourth moneylender was a widowed member of one of the wealthier landowning families of the village. She no longer engages in extensive moneylending activities because she recently joined a local Taoist religious society which frowns on usury.

Traditionally, the attitude of the villagers towards borrowing money was very cautious. The villagers had learned from long experience that borrowing was the first sign of a declining family and almost inevitably led to the loss of property. This was because interest rates were so high that there was little hope of repaying the loan. There seems to have been a definite weakening in this traditional attitude in the two decades before the war, when many villagers mortgaged or sold land. Perhaps this can be explained by the fact that the villagers demands for new goods and services increased faster than their incomes. It might be a general rule that some breakdown in traditional attitudes of thrift occurs in the period when the first new commercial and industrial influences from urban areas penetrate peasant villages. At this time much property is sold to gain money for new goods and services. Only later, in the takeoff period of economic growth, are the new economic opportunities that allow sufficient income for the new standard of living made available. This is apparently what happened in Ping Shan.

It was not until after the war that Chinese and British banks from Kowloon and Hong Kong began to establish branches in Yuen Long, and in 1962 the villagers were just beginning to have contact with such economic devices as checking and savings accounts. Some of the wealthier and better educated villagers have opened checking accounts, but most villagers remain ignorant about banking procedures and are generally suspicious of banking operations. Consequently, they continue to hide their money in the house walls or under the floor, where it is "safer."

Very few villagers have borrowed money from the Yuen Long banks. They do not know how one would go about getting a bank loan, and they are afraid of the red tape involved as well as the impersonal relations with the bank staff. There was also a great deal of misinformation about banks circulating in the village. Some villagers said that they had "heard" that bank interest was even higher than the traditional interest rates, and that one had to hire a lawyer to draw up a contract before one could borrow from the bank. They considered these procedures to be too expensive and "too much trouble."

Nevertheless, some of the villagers are beginning to open bank accounts, and at least one Ha Fu family was purchasing a truck on a time-payment plan. It seems that gradually the villagers will become accustomed to banking procedures and make greater use of the new facilities. These new financial patterns are not totally unfamiliar to the villagers because even in traditional times they deposited funds in some of the market town stores for safety and gradually drew on this account to make purchases in the store.

There is general agreement among the villagers that it is harder to borrow money now than before. One villager expressed his views in the following way: "Now it is harder to borrow money. Before the war, people kept their promises, but nowadays people cannot be depended on—they are 'foxier.' In the old days, everyone in the village trusted each other. Everyone always paid their debts because everyone had roots here and there was no place else to go. Nowadays people can move off to the city to escape their debts and avoid social censure."

VII

The Social and Cultural
Effects of
Economic Change

The effects of economic change and development on the social and cultural patterns of the village form an interesting theoretical problem that cannot be ignored. As Hoselitz (1960:26) has said, the process of economic development "involves not merely a reshaping of the 'economic order' but also a restructuring of social relations in general, or at least of those social relations which are relevant to the performance of the productive and distributive tasks of the society."

The theoretical problem of determining the social and cultural effects of economic change has been cogently outlined by Nash (1955:277) and encompasses, among others, the following questions: What is the effect of the new occupational roles, where recruitment is by universalistic standards, and status is based upon achievement rather than age, sex, and kinship? Does the villagers' participation in new occupational roles necessarily lead to the breakdown of extended family patterns and unilineal kinship groups? Does participation in an industrialized economy, which is characterized by relatively impersonal social relations, inevitably lead to basic changes in the character of interpersonal relations in a peasant society? Does participation in a capitalist industrial economy necessarily lead to basic changes in value orientation? If not, can traditional and modern patterns coexist in the same society? Although my analysis of social and cultural change in Ping Shan and its relation to economic change is hampered by the lack of good historical evidence, some tentative answers can be found to these questions.

CHANGES IN MARRIAGE AND
FAMILY PATTERNS

There is no doubt that one of the social and cultural effects of the economic development in the colony is a change in the family and marriage patterns in Ping Shan. Basically, the traditional pattern of the extended family (as an ideal) and arranged marriage is giving way to one of a Western-type nuclear family based upon free marital choice. In general, this pattern of change is a continuation of the following trends, which were observed throughout China before and after the Communist Revolution (Lang, 1946; Levy, 1949; and C. K. Yang, 1959a) : (1) a shift from arranged, "blind" marriage to courtship patterns and free marital choice; (2) the rising status of women in the family; (3) the weakening of extended family structures owing to greater solidarity between husband and wife and the increased status of the daughter-in-law; (4) the decline of the old Confucian pattern of respect due the older generation, and the rise in status of younger members of the family; (5) the decline in family solidarity owing to increased conflict between the older and younger generations; (6) the increasing importance of nonkin and nonfamilial relationships; and (7) the loss of the traditional functions of the Chinese farm family as an integral productive unit, and the declining importance of the family as the center of personal sentiment and loyalty.

The first of these trends, a shift from arranged marriage to courtship patterns and free marital choice, is already evident in the urban areas, where courtship patterns are well developed, and where young people frequently have dates (termed "walking hand in hand" in Cantonese), on which they go to the country, to a restaurant, or to the movies. In the villages, these modern patterns of courtship are just being introduced and are not generally accepted by the older generation. The young people, however, are constantly exposed, by local and foreign motion pictures, by magazines that are the Chinese equivalent of *Popular Romance,* and by the "soap operas" on the radio, to the ideals of romantic love and free marital choice, and most of them subscribe wholeheartedly to these ideals. The difficulty is that courtship patterns have not developed as rapidly in the village so that, although most young people now believe that it is "right" to choose one's own spouse, they do not know how to go about forming such matches.

The opportunity for implementing the ideals of romantic love and for learning courtship patterns comes when the young people, attracted by job possibilities, move into the city. Almost without exception, they imitate the urban patterns and ultimately choose their own marriage partners. The reason for this emulation is not an economic one, but simply that the urban patterns are more modern and prestigious. On the other hand, it seems very probable that economic factors were important in the initial adoption of Western marriage patterns by the urban population, since free marital choice, which is closely associated with the nuclear family structure, was undoubtedly more suited to economic conditions in the city than was the traditional family pattern. It may be that economic factors were more important in changing patterns in the city, but that simple emulation was more important in the villages.

The second trend in the changing marriage and family patterns is the rising status of women. This can be attributed largely to the new job opportunities that the colony's economic development has given women, particularly women from the villages. Factory jobs have attracted young unmarried women to the city, where, as I have noted above, they not only adopt Western courtship patterns, but are also exposed to modern ideas concerning the role of women in society. Independent incomes have strengthened their position in the family, as compared to the old situation where women were financially dependent on the men, and in many families a daughter is able to make substantial financial contributions. Sometimes a daughter helps pay for the education of her brothers, and in some cases the entire burden of supporting the family is on her shoulders.

The family structure of the village is also being changed by the increased employment opportunities available to young men in the city. Village sons working in the city often marry city girls and bring their "city wives" (as some of the older villagers contemptuously refer to them) back to live in the village. These modern-minded girls have definite ideas of independence and often dominate their mothers-in-law, quite the reverse of the traditional situation. Since most of the marriages made outside the village are "love marriages," the most important tie in the family structure is gradually becoming the husband-wife tie, rather than the parent-son tie, which was the crucial structural relationship in the traditional patrilineal extended family.

Economic forces have further affected the family patterns in the village by undermining the authority of the father. The father's position is initially weakened by the bifurcation of social and cultural values between the generations; it is further weakened when their sons, particularly those from the wealthier families who have received good educations, begin to find high-status and high-salaried positions. The increased financial power of the sons frequently enables them to achieve a dominant position in the family. Of course, conflict and hostility between father and son, since it is a reaction inherent in the old patrilineal extended family structure, has always been characteristic of the Chinese family, but it has now increased to the point where it is quantitatively, if not qualitatively, different from the traditional situation.

One final effect of the colony's economic development is the diminishing importance of the farm family in the village as a largely self-sufficient productive unit. With new opportunities available outside agriculture, more and more young men from farm families have refused to continue in their fathers' footsteps, and an increasing number of farm families now have members working in nonagricultural occupations. Thus the continuity of the farm family from generation to generation is seriously threatened.

It should not be construed from the above that the village family and marital patterns have already been completely transformed by these economic, social, and cultural influences; this is far from the case. Most of the older generation still conform to the traditional patterns, and most sons still, overtly at least, show respect for and obedience to their fathers. The women have not yet achieved full equality either in the family or in village society; they are still considered socially inferior, and daughters are still considered less important than sons, not "real" members of the family. At present, there is every kind of marriage arrangement in the village—ranging from marriages totally arranged by parents to completely modern marriages based on free choice. The farmers are the most conservative section of the population and still practice traditional family patterns, including arranged marriage, whereas the outsider families are the most progressive, conforming almost wholly to urban norms. Marriage and family patterns are thus beginning to give way to the modern Westernized patterns of the urban Chinese, but as yet this process is only about half completed; the next generation may finish the job.

But even if village family patterns completely conform to urban Chinese patterns in the next generation, this does not mean that they will become a blueprint of Western norms. From general and limited observation (though not intensive study), it appears that even highly Westernized urban Chinese families still retain traditional elements that differentiate them from Western families. The urban Chinese woman does not seem to have as much status as the Western woman; the husband still has more control over family finances than does the husband in the West; and the husband-wife tie still does not seem to be nearly as strong as it is in Western countries. There is still a definite separation between the world of women and the world of men. For example, after marriage the husband and wife do not go out very often together, except for a family tea on Sunday. Also, a modified extended family pattern continues, out of necessity if not choice. The lack of well-developed social security benefits and old age pensions makes it essential in most cases for old people to live with the family of one of their sons, since few families have sufficient wealth to maintain a separate residence. Full documentation of these differences would require a more intensive study of urban social patterns in Hong Kong. In the village these differences from the Western nuclear family will probably persist longer and be even more pronounced than they are in the city.

CHANGES IN LINEAGE ORGANIZATION

The changes brought about in the lineage groups by modern economic influences is one of the most theoretically interesting aspects of economic development in Ping Shan. Next to the Chinese family itself, the traditional Chinese lineage was the epitome of particularism, functional diffuseness, and collectivist orientation—qualities of social relations that are thought to be incompatible with a modern industrialized economic system of Western type.

Fortes (1953:24), in discussing unilineal descent groups, has stated: "Where these groups are most in evidence is in the middle range of relatively homogeneous, pre-capitalist economies in which there is some degree of technological sophistication and value is attached to rights in durable property." Freedman (1958) has shown that Fortes has probably overemphasized the association between social homogeneity and unilineal descent groups. The Chinese lineage existed in a traditional society which was highly differentiated in terms of wealth, prestige, power, occupation, and social class, to an extent perhaps not matched by the African societies on which most unilineal descent group theory has been based. Nevertheless, most social anthropologists would agree with Fortes' statement (1953:24) concerning the effects participation in a modern economy on unilineal descent groups: "On the other hand, there is evidence that they break down when a modern economic framework with occupational differentiation linked to a wider range of specialized skills, to produce capital and to monetary media of exchange is introduced." Freedman (1958:140), however, is not so sure of this conclusion, and he ends a most remarkable and accurate study of the Southeastern Chinese lineage organization by speculating as to how this particular type of unilineal descent group will fare in Hong Kong under a social, administrative, and economic framework that is so different from the traditional society. The following remarks are directed to this problem.

The most obvious and important change that has taken place in the Ping Shan lineage over the past sixty years is the loss of most of the functions that this unit performed in the traditional society. As in most areas of China during traditional times, the hsien magistrate, located in Nam Tau, seems to have seldom interfered in local affairs if taxes were paid and if there were no major rebellions that threatened the government. This left a power vacuum on the village level that precipitated fierce struggles over power, wealth, and prestige between the powerful lineages in the New Territories. It seems that in the old days the only way a lineage like Ping Shan could defend its property and social honor was to fight for them, and thus the lineage functioned as an important military unit; every able-bodied male over sixteen years of age could be mobilized to protect the rights and honor of the group in disputes with other powerful lineages in the area. From the accounts given by villagers, interlineage feuds, which often developed into bloody wars that lasted for years, were apparently not uncommon in this region. The lineage also functioned as an important political unit, making decisions for the group as a whole and maintaining internal order. In such circumstances, it is clear that the lineage was the most important group (next to the family) in a man's life: his personal safety, the protection of his rights and property, and his position in the wider society all depended in large part on his membership in a particular lineage group.

The lineages of the New Territories lost these important political functions with the incorporation of the New Territories into the colony in 1898. Soon after taking over the New Territories, the British made it quite clear that they would no longer tolerate the feuds, wars, and other breaches of the peace that had formerly been the rule rather than the exception. This determination was demonstrated to the inhabitants by force of arms when the British occupied the area, defeating in the process an irregular army raised by the powerful lineages of the New Territories and led by the Tangs (Ping Shan was a leader in organizing armed opposition to the British in 1898). Local District Offices were established throughout the New Territories, and police stations were built in the most troublesome areas (including Ping Shan). Peace and order were enforced by the government, thus depriving the lineage of one of its most important functions—protecting the group's rights against the other lineages in the New Territories.

Other inroads into Ping Shan's political power by the government have occurred over the years. One of the most important changes brought about by the new administrative and legal system was the gradual weakening of the power of strong lineages over the smaller lineages, which they once dominated and exploited. An important step in this direction was taken when the land survey was carried out at the turn of the century. The powerful lineages were deprived of large amounts of land which they claimed they owned but for which they held no valid deeds. This land, as has been mentioned above, was given for the most part to the tenant farmers who were tilling the land. The effects of this informal "land reform" was to give the smaller, satellite villages a measure of economic independence. Within the village, the presence of the British prevented the large lineages from exploiting the Ha Fu groups as they had done in the past.

Another important change in Ping Shan lineage organization that has taken place in the last sixty years is that it is no longer an important reference group for social prestige. In the traditional society the lineage was, next to the family, the most important unit in the stratification system, and it was primarily from one's kin group that an individual received his status in rural society. Ping Shan competed intensively for prestige with other lineages in the area, especially with other branches of the Tang clan. Social prestige was gained by having members of the village pass the imperial examinations and enter the gentry, the official elite of Chinese society. In the front of the Ping Shan ancestral hall are remnants of granite memorial stones, on which are engraved the names of those members of the lineage who achieved official positions in the traditional government. There are also some remains of circular flag pole holders which used to hold the flags of the official members of the lineage. In the outer hall of the compound of the Zunn Tak Hall branch of the Six Families there are gilt and red wooden banners on which are engraved the names of members who had passed the official examinations. In traditional times, these signs were carried in wedding processions, usually in front of the sedan chair sent to fetch the bride, proclaiming to all the countryside the honor and prestige of the group.

After the New Territories were incorporated into the colony, the prestige function of the lineage was no longer so important. The traditional prestige rankings of the lineages did not mean much to the British administration, whose officials ideally treated all citizens and all groups as equals before the government and before the law. Furthermore, after World War II, many outsiders moved into the New Territories who knew little about the traditional prestige of the old lineage groups. No longer are the banners of Zunn Tak Hall carried in wedding processions, and the old memorial stones and flag poles have been swept aside to make room for a basketball court. These traditional symbols of prestige, remnants of a past social order, no longer have much significance for the villagers. Social prestige is increasingly measured in individual terms, such as personal attainment and wealth, rather than in terms of membership in a particular kin group.

There has also been a decline in the degree to which the lineage has the power to regulate its own internal affairs. Formerly, all internal affairs, such as making decisions, settling disputes, and the like, were handled by the elders and the prominent gentry members of the group. Over the past fifty years the government courts and the police have increasingly interfered with the lineage's self-regulating power, and nowadays they settle most of the group's disputes. The government has also interfered with the management of the group's common property by appointing trustees for the ancestral estates and by taking steps to prevent the kin groups from being exploited by dishonest elements within the village. Thus, aside from the management and ownership of the ancestral estate, the lineage no longer fulfills many of its previous corporate functions.

In more general terms, it seems clear that the kin groups are simply no longer the focal point of the villagers' lives. The main orientation of the villagers nowadays tends to shift away from village and kin group affairs towards new interests—economic, political, and social—that center in the market town and the wider society of the colony. Many of the younger men of the village are much more concerned with their jobs and business affairs than they are with the affairs of the kin group. This was probably always true to some extent, but in the past few decades it has led to a decided deemphasis of the kin group. Many of the younger educated men of the village informed me that they would rather divide the ancestral property and be done with lineage affairs because disputes over the common property caused too much trouble and conflict in the village.

The increasing conflict over the disposition and management of the common ancestral lands has already been mentioned (see above, pp. 110–111). Conflict between lineage segments is probably nothing new in Southeastern China, since this kind of conflict is inherent in the nature of a segmentary-type of society. But what is occurring at present in the village seems to indicate a definite weakening of lineage solidarity. When a member of the Six Families suggests that all the land of the group be divided among private individuals, this threatens the very existence of the lineage, since the common landholdings are at present about the only thing that is holding the ancestral groups together. Once this property disappears, the lineage will cease to be an important structural feature of Ping Shan society, because the lineage has already lost most of its other important functions, and sentiment and the ancestral cult alone do not seem to be bonds that are strong enough to hold the group together in the absence of common economic interests.

Increasing conflict, which threatens to tear apart the lineage, seems to be the result of a changing value orientation. Collectivist values, which in the past stressed loyalty to the kin group as well as the family, are apparently giving way to a more "individualistic orientation," which emphasizes loyalty to one's own immediate family and de-emphasizes loyalty to the group. The reasons for this shift in value orientation, if indeed there is such a shift, are difficult to explain. One part of the explanation might be that the lineage groups, based as they are on traditional sentiments and values, have simply ceased to be meaningful in the new social, cultural, and economic conditions. Such sentiments and loyalties are considered to be old-fashioned and out-of-date, as well as unimportant. Another part of the explanation might be that the increased occupational specialization and individual social mobility required by the new economy and the new society are simply undermining the older system which rested upon a collectivist orientation and upon ascribed status and particularistic relationships.

The above are some factors which tend to weaken the lineage. organization of Ping Shan. If these factors are emphasized, it would seem that eventually the lineage organization will cease to exist in Ping Shan, or if it does survive it will be only a pale reflection of former times, an anachronistic survival in a changed social and cultural universe.

On the other hand, even though the lineage is at present faced with loss of function, increased conflict, and a decline in sentiment and loyalty, there are many factors which tend to maintain its existence. One such factor, already mentioned above, is that there is so much suspicion and distrust among lineage segments that it is difficult to get everyone to agree to the sale of ancestral property, so that the economic basis of the lineage is preserved more or less in spite of itself. As long as this situation continues, the estates will not be divided, in spite of increasing property values and the inefficiency of the present system for managing ancestral estates.

Common residence is another factor which functions to preserve the lineage organization. As Murdock has pointed out, residence rules are the basis for the formation of kinship groups, and change in social organization frequently comes about because of changes in residence patterns: "Rules of residence reflect general economic, social, and cultural conditions. When underlying conditions change, rules of residence tend to be modified accordingly. The local alignment of kinsmen is thereby altered, with the result that a series of adaptive changes is initiated which may ultimately produce a reorganization of the entire social structure" (Murdock, 1949:17).

In a modern industrialized country like the United States, only small nuclear families capable of rapid and extensive social and geographical mobility are suited to the economic organization of the society. This seems to be a requirement for all industrializing societies, and usually the first effects of industrial growth in the urban sector is to attract rural dwellers to the cities to work in the factories. Such a shift in residence from the villages to the cities leads to the scattering of the members of rural-based kinship groups and ultimately weakens the solidarity of such groups.

This general rule also holds true in China, but in Ping Shan and most other New Territories villages the common residence pattern is still preserved. This is because although many villagers now work in the market town and the cities, very few of them have moved away from the village to take up permanent residence in Kowloon or Hong Kong. The reasons for this have already been mentioned: living conditions in the countryside are cheaper and better than those in the crowded cities; and since the villagers usually own houses in the village, it would be economically foolish for them to move to Kowloon or Victoria. Kinship and communal ties in the village also act as a force in maintaining the common residence pattern. However, even these factors would probably not be sufficient to prevent people from leaving the village were it not for the additional fact that the village is so close to the city that, with the improved transportation facilities, it is convenient to return to the village frequently. Thus, because of special conditions in the colony, the economic factors that in other circumstances would probably erode the solidarity of the lineage by changing the patterns of residence have not had this effect in Ping Shan. Lineage members still reside together in the same community, as they have always done, and traditional contiguity is maintained.

There are, therefore, factors which tend to weaken and destroy the lineage organization of Ping Shan, as well as factors which tend to maintain it. In 1962 these opposing forces seem to have achieved a balance, but it is too soon to tell how long this state will continue.

There is not enough evidence at present to predict with any certainty that the lineage organization will disappear in the near future. In 1962 the lineage was still very much a going concern, in spite of the fact that it had lost many of its former functions and internal conflict had reached a critical stage. Very little common property had been sold, and it was at least problematical whether any more would be sold in the immediate future. The worshipping ceremonies at the ancestral graves and in the ancestral halls were still performed as they always have been and, as far as I could tell, they were attended by just as large a percentage of the lineage members as ever. It is possible, of course, that the meaning of the ceremonies had changed in the minds of the members participating, but this is very difficult to determine. The lineage was extremely important in the lives of the villagers, and the ancestral land and other kin group affairs were still of much concern to them.

There seems to be no compelling reason why the lineage organization of Ping Shan cannot continue in its present modified form into a more fully industrialized and Westernized society. It must be remembered that the Chinese lineage has existed for centuries in a highly differentiated society and economy, so that it may not be as difficult for it to adapt to the new economy and society as it would be for lineage organizations of more homogeneous societies. Most of the changes that have occurred in lineage organization over the past sixty years in Ping Shan are the result of the incorporation of the lineage into a new social, legal, and administrative framework and have not been caused by economic factors. The one economic force that could have had the most effect on the lineage system—change in residence caused by participation in urban occupations—has been blunted by the special conditions that exist in Hong Kong.

One point should be emphasized: whether the lineage structure continues to exist in Ping Shan is largely a matter of choice by the villagers. As Firth (1951:40) has pointed out, the concept "social organization," which is defined as "the systematic ordering of social relations by acts of choice and decision," is a necessary adjunct to the concept of social structure. The villagers have several choices as to how they will reorganize the elements in their social structure. There have already been suggestions made in the village that the lineage organization should be converted into a modern corporation and placed under the supervision of the government. There is some possibility that eventually the lineage organization will evolve into a group of this type, but if such a course of action should be taken, the organization would, of course, have to be greatly modified. The leadership of the group would certainly have to be placed in the hands of managers with modern education, and the elders would no longer have as much to do with the management of the ancestral property. However, income from the property could still be used to finance the ancestral ceremonies, with the balance distributed to the individual members of the group. Such a transformation of the lineage organization into a corporate group more compatible with the new economic conditions would be a very complicated task, but not an impossible one. There is some evidence that this type of change took place during the early part of this century in the transformation of the Hop Yick Company from a market organization controlled by a Kam Tin lineage group into a modern business corporation.

THE DECLINE IN TRADITIONAL RITUAL AND CEREMONY

Another social and cultural effect of economic change in Ping Shan has been the decline in the importance of ritual and ceremony. In the traditional culture, families spent as much as they could possibly afford on ritual occasions, such as marriages and funerals, and on the major festivals of the religious calendar. This is because the status of the family was validated by the elaborateness of its celebrations. Today, however, there is a definite reluctance on the part of the villagers to assume this financial burden, and in almost every instance traditional patterns of ritual and ceremony are being changed to conform to the simpler customs that are prevalent in urban areas. Whereas it was almost mandatory in traditional times to invite at least one member of each family in the village to wedding banquets, now it is more common to invite only the members of one's immediate kin group. Similarly, the traditional customs regulating the amount and kind of food exchanged between two families engaged in forming a marriage have lost much of their meaning, and now it is common for the bridegroom merely to give a sum of money to the bride's family to buy the traditional wedding cakes. Other traditional ceremonies, such as Dragon Boat Races and the yearly opera that the Ping Shan villagers used to give, have been entirely abandoned.

There seem to be several reasons for the decline in traditional ritual and ceremony. One is that the villagers have become increasingly involved in groups outside the village, with the result that village society as a reference group for confirming social status has declined in importance. In the wider society of the colony, social status is largely determined by education, occupation, and personal wealth, and hence the traditional means of validating status in the village are no longer as meaningful as they once were.

Another reason for the decline in traditional ritual and ceremony is that many villagers feel the old customs are "too much trouble," and they no longer care to spend the time and money on ritual patterns that are increasingly irrelevant in the new society. The disappearance of traditional ceremony and social ritual appears to be a manifestation of what Kroeber (1948:211–213) has called "cultural fatigue": the villagers are simply tired of the old patterns.

A third reason for the breakdown in traditional ritual patterns is that village families are now greatly concerned with bettering their own levels of living. Faced with alternative means of expending limited funds, the villagers choose to educate their children and to purchase the new material comforts of life, a trend which seems to indicate a definite change in value orientation. Status in the social networks outside the village is now more important than status in the village, and consequently the old patterns for validating status are being replaced by new status symbols that are more meaningful in the modern social context.

CHANGES IN KINSHIP RELATIONS

In traditional times, kinship ties were by far the most important relationship in the villagers' lives. Now, however, many villagers are working in the towns and cities, and their relationships with fellow workers, friends, and business associates are becoming increasingly important, in many cases more important than their relationships with kinsmen and relatives. This change in the pattern of social relationships has been eased somewhat by the extension of kinship terms into a nonkin context. Usually, unrelated men with whom the villagers have some kind of social relations are addressed by kinship terms such as "uncle," "grandfather," and "brother," depending upon the age and social status of the person addressed and his relationship to the speaker. For example, the highest Chinese official in the Yuen Long District Office is addressed by the villagers as "Grandfather Jeung," in deference to his high position. Most young men in the market town call each other by the term "brother," whether or not they are related. The more formal term *hsien-sheng* ["Mr."], which is now commonly used in the city, is rarely used by the villagers, primarily because its impersonal tone makes them feel uncomfortable.

Kinship relations have not been entirely replaced by nonkin relations outside the village context. Many villagers obtain job introductions from kinsmen or relatives, and many receive special treatment or favors from relatives or friends. When the villagers operate outside the village context, any tie they may have with other persons, whether it be kinship, relationship by marriage, or simply friendship, is activated if it is to their advantage. In general, there seems to be a definite change from kin to nonkin relations, but the nonkin relations tend to be based on kinship models.

THE EFFECTS OF ECONOMIC CHANGE ON SOCIAL STRATIFICATION

One important effect of economic development on village social patterns is the change that has been brought about in the system of stratification. The economic position of the farmer, owing to his increased prosperity, is now almost equal to that of the former landlord groups. On a broader scale, the former tenant villages in the Yuen Long Valley are now approaching an economic status equal to that of the landlord villages, such as those of Ping Shan. This economic leveling between farmer and landlord can be attributed largely to the fact that rents have not risen as rapidly as the value of the produce of the land. A leveling of status has also occurred between the Ha Fu and the Tang within the village, with the Ha Fu now better off economically than the poorer Tang groups.

In addition to a leveling of economic status in the rural society, the economic development in the colony has also brought about a fundamental change in status symbols. Traditionally, the status of a village family has depended on the amount of land and the number of houses owned, in addition to the size of the ancestral estate in which the family had a share. Nowadays, with most of the wealth in the village derived from salaries and from brokerage deals by the political leaders of the village, a family's wealth is largely hidden or is expressed in different terms and is rarely invested in land. For example, the village political leader, Tang Lai-ming, is the wealthiest man in the village (with an income in excess of $100,000), but he owns no land and only two houses. His status is determined largely by the nature of his occupation, the size of his salaried income, and his visible level of living. Although many of the more conservative villagers still tend to classify a man socially on the basis of his private landholdings, there is evidence that status will be increasingly determined by occupation, salary, and level of living. This will be a major change from the traditional days when land was so important for status that villagers struggled for a lifetime to save enough money to purchase a small lot.

VIII

Western Treaty Ports and the Rural Chinese Economy

The conclusion reached in this study, that the rise of a Western-type capitalist economy in the colony has favorably affected the economic conditions of the rural villagers of Ping Shan over the past half-century, contradicts the orthodox interpretation of modern Chinese rural economic history, which holds that treaty port industry and commerce were among the principal factors responsible for the bankruptcy of the Chinese countryside during the period prior to the Communist Revolution. Writers on the Chinese economy during the 1920's and 1930's were apparently strongly influenced by a Marxist–Leninist interpretation of the effects of capitalist industrialization on peasantries and tended to adopt a similar interpretation of twentieth-century rural Chinese economic history. In this concluding chapter, I intend to examine this orthodox interpretation in the light of information from the Ping Shan study and other data on the modern history of China's rural economy. I hope to show that the Western treaty ports, like Hong Kong, were not as uniformly detrimental to the economic interests of the Chinese peasantry as most writers have believed.

Marx took it for granted that in agriculture, just as in industry, large-scale production was inevitable because it was more efficient.[1] Indeed, basing his views on what was happening to the English peasants in the nineteenth century, he thought he could perceive the

[1] Among the most important sources for the Marxist theory of the effects of capitalist industrialization on peasant economies are the following: Engels, 1958, 1955; Marx, 1955 (especially chapters 15, 25 and 26); Kautsky 1898, 1931 (especially chapter 1); and Lenin, 1946. Some important commentaries on the Marxist theory can be found in Mitrany, 1951 (especially chapter 2); Laidler, 1920; and Lichtheim, 1961.

destruction of small-scale peasant farming in the Europe of his day. The peasants of nineteenth-century England were experiencing severe economic difficulties owing to the industrializing process. The rise of capitalist industry and the resulting influx of machine-made goods into the countryside were destroying certain of the peasants' cottage industries on which they depended to supplement their meager agricultural income. The enclosure of the common lands made it impossible for them to raise domestic animals along traditional lines. Since almost all of their capital was invested in their small farms, they had to borrow money to carry on farm operations and were eventually forced to sell their land under the squeeze of the tax collector on one side and the moneylender on the other. Since small-scale peasant production supposedly could not compete with the efficient large-scale capitalist farms that Marx thought must come into being, the peasant farmer was doomed. Capitalist industrialization in the eyes of Marx was anathema to traditional peasantries.

Marx's predictions as to capitalism's effect on peasants were no more accurate than his predictions about the industrial sector of European economies. When it later became apparent to Marxists that large-scale capitalist farming was not prevailing in Europe and that the peasantry was not being destroyed, they explained these contradictions by claiming that although agricultural production was not increasing in scale, the concentration of land ownership and the growth of tenancy resulted in substantially the same thing (Kautsky, 1898). According to these later Marxists, everywhere in Europe the peasant farmer was losing the ownership of his land. Because he was an inefficient producer and because of the destruction of his handicraft industries, the peasant had to borrow from the moneylender, and since he could not hope to repay these loans he would eventually have to sell his land. Behind the scenes, capitalists and moneylenders were buying the land of impoverished peasants, who then became the tenants of these absentee landlords. Even though the farm unit remained the same, the farmer was no longer an independent peasant. According to later Marxist-Leninist opinion, the rise of capitalist industry inevitably doomed the peasantry by splitting the rural population into two sections: 1) a small minority of capitalist farmers and large landlords, and 2) a vast majority of rural landless proletarians.

The same inexorable economic laws were also held to be applicable to the underdeveloped countries which the capitalist West exploited, and the Marxist-Leninist thesis has in fact been a popular interpretation of the effects of Western imperialism on Asian peasant societies such as India, China, and Japan. This theory became the dominant interpretation, held by Marxists and non-Marxists alike, of the economic history of rural China in the half-century preceding the Communist Revolution in 1949.[2]

The overwhelming opinion of Chinese writers on their country's rural economic history in the modern period is that the influence of Western industry and commerce, centered in the treaty ports, was detrimental to China's rural economy and was leading to the economic and social bankruptcy of the countryside. One of the major themes in the Chinese rural economic literature of the 1930's is the decline of traditional handicraft industries owing to the competition of machine-made goods from abroad and the modernized coastal centers (see Hou, 1965:1, 165).

This view has been and is now the interpretation sanctioned by the Chinese Communist Party. Lin Yi (1963:15, 37), a Chinese Communist writer, succinctly summarizes the Party's views in his *Short History of China: 1840–1919* as follows:

The Capitalist countries started, in the 1840's, to set up industrial enterprises in China in order to directly exploit her raw materials at give-away prices. . . . A large number of peasants and handicraftsmen had no alternative but to go and work for the foreign capitalists, their own enterprises having been bankrupted by the dumping of foreign goods on the Chinese market. . . . The opening of the free ports and the tariff agreement gave the foreigners unlimited opportunity to push the sales of their goods and grab new raw materials. British textiles flooded the Chinese market, penetrated the countryside, bringing ruin to the peasants' cottage industries. . . . Under the battering blows of foreign capitalism, China's self-sufficient feudal economy started giving way, and a semi-colonial and semi-feudal economy began to take shape.

This theme was stressed repeatedly in the Chinese rural economic literature of the 1930's (see Chen, 1936), and the Marxist influence is nowhere more evident than in the widely known book *Agrarian China* (Institute of Pacific Relations, 1939). This book, with an Introduction by Tawney, a prominent English economic historian (and a

---

[2] A sample of Chinese writing on the rural economy can be found in *Agrarian China* (Institute of Pacific Relations, 1939). Other important sources are the series of studies issued by the Nankai Institute of Economics in Tientsin by H. D. Fong (see Bibliography). Additional information can be found in the following journals: *Annual Reports of the China International Famine Relief Commission* (in addition to other publications by this organization); *Monthly Bulletin on Economic China; Nanking Social and Economic Quarterly; Quarterly Journal of Economics* (in Chinese); *Chinese Economic Journal; Chinese Economic Bulletin;* and *Journal of the Chinese Association of Land Economics* (in Chinese). See also the writings of Buck, Tawney, Cressey, Ho, and Chen cited in the Bibliography.

Fabian Socialist) who apparently influenced Chinese thinking, consists of translations of important articles on the rural Chinese economy written by Chinese workers in the field. Two themes dominate most articles in the book: (1) the exploitation of poor peasants by large landlords; and (2) the adverse effects of Western industry and commerce on the rural economy. It is an understatement to say that many of these articles carry an ideological bias (see Institute of Pacific Relations, 1939:73–79, 157–160).

Elsewhere, Chen Han-seng (1939) argued that industrialization in China, under what he called "semi-colonial circumstances," had the effect of lowering the standard of living of the rural population in general, particularly that of the middle and poor peasants. Franklin L. Ho (1936) a non-Marxist pioneer in the study of China's rural economy, in a preliminary paper read before the Sixth Conference of the Institute of Pacific Relations in 1936, claimed that rural China had shown an uninterrupted decline since her contact with the industrialized Western societies.

H. D. Fong (1933, 1934, and 1936), another non-Marxist pioneer in the field, in a series of studies on the rural handicraft industries of China issued in the 1930's by the Nankai Institute of Economics in Tientsin, mentioned the decline of China's three basic rural industries: cotton spinning, silk reeling, and the preparation of tea (1933: 13–15). He said that, because of the "growth in the import of foreign spun yarns, the hand spinning of cotton yarn, formerly a widespread domestic industry all over the rural districts, has now become almost extinct," (1933:13). The decline of hand reeling of silk, according to Fong, was no less remarkable than that of cotton spinning; and the preparation of tea, another widespread rural industry, showed an equally rapid decline. Moreover, Fong said, other less important rural industries had also suffered (1933:16–18). The rapid increase in the import of foreign paper brought about a decline in the native paper-making industry. Native flour milling, formerly a rural industry, also declined in the face of competition from machine-milled flour from home industry and foreign mills. Oil pressed from rape and other vegetables for domestic lamps was almost wholly replaced by kerosene imported chiefly from the United States. As an indication of rural China's growing dependence on kerosene, Fong cited figures that showed an increase in the importation of kerosene from 23 million gallons in 1886 to almost 146 million gallons in 1932 (1933:17–18). The destruction of these rural industries was attributed both to foreign imports, in the case of kerosene and paper, and to the products of the treaty port industries, in the case of cotton yarn and flour. The destruction of the silk and tea industries was caused by the replacement of Chinese products on foreign markets by silk from Japan and tea from India, Ceylon, the East Indies, and Japan (1933:18).

On the basis of his studies, Fong stated that, "although this conclusion [that industrialization ultimately destroyed the rural industries] with regard to the industrial conditions in England about a century ago cannot be applied with equal force to a still medieval country like China, yet the disappearance of rural industries in China, under modern industrializing influences of the Western trading nations, cannot be denied" (1933:13).

Among the most influential interpreters of modern China's rural economic history was the Chinese anthropologist Fei Hsiao-tung, who, in *Earthbound China,* a book written jointly with Chang Chih-i and published in 1945, put forth the thesis that the introduction of Western industry and commerce in the coastal treaty port cities had upset the precarious balance of the rural economy and was leading to the economic ruin of the peasantry. His thesis was, in brief, that the peasants depended upon traditional handicraft industries diffused throughout the countryside to supplement their inadequate agricultural income. With the rise of both foreign and Chinese industries in the treaty ports and the gradual penetration of their industrial and commercial influences into the interior, the traditional handicraft industries were being destroyed. Once these were gone, the peasants were left with only agriculture, from which they could not gain an adequate livelihood. When periodic emergencies appeared or when the peasants had to finance a marriage or a funeral, they were forced to mortgage land to moneylenders from the towns, who in many instances were commercial middlemen obtaining their capital from modern commerce and industry. Since the peasant could not hope to repay these loans, taken at the traditionally high rate of interest, he eventually lost the ownership of his land and became the tenant of the landlord-moneylender. As tenants paying high rent, the peasants were further impoverished, forming a rural proletariat of landless agricultural laborers. At the same time, land ownership was concentrating in the hands of absentee landlords, leading to a bipolarization of classes in the countryside. The concentration of land ownership, said Fei, had already taken place in those areas of China, such as the Yangtze River Delta and the Pearl River Delta, where urban capital had flowed into the land market and where the rural industries had been destroyed or badly damaged by the influx of machine-made goods. Fei saw this process of land concentration and tenancy spreading out from the urban areas on the coast into the back regions of China like a cancerous growth.

This interpretation of the effects of Western treaty port industry and commerce on the rural Chinese economy was, then, a general one, held by many China scholars, Marxist and non-Marxist alike, in the 1930's, and, except for the work of Chi-ming Hou (see Hou, 1965), it has remained virtually unchallenged. This thesis, however, fails to explain what has happened to the rural economy of Ping Shan and the New Territories over the past half-century. Objections might be raised that Hang Mei village, a suburban village in a British colony, is a special case to which the thesis was not meant to apply and that it is improper to test the theory using data from this area. I admit that the villages of the New Territories have had the advantage of existing in an island of stability whereas other rural areas of China have been torn and disrupted by war in the twentieth century, but I also maintain that in matters directly pertinent to the testing of this theory Ping Shan and the New Territories are valid test cases. The villages of Ping Shan received no special economic advantages simply because they were situated inside the boundaries of Hong Kong. The New Territories economy was allowed to pursue its own course in a *laissez-faire* fashion and was not subject to intensive government control or interference. In pre-Communist days the border of the colony was not very important, and both people and commerce moved freely across it. In economic terms, then, the affect of the Hong Kong economy on the Ping Shan villages was substantially the same as its affect on the villages across the Sham Chun River, within China proper, and it is legitimate to use this case in testing this theory, especially since the ill-effects of treaty port industry and commerce were supposed to be most evident in those villages directly adjacent to the cities.

Whether one accepts the Ping Shan material as relevant or not, my questioning of the orthodox interpretation does not rest on this study alone. Evidence from other villages within China, historical information on the rural Chinese economy as a whole, and evidence from the writings of some of the very authors who have most forcibly put forth the thesis, lend support to the insight given by the Ping Shan study: the orthodox interpretation of the effects of treaty port industry and commerce on the rural Chinese economy during the first half of the twentieth century, although valid in some respects, is overgeneralized and, in the following respects, misleading. First, Fei and other proponents of the orthodox thesis tend to blame too much of the concentration of land ownership in China on the effects of modern industry and commerce. Landlords owning large amounts of land are by no means a modern phenomenon and were present in some areas of China long before Western economic contact. Moreover, there is little reliable evidence to show that the industrialization and commercial development that occurred in the treaty ports actually increased the concentration of land ownership in rural China to any appreciable extent, or that the concentration of land ownership around the treaty ports was higher than in other parts of China which were relatively isolated from modern economic influences. Second, the importance of handicrafts to the village economies of China as a whole has also been overemphasized. Handicraft industries were certainly of crucial importance in some areas; but in other areas they were of much less significance to the peasants. Furthermore, many writers in the orthodox vein have overstressed the destructive effects of Western economic influences on the rural handicraft industries of China in the modern period. In certain areas of China which depended heavily upon traditional handicrafts, the decline of handicraft industries because of their inability to compete with manufactured goods from coastal centers undoubtedly damaged the rural economy. But not all, or even most, traditional Chinese handicraft industries were severely damaged by the influx of modern manufactured products; and in areas where handicrafts were not of crucial importance to the rural economy, the damage they suffered was not a mortal blow to the total rural economy. Third and finally, it seems inaccurate and unfair to blame all of rural China's economic difficulties on foreign commerce and industry. The basic difficulty in rural China during the past century was that too many people were trying to make a living off too little land using a primitive technology. Observations in Ping Shan and data from other rural villages near coastal centers of industry and commerce suggest that the treaty ports, rather than aggravating this situation, actually alleviated it to some extent. In some areas of China, the treaty ports provided jobs for the surplus population that could never be fully employed in agriculture. Rather than contributing to the bifurcation of rural Chinese society, in some cases treaty port influence actually brought about a levelling of classes. And, to some extent, the modern centers of commerce and industry stimulated the rural economy by providing new markets for handicraft goods and commercialized agriculture.

Before proceeding to marshal detailed evidence to support these assertions, I would like to clarify several points that might easily give rise to a serious misunderstanding of my position. I am *not* out to prove that Fei and other proponents of the orthodox interpretation of modern China's rural economic history are totally wrong in their thinking. I do not doubt that the process they describe was occurring in some parts of rural China: some handicraft industries *were* seriously damaged by competition from manufactured goods produced in the treaty ports and imported from abroad; in areas where handicrafts were important and could not meet the competition from manufactured goods, the poorer parts of the rural population did suffer; and it is conceivable that this did lead to the concentration of land ownership in certain areas of China. I have to accept certain elements in this thesis as true because of the weight of testimony and because this process was operative to some extent in the history of the Ping Shan economy over the past fifty years. I do, however, claim that the orthodox interpretation is oversimplified and misleading, and that the complex economic history of a variegated subcontinent containing a million villages or more cannot be forced into this orthodox framework without doing great violence to the data. The realities of the rural Chinese economic situation in the modern period are more complex than this; and it adds no credit to the valuable insights achieved by Fei and other proponents of the orthodox thesis to have all thinking on this important aspect of Chinese history forced onto this Procrustean bed. The orthodox thesis is widely held as *the* interpretation of the effects of modern economic influences on rural China, and is not a "straw man" that I have set up for the sake of argument. By challenging this position I am not trying to establish a new orthodoxy by taking the obverse position and claiming that in all cases modern economic influences were beneficial to the Chinese rural economy, for clearly they were not; eclecticism is not as satisfying as a monolithic explanation, but it is infinitely closer to reality. Borrowing a page from Chi-ming Hou's book (1965:221), I might add that I am not so presumptuous as to suggest that I am always right in the following analysis and argument, but an important purpose will be served if this leads to the questioning of traditional views on the effects that treaty port industry and commerce had on the rural Chinese economy. One last note: in no sense is this argument meant as a political or ideological diatribe; I do not mean to imply that writers who subscribed to the orthodox Marxist-Leninist interpretation were or are necessarily Marxist in their political beliefs and actions. Furthermore, in discussing the effects of treaty port industry and commerce on the Chinese rural economy, I am talking only about the period from roughly 1900 to the late 1930's, a limited time perspective, and am not making judgments as to the ultimate and long-range effects of the treaty powers on the rural Chinese economy or on Chinese society as a whole.

Getting down to specifics, according to Fei, the ill effects of treaty port economic influences were most severe in rural Chinese villages directly adjacent to the treaty ports. If this is the case, then these ill effects should certainly have been noticeable in the New Territories, which are comparable to other Chinese rural areas adjacent to treaty ports, and which have been increasingly affected by the Hong Kong economy over the past half-century. However, the New Territories example indicates that this commonly held theory is simply not borne out by the facts, for the economic influence of Hong Kong, which has been one of the most active centers of Western-inspired industry and commerce, has neither led to the impoverishment of the villagers by destroying their handicraft industries nor divided the rural society into absentee landlords and a landless rural proletariat.

In the first place, in many areas of South China and in the New Territories, handicraft industries were situated primarily in the towns and cities, and were not of great significance in the rural villages. It is, then, largely irrelevant to argue that the influx of machine-made goods destroyed the villagers' major source of supplementary income. More important than this question of relevance, however, is the fact that under the influence of Hong Kong's economic development handicraft industries in the rural villages and market towns of the New Territories have not been destroyed.

In the second place, Fei's suggestion that the nonproductive use of capital derived from the new economy has led to the concentration of land ownership and a high rate of tenancy in areas near Western industrial and commercial centers has simply not proven true in the New Territories. Land ownership has traditionally been concentrated in the hands of old, established lineages like the Tangs, and this remains true even today. Although some land has been sold to urban interests, this land has been used for industrial and economic expansion, which has ultimately benefitted the peasants. Rather than contributing to the growth of tenancy to any important or recognizable extent, modern industrial influences have actually led to a general levelling of class status between tenant farmers and former landlord groups; instead of leading to the formation of an impoverished, rural, landless proletariat, Hong Kong's economic development has helped to create a prosperous farming population.

The orthodox thesis is contradicted not only by evidence from the Ping Shan study but also by evidence from elsewhere within China. Even Chen Han-seng, a harsh critic of Western economic influence in rural China and a major proponent of the accepted theory, presents, in a book (1939) purporting to show the ill effects of Western industry and commerce, data that could support a quite different conclusion. Writing on the Chinese tobacco industry, he describes the formation of the British American Tobacco Company in 1902, after the Treaty of Shimonoseki (1895) made it possible for foreign merchants to set up factories in treaty ports such as Shanghai, Hankow, Tsingtao, Tientsin, Mukden, and Harbin. At first the company had to import tobacco from the United States for its factories because at that time tobacco suitable for cigarette manufacture was not grown in China. This was a transitory phase, however, and in 1913 the company, with the assistance of Chinese agents and using American seed, established tobacco-producing regions in China (1939:5). Later, Chinese tobacco companies, like the Nanyang Bros., distributed American seed tobacco free of charge to peasants in several provinces. They taught the peasants how to raise suitable tobacco and promised them good prices for their crops. The tobacco regions selected were, according to Chen, all situated along modern railroad lines leading to the coastal industrial cities (1939:6).

Chen remarks that the introduction of commercial crops like tobacco "speeded up the introduction of the new railway system in China" (1939:7). It certainly stimulated the peasant economy by supplying cash income to the tobacco-growing peasants. Farmers who had originally grown "native" tobacco switched to American tobacco; peasants who had never grown tobacco reduced their grain-crop acreage to plant tobacco (1939:8).

Cigarette manufacturing in China, by both foreign and Chinese firms, rapidly grew into a sizable industry. The first Chinese company was established in 1905, and by 1927 there were 186 Chinese-owned plants (Chen, 1939:16). Under the continued stimulus of the growing cigarette industry, the cultivation of American tobacco spread among the farmers. By 1934, China (including Manchuria) was planting about one million *mow* in American tobacco. Two million peasants, or 300,000 families, were by this time engaged in the production of a crop which yielded a value of at least thirty million Chinese dollars (Chen, 1939:17). Although the production of American tobacco was not of crucial importance when seen against the total background of Chinese agriculture, this case does suggest that Western-inspired industry based in the treaty ports was not as uniformly harmful to the rural economy as some writers, including Chen, have implied. Chen claims that, because the peasants had insufficient capital to finance tobacco cultivation, they fell into the clutches of moneylending local gentry and Chinese middlemen, (1939:10). To me, however, Chen's thesis is not very convincing, particularly since the peasants were given the tobacco seed and fertilizer free of charge. From what I learned about the business acumen of the Ping Shan villagers, it is difficult to imagine all those peasants switching to tobacco cultivation if they did not make substantial profits.

Even in the cotton weaving industry, supposedly hard hit by the competition of the coastal textile factories, the picture is not simply one of uninterrupted decline (see Fong, 1936). The rural handloom weaving industry, which according to Fong still accounted for four-fifths of the cotton yarn consumption in China during the 1930's, was situated chiefly in the northern part of the country, especially in three areas—Wei Hsien in Shantung Province, and Kaoyang and Paoti in Hopei Province—with lesser centers scattered in other parts of the country (Fong, 1936:692). In a study of rural weaving in Kaoyang, Fong (1935) related the history of this industry over several decades of the modern period. Village weaving had existed in Kaoyang for a long time, but the creation of a substantial weaving industry began around 1906 with the establishment of a Textile Training Institute at Tientsin. Some Kaoyang residents acquired training at the institute and then returned to Kaoyang to set up a modern weaving industry (Fong, 1935:5–7). Machine-spun thread and Japanese iron looms were imported into the district from Tientsin between 1908 and 1914, and this stimulated commercial expansion in the district to service the weaving industry. A wholesale yarn market was established in 1913 to sell yarn imported from Tientsin spinning factories, and machine dyeing and calendering plants, native dyeing and calendering plants, printing plants, and the like were also established in conjunction with the weaving trade (Fong, 1933:54–55). The industry prospered after 1914 when the importation of goods from abroad became impossible and an unprecedented demand was created for native fabrics (Fong, 1935:5–7).

This wave of prosperity did not last long because after World War I foreign imports once more appeared on the domestic market. Also, from 1920 to 1924, the number of power looms in China increased from 16,993 to 29,234, and this represented further competition for the Kaoyang industry (Fong, 1935:9). Finally, the rise of rural weaving in a neighboring district also contributed to a decline by cutting into Kaoyang's business. This decline, however, was not permanent; in 1926 the improved Jacquard loom and new rayon fabrics were introduced, and these led to a new period of prosperity that lasted until 1929 (Fong, 1935:12–13). In 1930, however, rural weaving in Kaoyang entered another period of decline. Production dropped from 80,000 bales of cotton yarn and 12,000 boxes of rayon yarn in 1929 to 30,000 bales and 8,000 boxes in 1932, with a still greater decline in production in 1933 (Fong 1933:59).

Fong gives several reasons for the decline of the Kaoyang handloom industry in the 1930's: (1) the dumping of Japanese and Russian goods on the Chinese market; (2) the growth of the domestic power loom industry; (3) the civil war in the countryside, with the resulting chaos and decline in the domestic market; (4) the beginning of the Japanese invasion; (5) the beginning of the worldwide depression (1933:59; 1935:12–13); and finally (6) the backwardness of technique and business "know-how," which was responsible for the decline of many Chinese rural industries (1933:44).

The Kaoyang case illustrates the complex and varied factors that affected Chinese rural industries in the first half of this century. The weaving industry in Kaoyang was at one point largely stimulated by modern Western and Chinese industrial enterprise in the treaty port cities. If there had been no contact with treaty port centers, the industry would not have flourished as it did. Its ultimate decline in the 1930's can be attributed to a number of complex factors, not solely or even mainly to economic competition from the coastal industries.

Hou (1965:172–181) even argues that in spite of the great development of the cotton textile industry in China prior to 1937, the commercial hand-spinning industry did not suffer a serious decline, and the hand-weaving industry "must have witnessed growth." Furthermore, spare-time weaving for home consumption, a widespread industry in peasant households throughout rural China, according to Hou, must have resisted competition from foreign cloth to an even greater extent, especially in the interior regions of China where transportation costs reduced the competitiveness of modern textiles. Hou's evidence suggests that the traditional sector of the Chinese economy was able to coexist with the modern sector because modern technology held no advantage over the traditional industries in terms of unit cost. Modern manufactured goods were able to compete with the traditional products mainly in the area of higher-priced goods, or in the production of specialized goods beyond the capability of the handicraft industries, although most of the Chinese rural inhabitants continued to use the traditional handicraft products because they could not afford the more expensive manufactured goods from the treaty ports.

Fong stresses the backwardness of technique as perhaps the main reason for the decline of China's basic rural industries, silk and tea, as well as of other industries like straw plaiting and pottery manufacture (1933:44). This is also given primary importance by Allen and Donnithorne in their explanation of the decline of Chinese silk and tea industries (1954:52–57). They point out that Western demand stimulated a tea export industry that had ancient origins in China. Tea was the commodity that made up the bulk of China's exports to Europe before the modern era, but in the 1870's the export of tea began a process of decline that has continued to the present. The reason for the decline is that Chinese tea was driven off the world market by tea produced in other Asian countries. The same reason is responsible for the decline in the export of other Chinese rural products. Like tea, silk was made a major export industry largely through Western treaty port entrepreneurship. Hand-reeled silk and tea suffered a decline after the 1880's; tea because of China's lack of progress in modern methods of growing tea, and silk because of the competition from foreign filature silk. But, Hou says, in the case of silk, if the base period is taken as the 1840's, when foreign economic influences on China began in earnest, tea exports show a rise from 8,000 piculs a year to 19,300 piculs a year in 1932 (1965:169–170).

Donnithorne and Allen give many examples of the favorable effects of Western commerce on agriculture and the rural industries of China. For example, Western entrepreneurs created an export market for many Chinese products such as hides, soya oil, bean press cakes, and eggs (1954:80). In addition, some already existing handicraft industries were developed through Western initiative into sizable export industries. When Chefoo was opened to foreign trade in 1862, the traditional straw-plaiting industry was already well established, but with the development of an export market it flourished. By 1891 it was described as the "chief industry of parts of the province" and brought additional income to many peasants during the agricultural slack season (1954:84). Western enterprise may have harmed some of the traditional rural industries, but at the same time it stimulated others, and thus the question of determining the effects of Western and treaty port industry on the rural economy is more complex than many writers in the 1930's suggested.

Chi-ming Hou (1965:169), working from the viewpoint of an economic historian, has concluded that, contrary to the orthodox interpretation of modern China's economic history (which held that foreign trade and investment in China was detrimental to the traditional sector of the Chinese economy), there was an actual increase in the value of exports of Chinese handicrafts, from 1875 to 1931, to meet a rise in external demand for traditional Chinese products.

If some Chinese rural handicrafts were harmed by competition from foreign and treaty port industries, and this seems to be an established fact, the question remains just how serious a blow this was to the rural economy as a whole. Was the damage done serious enough to lead to the large-scale impoverishment of the peasants and to the bifurcation of class structure in the countryside? To answer these questions it is necessary to reach some judgment as to the overall importance of the handicraft industries in the rural economy.

In attempting to do this, we are handicapped by the same lack of reliable data that makes research into any aspect of modern Chinese rural economic history difficult. However, the data gathered by Buck in his survey of the Chinese farm economy do allow some provisional estimates of the importance of rural industries to farm families. Buck's survey results (1937:298) show that the net income from sources other than farm enterprises amounted to an average of 14 per cent of the total income of the farm families in his sample. He also found that 22 per cent of the farm families engaged in home industry; 16 per cent in merchant activities; 14 per cent hired out as farm laborers; 11 per cent engaged in unskilled labor; 7 per cent in skilled labor; 5 per cent in professional occupations; 2 per cent in scholarly activities; 1 per cent served as officials; and 1 per cent as soldiers (1937:298). If an average of 14 per cent of farm family income was derived from subsidiary work and if only 22 per cent of the families engaged in home industry, then income from home industries represented roughly only 14 per cent of the income of about one-fifth of the peasants, or about 3 per cent of the Chinese peasantry's total income. Even if all home industries were eliminated by the influx of industrial goods, an assumption clearly contrary to fact, this would have deprived the peasantry of only 3 per cent of their total income. This deprivation is hardly significant enough to force large numbers of peasants into bankruptcy, and it hardly warrants the overwhelming importance that many writers have attributed to it. Although the destruction of certain home industries in restricted areas that relied heavily on handicrafts may have caused economic hardship in these areas, especially among the poorer peasants dependent upon this income, from the point of view of the entire rural economy it seems to have been a relatively isolated and limited factor.

If we assume from the foregoing analysis that the rise of Western and Chinese capitalist industries did not affect rural handicrafts as adversely as has heretofore been believed, and if we further assume that the damage to the handicraft industries that did occur was not sufficient to bring about the impoverishment of the Chinese peasants as a whole, what about the other element in the thesis we have been discussing—the concentration of land ownership and the bifurcation of the rural population into landless laborers and wealthy landlords? Is this element of the theory any more valid than the argument concerning handicrafts?

In discussing land ownership in China, we are again faced with a lack of reliable data. Franklin Ho, one of the prominent Chinese rural economists in the pre-Communist period, tells of several attempts to carry out a cadastral survey in the '20's and '30's, none of which was successful (1936:47–51). The cadastral survey on which the land tax was based dates from the year 1713, and even these records were for the most part lost during the subsequent one and one-half centuries of internal warfare, particularly during the Taiping Rebellion. From

Ho's discussion it seems clear that little was actually known about the distribution of land ownership in China during the 1930's, and we must proceed with this difficulty in mind.

Various estimates have been made of the distribution of land ownership during the pre-Communist period. Statistics published by the Department of Agriculture and Commerce for 1918 suggest that at that time about 50 per cent of the peasants were occupying owners, 30 per cent were tenants, and 20 per cent were part-owners of their farms (quoted in Tawney, 1939:xiii). C. C. Chang gave figures in 1930, which showed that 51.7 per cent of the peasants owned their land, 22.1 per cent were part-owners, and 26.2 per cent were tenants. The National Agricultural Research Bureau published another estimate in 1935 that gave 46 per cent owners, 25 per cent part-owners, and 29 per cent tenants.[3]

Probably the most reliable figures on land ownership among Chinese farmers are those obtained in Buck's surveys of the rural economy. His figures show that during the period 1929–1930, 93 per cent of the land was privately owned (1937:193). Of the privately owned land, almost three-fourths was owned by the farmers themselves, with the balance being rented. For China as a whole, 54 per cent of the farmers owned their own land, 29 per cent owned some land and rented additional land, and only 17 per cent were full tenants. Conditions varied in different parts of China: in the Wheat Region of North China, 76 per cent of the peasants were full owners, 18 per cent part-owners, and only 6 per cent tenants; in the Rice Region of Central and South China, 38 per cent were owners, 37 per cent part-owners, and 25 per cent full tenants (Buck, 1937:196). As Cressey (1955:107–108) remarks, it is clear from Buck's study that for the country as a whole the importance of land concentration and tenancy as the fundamental problem in the rural economy has been vastly overestimated by Chinese writers. R. H. Tawney at one time supported this view. He stated in 1929 that "there is no landed aristocracy in China; when great estates are formed, they normally disappear in a few generations by division among heirs; and while in parts of the country small absentee landlords are numerous, large landlords, though they exist in certain regions, are few" (1929:23). Tawney goes on to say that landless agricultural workers probably form only a small minority of the rural population, and that, "whatever rural problems [there] may be, they are not complicated by the existence of a landless proletariat" (1929:24–25). These data on land ownership certainly do not support the generally accepted interpretation that Western capi-

---

[3] *Crop Reports*, Vol. III, April 15, 1935, No. 4.

talist industrialization of the treaty ports had led to the impoverishment of the peasants and to the division of rural Chinese society into a
small group of landlords on the one hand and a large group of
landless peasants on the other.

A possible argument might be that these figures do not show the
trends in rural China toward land concentration during the 1930's.
Tawney, writing in 1939 in his introduction to *Agrarian China*, takes
this position. He writes that "there is reason to think . . . that, in the
twenty years which have elapsed [since 1918], occupying ownership has
lost ground, and tenancy advanced. . . . Whatever the explanation of
the concentration of landed property, the fact of concentration can
hardly be questioned. It is more marked in the south than in the
north, and in the neighborhood of Shanghai or Canton, where 70 to 90
per cent of the holdings are thought to be rented. Over a large part of
China, however, tenancy of one kind or another undoubtedly pre-
dominates, and it appears everywhere to be increasing" (p. xiii). One
might wonder at the complete change in Tawney's interpretation over
a decade. A possible explanation is that during this decade Tawney
was influenced by the flood of articles by Chinese writers, almost all of
whom gave a Marxist-Leninist interpretation of the changes occurring
in the rural economic situation. The series of articles in *Agrarian
China* (Institute of Pacific Relations, 1939) are a good example of this
tendency; they speak again and again of powerful feudal landlords
and of poor, exploited and impoverished peasants. To an observer it
appears that most of these writers were dedicated more to proving the
necessity for revolution in a "feudal society" dominated by rich
landlords than they were to an objective assessment of the processes
operating in the economy. By 1939, it appears, Tawney was reflecting
the opinion of the overwhelming mass of Chinese writers on the
subject.

There is, however, little reliable evidence to prove that there was an
increasing concentration of land ownership during this period. Most of
the Chinese investigators did not make extensive surveys of land
ownership; they preferred to speak of, for example, "ten representative
villages in such and such a province where 2 per cent of the population owns 80 per cent of the land." In the absence of reliable data,
then, arguments on this topic must remain inconclusive. There is,
however, indirect evidence that tends to weaken the land-concentra-
tion thesis. Buck notes that land values either declined or remained
stable after 1925 because of unfavorable conditions in the countryside.
The major factor was, Buck said, the peasants' agitation against
landlords during this period, which "reduced the demand for land
and even encouraged owners to sell their property. Investors preferred

to make investments in industry, securities or bank deposits rather than risk their money in land" (1937:333). In more than one area of the country landlords were deserting the countryside and escaping to the safety of the cities. As Lee Siao-ming put it, "Many of the well-to-do landlord families of Foping have sold their land and made their way to larger cities such as Tientsin and Peiping" (Institute of Pacific Relations, 1939:21). Fei, in his study of Kaihsienkung, also mentions that, because of Communist agitation and the resulting insecurity of land rents, there was a scarcity of capital in the rural districts and that "at present . . . there is already a tendency for urban capital to move into the treaty-ports instead of into the rural districts" (1939:284). If landlords were so afraid of peasant unrest that they sold land or ran to the cities, it is difficult to see a process of land concentration taking place in rural China. The lack of concrete evidence to support the argument for land concentration during this period and the suggestive evidence concerning land values and the outflux of capital from the rural areas lead me to question to contention of most Chinese writers on this subject.

Tawney and other writers claimed that tenancy was highest in those areas of the country nearest the large treaty port centers, where industry and commerce supplied capital for land purchases and where the peasants were supposedly hardest hit by the influx of manufactured articles. Let us examine the evidence for this hypothesis. The best data on this subject are again presented by Buck. Buck has produced a map of China divided into eight regions and showing in detail the percentage of tenancy in each; the resulting pattern does not confirm the opinion that land concentration was highest in areas near the treaty ports. For example, the highest regional percentage of rented land (49 per cent) occurred in Szechuan Province, far from the influence of the coastal industrial cities, whereas in Kwangtung Province only 47 per cent of the land was rented. Also, the Southern Yangtze Rice-Tea Region had a higher percentage (42 per cent) of rented land than the Lower Yangtze Delta Region (39 per cent), the area immediately adjacent to the greatest center of Western commerce and industry in China, Shanghai. In addition to the regional breakdown, Buck's map also includes figures showing the distribution of tenancy in local areas all over China. Evidence supporting the hypothesis that land concentration was highest near the coastal centers of commerce is indicated by the 99 per cent tenancy rate for the Pearl River Delta region around Canton, and by the generally high figures that are found in areas along the southern coast. However, these are offset by the high tenancy rates in areas scattered all over central and south China far from the treaty port cities, and by the fact that there are also areas with low tenancy rates along the southern and southeastern coast. The areas around Tsingtao and Tientsin, other important treaty ports, had relatively low percentages of rented land. The conclusion indicated by Buck's figures is that land concentration was highest, not necessarily near treaty port cities (Buck, 1937:195), but in the most fertile farming regions of China; and this was probably a situation that existed before Western contact. Thus, the contention that there was an increasing concentration of land in pre-Communist China seems to receive no absolutely firm support from the available evidence.

Other important sources of information on the Chinese rural economy are the studies of Chinese villages that were carried out in the period prior to the Communist Revolution. If Western economic influences emanating from the treaty ports were destroying the handicraft industries, impoverishing the peasants, and leading to the bifurcation of classes in the countryside by increasing land concentration and tenancy, this process should have been noticeable in those villages studied during this period that were situated close to the treaty port industrial and commercial centers. This first-hand material is a useful supplement to the general evidence considered so far in our discussion.

A relevant case from North China, in many ways comparable to Ping Shan, is the village of Taitou in Shantung Province, described by Martin C. Yang. Taitou is located near a market town, only sixteen miles from the city of Tsingtao, an important coastal treaty port in North China that had been developed by the Germans. As M. C. Yang describes it, before the war Tsingtao was "a center of commerce, industry, and transportation and thus [played] . . . an important role in the growing trade between rural China and the manufacturing centers in distant parts of the world" (1948:1). Like Ping Shan, then, Taitou, although not within a foreign enclave, was an example of a village near a coastal treaty port and directly subject to its economic influences. If Fei and other writers are correct, the ill effects of treaty port commerce and industry should have been visible in Taitou.

It is clear, however, from M. C. Yang's account that no such ill effects were evident in the village. In the first place, Taitou was overwhelmingly agricultural in character, with almost all the peasants cultivating their own land (1948:1). The village did not seem to depend greatly upon decentralized handicraft industries for a livelihood and was not impoverished. There was no serious problem of tenancy, and concentration of land ownership was conspicuous only by its absence. In fact, an opposite process of land ownership, one of decentralization, seems to have been more characteristic of Taitou: M. C. Yang mentions that there were two or three families who in 1935 had owned from 80 to 90 *mou* of land each, but that by the 1940's these estates had been split up among heirs (1948:16). Land sales consisted, as they always had, of small bits and pieces sold to fellow villagers, and there is no mention or indication that commercial or industrial capital from Tsingtao had entered the village land market.

Some of the Taitou villagers engaged in nonagricultural industries during the slack agricultural periods, but none made their living solely from handicraft activities. Among the supplementary industries were a new foundry run by two brothers who had learned their trade in Tsingtao; a woodworking shop; and three or four small weaving establishments. M. C. Yang mentions some decline in the spinning and weaving activities in the village. Traditionally, the villagers spun, wove, and dyed cloth to make their own clothing, but with the economic development of Tsingtao they shifted to factory-made cloth for all except work clothes. The business of the three or four cloth weavers in the village was undoubtedly hurt, but even so, like most Chinese handicraftsmen, they were still in business at the time Yang wrote. One compromise which allowed them to remain in business involved their buying factory-spun yarn and weaving it on the old looms (1948:26), an adaptation made in other parts of China.

It seems clear from the Taitou example that some harm was done to the rural industries; but from the point of view of the total village economy, no serious consequences resulted: no process of rural impoverishment or land concentration owing to the effects of modern industrial and commercial influence was noticeable in the village. As M. C. Yang remarks, particularly to those who might accuse him of overlooking landlords, usurers, and crooked village gentry, "One cannot assume that because abuses exist in some parts of China, they must be found also in Taitou, and that if life is dark in some village, it must be the same in this one" (1948:xii).

Another relevant study of the Chinese rural economy was done by C. K. Yang (1959b), who focused on the village of Nanching, situated five miles from the city of Canton on the Pearl River Delta. Nanching is only about 80 miles from the New Territories and is similar to the Ping Shan villages in its basic social, cultural, and economic features. Yang says that Nanching "was typical of the villages near large southern cities in the pre-Communist period" (1959b:9); if Fei's thesis is correct, the ill effects that he predicted should certainly have been evident in Nanching.

In the early part of this century, Nanching was connected to the city of Canton only by narrow flagstone paths. These inadequate transportation facilities limited urban contact and allowed the village to retain its essential rural character (1959b:7). However, in the 1920's, Canton began a period of commercial expansion, and, with the development of transportation facilities, Nanching began to feel the economic influences from the nearby city and the outside world. Like Ping Shan, Nanching was situated near a market town which brought urban and commercial influences directly to the village, and Yang mentions that Nanching villagers could travel and transport goods to Hong Kong well within a day (1959b:8). Yang summarizes the influences of the urban centers on Nanching as follows (1959b:74–75) :

> The urban centers . . . operated as a safety valve for the hard-pressed elements in the countryside and for the overstrained agrarian economy. On the other hand, when the urban economy was plagued by a depression or disrupted by political and military disturbances, the unemployed or otherwise economically dislocated persons could return to the village where their kinship roots lay and where the soil would provide subsistence until times became better again for them to return, to the city. The urban and the village economies thus helped each other regain balance when either was struck by a crisis.

This last statement would also hold true for the villages of Ping Shan and for Hong Kong, and it is precisely one of the major points of my argument. It seems clear from Yang's remarks that the overall effects of the coastal centers of industry and commerce were beneficial to Nanching's economy because they provided an outlet for surplus rural population which could never be fully employed in agriculture. If it had not been for the employment opportunities available in Canton and Hong Kong, the economic situation in the village would certainly have been much worse than it was.

Contrary to the orthodox thesis, Yang found that the industrial development of Canton did not impoverish the peasants by destroying their handicraft industries, primarily because in Nanching, as in Ping Shan, handicrafts did not seem to have been very important. Yang does, however, mention the decline in handicraft industries in Canton and nearby towns, and discusses the indirect effect of this decline on the economy of Nanching (1959b:64) :

> Whereas ruinous competition from machine-made goods from both Chinese and foreign sources had directly impoverished rural populations in parts of the country where home industry was well developed, its effect on Nanching was only an indirect one. The reduction of handicraft industries in Canton and the neighboring towns created unemployment, thus making it harder for the people from Nanching to find work in towns and cities when it became difficult to make a living at home.

The indirect effects of the decline of urban handicraft shops need more data to be firmly established but, in any case, this argument was *not* one of primary concern to most writers on the rural economy. Moreover, from Yang's account, it appears that the villagers did not have too much trouble finding work in Canton and Hong Kong, and that the modern commercial and industrial enterprises offered employment opportunities which helped to offset any harm done to handicraft shops in the cities.

The evidence that Yang presents on the land situation in Nanching is inconclusive, since he lacked not only information on the history of land ownership in the village but also exact figures on the distribution of land ownership in 1949. According to Yang, the degree of concentration in 1949, while substantial, "did not tally with the generalization of the Chinese Communist Party that the landlords and rich peasants who constituted 10 per cent of the rural population owned 70 to 80 per cent of the land" (1959b:46). Nanching had three large landowning families who owned 120, 70, and 60 *mou*, respectively, as well as two other families who owned 30 *mou* each (1959b:44). Yang says that the property of the largest landowning families had been acquired during the past 50 years, but that "there were no records to show how many large landlords there had been in former times or the extent of their aggregate possessions of land as compared with the present situation" (1959b:76). He notes that the "protracted war against the Japanese invasion of 1937–45 and the inflationary postwar years" had varying effects in different areas of China, but that in Nanching it led to the decentralization of land ownership (1959b:45, 76). However, Yang says that this trend was confined to the war and postwar years and did not represent a long-term tendency over the past half-century.

Yang says that the "one discernible change in land ownership in Nanching" was that many villagers, attracted by economic opportunities, went to the cities to live and work, and then used their earnings to buy small plots of land in the village. According to Yang, in 1948 the village had a population of about 1,100 persons, divided into 230 households (1959b:14). He notes that before 1933–1934 there were about 100 families who had one or more members working and living in the towns and cities, and that as late as 1948–1951 there were still 40 to 50 such families (1959b:71). Some village families bought small bits of land in the village with their earnings from urban employment. Yang sees this trend as one which reduced both the ownership of land by and the income of the "tillers of the soil," and he says that it explains in part the high percentage of tenancy in the village. Moreover, he claims that "these were typical phenomena in a village so near a big city, phenomena that had long attracted the attention of students of rural problems of modern China" (1959b:76).

I assume that by this statement Yang feels he is lending support to the orthodox interpretation of the effects of urban economic influences on the rural economy. It seems to me, however, that this is stretching the thesis a bit far. In the first place, if the situation in Nanching was similar to that in the villages of Ping Shan, most likely some of the members of the farm families of the village also had short- and long-term jobs in the city. In the second place, the "typical phenomena" of which Fei, Tawney, and others were speaking did not include the purchase of small plots of land by village families that had a member or two working in the city; on the contrary, Fei and the others were talking about land purchases by large absentee landlords and merchant-moneylenders who had gained their capital from modern commerce and industry. Finally, this statement is inconsistent with an earlier one by Professor Yang that "the majority of these landowners [villagers who bought land with money earned in the cities] kept their families in the village; they were not absentee owners who drained wealth from the village" (1959b:74). In short, it seems clear that, although the data on land ownership are inconclusive, they do not support the thesis that there was a tendency for land to concentrate in the hands of absentee landlords.

Yang says that he "had no accurate basis for a statistical comparison of the present village economy with that of former periods," but that two bits of evidence seemed to confirm the villagers' view that life was harder than in previous periods. Yang notes that the newer houses in the village were generally of poorer quality than the older houses, and that many of the ancestral temples of the village were in extremely poor condition. Yang is justifiably cautious in assessing this evidence, but he does go on to say that it is an "indication that the economic condition of the village as a whole had deteriorated compared to that of half a century ago" (1959b:78).

On the basis of what I observed in the villages of Ping Shan, I must disagree with Yang that this type of evidence is necessarily an indication of a decline in prosperity. Like the newer houses in Nanching, those currently being built in Ping Shan do not compare favorably with the older houses. The reason for this, however, is not that the villagers cannot afford better housing; it is simply that they consider the older homes out of date and prefer "modern-style" houses, even though most of these are poorly constructed. Similarly, the ancestral halls in Ping Shan are in poor condition not because the villagers are unable financially to repair them, but because they are no longer as interested in the ancestral halls and thus permit them to run down until a good occasion arises for remodelling them. It seems, then, that the evidence cited by Yang to show a decline in village prosperity does not show this at all, since the same conditions exist in Ping Shan, where the economic situation of the villagers has clearly improved. It may be that the villagers of Nanching, like some of the Ping Shan villagers, simply enjoy talking about the "good old days," when life was supposedly much better than it is at present.

If we look at the evidence from Nanching, a village similar to the villages of Ping Shan in many ways and which Yang believes to have been typical of suburban villages in South China before the revolution, it seems clear that the orthodox interpretation of modern Chinese rural economic history holds no better there than it does in Ping Shan. There were no important handicraft industries to be destroyed by manufactured goods; there is no firm evidence for the increasing concentration of land ownership in the hands of absentee landlords; and there is no convincing indication of a decline in village prosperity. On the contrary, the coastal centers of industry and commerce seem, on the whole, to have benefitted the village economy by providing both employment for the excess rural population and markets for the village vegetable-gardening industry.

A final source of evidence on China's rural economy in the pre-Communist period is the work of Fei himself. No other writer on the subject has been so influential with non-Chinese audiences as Fei Hsiao-tung, and no other writer has so clearly formulated and supported the thesis that I am in part arguing against in this book.

Fei's first major work on rural China was *Peasant Life in China,* published in 1939. It was in this study of Kaihsienkung, a village situated on Lake Tai in the lower Yangtze delta about 80 miles from Shanghai (1939:10–11), that he formulated the major elements in his argument. The economy of Kaihsienkung in the 1930's was overwhelmingly agricultural, with 274 out of 360 family heads engaged chiefly in farming (1939:139). The second major source of income for the villagers was the domestic silk industry, which, according to Fei, had been carried on here for centuries (1939:197). During the decade prior to Fei's study, this industry had been hard-hit by competition from better-quality Japanese silk on the world market; the worldwide depression of the 1930's also had an adverse effect, lowering the price of even the finest silk on the world market; and the introduction of modern factories for silk production in China and Japan created even greater competition for the rural industry (1939:16). According to Fei's analysis, the decline of the domestic silk industry had several effects in the village: (1) it led to shortages in the family budgets for food and other necessities; (2) it caused a delay in marriages and a cessation of ceremonial festivities; and (3) it increased usury in the village (1939:198). As the villagers were increasingly affected by the "deindustrialization process," Fei's term for the destruction of traditional decentralized handicraft industries such as silk (1939:280), they had to borrow from moneylenders, to whom they eventually lost the ownership of their land. This situation led to the concentration of land ownership in the hands of absentee landlords and to the drainage of rents from the village. Fei noted that this chain of events in Kaihsienkung "seems to confirm the general point suggested by Professor Tawney that the problem of tenancy is a function of the financial relation between village and city" (1939:186).

In his second major work on the rural economy, *Earthbound China,* written in collaboration with Chang Chih-i, Fei uses material from his research in Yunnan Province during the years of the Sino-Japanese War to develop his initial ideas into a more general theory of the history of the modern Chinese economy. He begins his book with a statement of admiration for Tawney's *Land and Labour in China* (Fei and Chang, 1945:5):

> Tawney's conclusions are valuable not so much because of the factual material but because he interprets the data against the background of the general economic changes taking place in China— changes which are comparable to those which occurred in Europe during the Industrial Revolution. . . .
> Information on most of the factors essential for presenting a complete picture of the agrarian situation is singularly lacking in the existing material. To construct a synthesis from the isolated data of social surveys, Tawney had to resort to conjectures based on his wealth of knowledge of the economic history of Europe. The parallel between the Industrial Revolution in the West and that which is likely to take place in the East is clear. One who reads Chinese material against the background of medieval Europe certainly will gain illuminating insights. Tawney's admirable summary of the Chinese economic situation, *Land and Labour in China,* remains the best treatise on China.

Fei then goes on to quote a favorite passage from Tawney's book (1932:37–38) which Fei mentions in several other works, and which forms the basis for his own interpretation of the dynamics of change in the rural economy:

> Occupying ownership is least prevalent in the proximity of great cities where urban capital flows into agriculture—in the Canton delta 85 per cent of farmers, and in the neighborhood of Shanghai 95 per

cent, are said to be tenants—and most general in the regions but little affected by modern economic developments. . . . It is reasonable to expect that, with the expansion of modern industrial and financial methods into regions as yet unaffected by them, similar conditions will tend to establish themselves in other parts of the country [quoted by Fei and Chang, 1945:6].

Fei says that this statement is essentially true, and that it was confirmed by his study of the village on Lake Tai. However, Fei qualifies his acceptance of Tawney's thesis based on European analogies by pointing out that the concentration of land ownership in China is not based solely upon fertility of the soil and the development of modern commerce, but that it depends upon the institutional arrangements of the villages and the importance of decentralized handicraft industries (Fei and Chang, 1945:6).

Fei states explicitly that the remainder of his book will explore the implications of Tawney's position in an attempt to formulate a "general statement of the way in which the concentration of landownership and the development of tenancy is effected by the decline in income of the peasants as a result of the Industrial Revolution" (Fei and Chang, 1945:16). The theoretical framework and methodology which Fei uses in formulating his thesis is similar to and based upon Robert Redfield's work in Yucatan (see Redfield, 1941), where synchronic studies were utilized to arrive at a diachronic formulation of processes of change. In Fei's words (Fei and Chang, 1945:16), "In order to study land ownership, four types of community were selected. They were selected to represent different degrees of concentration."

The body of Fei and Chang's book consists of a description and analysis of three villages in Yunnan Province: Luts'un, Yits'un, and Yuts'un. Luts'un was, according to Fei, representative of the traditional village in interior China, which had a simple form of economy with neither commerce nor industry playing an important part. The main occupation of the people was the management and cultivation of farms. The villagers were either petty landowners or landless laborers; there were no landlords with large holdings, and absentee owners were few and insignificant. Fei remarks that "in these fundamental ways Luts'un represents, in miniature, traditional China. It is also logically a prototype of the types of villages described later, where the development of handicraft industries and the commercial influence of the town complicates the structure" (Fei and Chang, 1945:19).

Yits'un, the second village described by Fei and Chang, was a fairly isolated village in interior Yunnan. The land around Yits'un was so barren that the villagers could not gain a livelihood from agriculture, and, consequently, they supplemented their income with rural industry of two types. The first, paper manufacturing, required substantial capital and was owned and operated by the few rich landowning families in the village. The second type of industry, basket weaving, was carried on by the poorer families. The development of Yits'un's rural industries was limited by deficient transportation facilities and the lack of raw material, but, even so, the development of the paper mills brought the owners enough capital to buy up land in the surrounding countryside (Fei and Chang, 1945:135–206).

The third Yunnan village described in *Earthbound China* is Yuts'un, situated 15 minutes from a town on a well-developed trade route between Burma and the city of Kunming (Fei and Chang, 1945:206–291). Because of its geographical location, this region was developed industrially and commercially, and was subject to the penetration of other modern influences during the war years. In this area, as in most other parts of China, population was dense and land was in limited supply, and thus many of the peasants engaged in rural handicraft industries to supplement their agricultural income. The rural weaving industry in Yuts'un, like that in Taitou, was well developed, with many women from village households weaving their own cloth, making the family's clothing, and selling the surplus fabric on the market. Nevertheless, Fei says that "in general, weaving is only a subsidiary occupation in the household. The women make as much money as they can out of it without considering it of vital importance" (Fei and Chang, 1945:240). And he notes in another place that this industry was not important in the family economy (Fei and Chang, 1945:244). According to Fei's analysis, the development of modern commerce in the towns and cities of this region brought sizable profits to merchant middlemen who used their capital to purchase land from impoverished peasants. This was the beginning of the process of land concentration, and 45 per cent of the rice fields and 39 per cent of the garden plots were owned by absentee landlords (Fei and Chang, 1945:227).

Finally, to complete the series of village studies which was supposed to show the course of economic change in rural China, Fei included Kaihsienkung, the village that he had studied earlier in *Peasant Life in China* (1939). Of the four villages studied in *Earthbound China*, Kaihsienkung had had the greatest degree of contact with modern commerce and industry. Here the ill effects of treaty port cities on adjacent rural areas were supposedly most severe: the peasants, impoverished by the decline of the silk industry, were being forced to sell their land to moneylenders and merchants from the urban areas, and thus the process of land concentration was well under way.

Put together, these four village types, said Fei, "show the process of economic development going on in rural China today" (Fei and Chang, 1945: 206). The hypothesis developed in this book, he said, "will require further research before its full validity is established. But the present study clearly supports this conclusion" (Fei and Chang, 1945:306).

Although I grant the brilliance of Fei and Chang's fieldwork, I believe it is still possible to dispute their methods and conclusions. There is a difference between *testing* an hypothesis and *illustrating* a theory; and it seems to me that Fei and Chang's formulation in *Earthbound China* is more an illustration of a preconceived notion than it is a test. For the fact remains, and Fei and Chang make this explicit, that these four villages were selected so as to demonstrate the process of land concentration as the rural population increases its contacts with modern economic influences (Fei and Chang, 1945:16–17). If this is the case, then how can this study be considered a validation of their thesis? The circularity here is obvious: selected data are arranged according to a preconceived idea of what the course of economic change in rural China "must" have been. Fei claims to have used the comparative method in this study (Fei and Chang, 1945:16), but the method he utilizes is essentially that of the nineteenth-century evolutionist writers. In the absence of historical information, the social evolutionists arranged coexisting societies throughout the world in an order leading from the simple to the complex, from the undifferentiated to the differentiated, and from social and cultural conditions least like nineteenth-century Europe to those most nearly approaching it. By so doing, these writers claimed to be discovering the laws of social change and development; in actuality they were only illustrating a preconceived notion of the course of social development. In the absence of historical data, there is no real proof or disproof of such formulations. Fei and Chang employ similar reasoning, albeit on a smaller scale. They have little or no historical information to prove that, in any of the villages they discuss, change took place in a pattern consistent with their hypothesis. Lacking such evidence, they follow the method used by Redfield *The Folk Culture of Yucatan,* selectively arranging a series of coexisting social and economic differences into a time sequence and ordered dictated by their theory. And the only way they can do this is by assuming the very thing they are trying to prove. Their study does not at all prove their theory of the direction of economic changes in rural China, a theory borrowed from Tawney who, in turn, was arguing mainly from European analogies; their work merely illustrates the theory.

Even in his study of Kaihsienkung, which is his most convincing example, Fei actually presents no historical evidence to prove his contention that the decline in the village silk industry forced the villagers to sell land to usurers from the city and thus led to the concentration of land ownership in the hands of absentee landlords. The only way that Fei could prove this would be to offer historical data on land sales and ownership in Kaihsienkung, and this he fails to do. He does say that about two-thirds of the subsoil of the village was owned by absentee landlords (1939:191). It may well be that Fei's postulated processes were operating at the time of his study, but he presents information in his book that would seem to lead to precisely the opposite conclusion. He tells us that the peasants in this area, influenced by the Communists' slogan of "land to the tillers," were refusing in many cases to pay their rent (1939:190), and that "at present, owing to the insecurity of rent, there is already a tendency for urban capital to move into the treaty-ports instead of into rural districts" (1939:284). In short, Fei fails to present convincing evidence that the concentration of land ownership in Kaihsienkung was a recent phenomenon brought about by Western-inspired industry and commerce. It would seem equally reasonable to believe that here, as in the villages of Ping Shan, land traditionally was concentrated, but we have no actual evidence to prove this contention either.

In summary, then, Fei's empirical studies seem at first glance to be a powerful argument for the thesis that Western treaty port industrial and commercial influences destroyed the rural handicraft industries, impoverished the peasants, and led to the concentration of land ownership in the hands of absentee landlords. Upon close scrutiny, however, Fei simply does not present the data necessary to prove this thesis, and I am led to conclude that this widely accepted interpretation of the effects of Western treaty port cities on the rural Chinese economy in the half-century preceding the Communist Revolution is at least open to serious question.

One of the main reasons that Chinese writers found a Marxist-Leninist thesis so attractive was that it laid most of the blame for China's ills on the Western nations that established and developed the treaty port cities. As our discussion of *Peasant Life in China* and *Earthbound China* has shown, Fei shared this tendency to blame the Western nations for China's troubles, and he expressed this view again in *China's Gentry,* which was published in 1953. In this book, Fei writes that the Western treaty ports, such as Shanghai, were "a gate by means of which foreign goods could come in; . . . they served as ratholes for dribbling away Chinese wealth. When I call the treaty ports 'economic ratholes,' I mean that they were fundamentally similar to the garrison towns, a community of consumers and not of producers" (1953:105). Fei regarded the treaty ports as "parasites," which brought about "the invasion of an industrialized economy into an economically inferior area, where a simple economy still prevailed" (1953:107). According to Fei, recent history has shown that the treaty ports did not promote rural prosperity; "on the contrary, the rise of modern Chinese cities has been paralleled by the decline in Chinese rural economy." Fei sees this rural economic decline and the impoverishment of the peasants as the main reason behind the Communist Revolution in China (1939:285), since the experience of the Chinese people with treaty ports, Fei says, led them to react against capitalism and ultimately to adopt a socialist ideology (1939:209).

Thus, the Marxist-Leninist thesis was attractive to writers in the '30's and '40's not only because it laid the blame for China's ills on the Western nations, but also because it provided an economic rationale for revolution that dovetailed nicely with the already-existing nationalist appeal for revolution. The majority of Chinese intellectuals went along with this thinking and seemed to have been easily convinced that one revolutionary stroke could solve all of China's pressing problems.

One can understand the appeal behind such reasoning, and no one can deny that the Chinese had many valid reasons to detest the treaty port cities as symbols of Western imperialism. But the effect of treaty port industry upon the rural Chinese economy is a matter of fact and must be discussed in factual and dispassionate terms. And the fact remains that the basic reason for the poverty of rural China in the first half of the twentieth century was not the growth of industry in the treaty ports, but simply that too many people were trying to make a living from too little land with too primitive a technology.

If this analysis is correct, then the effects of treaty port industry and commerce upon rural China in the pre-Communist period were much more complex than the orthodox theorists would have us believe.[4] In southernmost China, the effects of treaty port centers on adjacent villages were largely beneficial. Elsewhere, the treaty port cities did have some ill effects on the adjacent rural areas, although the extent of these differed according to the dependence of a particular village upon handicraft industry and its location. Villages like Taitou, where handicraft production was not important, were apparently little affected by modern industry and commerce. However, in places like Kaihsienkung, which depended heavily upon handicraft industries, the effects of the treaty port centers were severely felt, although these effects differed from time to time, with the rural economy alternatively prospering and declining according to the villages' ability to cope with

[4] Fei in his work is, of course, conscious of the diversity of rural China and is not as dogmatic as some other writers on the subject.

competition on the world market and competition from manufactured goods. Initially, many of these villages benefitted from Western enterprise because it created new export markets for traditional products; in the 1930's, however, many of them suffered a decline in income owing to the worldwide depression. Villages situated on the new routes of communication undoubtedly benefitted from the treaty port centers in that their crops and handicraft products could be easily transported to the newly created markets, whereas those situated in the interior, far from the railroads and other communication routes, were probably relatively little affected by the influence of the coastal industrial cities.

The total picture that emerges, then, is one of great diversity. China contained hundreds of thousands of villages, and, among them, one can find a wide range of rural economic conditions. A simple Marxist-Leninist interpretation of the effects of Western industry and commerce upon the rural economy is misleading; and, while valid in certain respects and by no means totally wrong, as a general hypothesis to explain changes in China's rural economy over the first half of the twentieth century, it is oversimplified.

Glossary

Ch'ao chou jen 潮洲人

Chap ng tsoh (chi wu tsu) 輯五祖

Chia chang 家長

Chia fen t'ien 家份田

Chi hsiu t'ien 祭修田

Dau-chung (tou-chung) 斗種

Fan ling (fen ling) 粉嶺

Fang 房

Feng shui 風水

Fui sha wai (hui sha wei) 灰沙圍

Ha fu (hsia fu) 下伏

Ha tsuen (hsia ts'un) 厦村

Hakka (k'o chia) 客家

Hang mei tsuen (k'eng wei ts'un) 坑尾村

Hang tau tsuen (k'eng t'ou ts'un) 坑頭村

Hok lo (ho liao) 厦佬

Hop yik company (ho i Kung ssu) 合益公司

Hsiang 鄉

Hsiang chang 鄉長

Hsiang i chü 鄉意局

Hsien [county] 縣

Hsiung ti 兄弟

Hung uk tsuen (hung wu ts'un) 洪屋村

Jong shan county (Chung shan hsien) 中山縣

Jui t'ai 瑞泰

Kam tin (chin t'ien) 錦田

Kiu tau wai (ch'iao t'ou wei) 橋頭圍

Kung so 公所

Lok ka (liu chia) 六家

Mien [face] 面

Mow (mu) 畝

Nan-wu hsien-sheng 南無先生

Nam tau (nan t'ou) 南頭

Ng fok (wu fu) 五服

Pen ti jen 本地人

Ping ha road (ping hsia lu) 屏厦路

Ping shan (p'ing shan) 屏山

Ping shan kung so 屏山公所

Ping shan jen 屏山人
Po an county (pao an hsien)
寶安縣

Sai kung (hsi kung) 西貢
Sai yeung ts'oi (hsi yang ts'ai)
西洋菜
San on county (hsin an hsien)
新安縣
Seak po tsuen (shih pu ts'un)
石埗村
Sey iap (ssu i) 四邑
Sha kong wai (sha chiang wei)
沙江圍
Sha tau kok (sha t'ou chiao)
沙頭角
Sha tin (sha t'ien) 沙田
Sham chun river (shen chen ho)
深圳河
Shan ha tsuen (shan hsia ts'un)
山下村
Sheung cheung wai (shang chang
wei) 上章圍
Sheung shui (shang shui) 上水
Su-po hsiung-ti 叔伯兄弟

Sung [food] 餸

Ta chia chang 大家長
Tai po (ta p'u) 大埔
Tang [surname] (teng) 鄧
Tanka (tan chia) 蛋家
Ti [subsurface] 底
Ti kwat (ti ku) 地骨
T'o p'i (t'u p'i) 土皮
Tong fong tsuen (t'ang fang
ts'un) 糖房村
Tsim sha tsui (chien sha tsui)
尖沙嘴
Tsu chang 族長
Tsuen wan (ch'üan wan) 荃灣

Wai jen 外人
Wai shan hall (wei hsin t'ang)
維新堂
Wan chai (wan tzu) 灣仔
Wu fu 五服

Yat t'ai hall (i t'i t'ang)
一體堂
Yuen long (yüan lang) 元朗

Zunn tak hall (ch'ung te t'ang)
崇德堂

Bibliography

Allen, G. C., and Audrey G. Donnithorne
  1954 *Western enterprise in Far Eastern economic development.* London: George Allen and Unwin, Ltd.
Anderson, Eugene N., Jr.
  1967 "The fish classification of the Hong Kong Boat People." Unpublished Ph.D. dissertation, University of California, Berkeley, California.
Baker, Hugh
  1964a "Marriage and the family," in *Aspects of social organization in the New Territories,* pp. 27–31. Hong Kong: Royal Asiatic Society, Hong Kong Branch.
  1964b "Burial, geomancy and ancestor worship," in *Aspects of social organization in the New Territories,* pp. 36–39. Hong Kong: Royal Asiatic Society, Hong Kong Branch.
  1964c "Clan organization and its role in village affairs: Some differences between single-clan and multiple-clan villages," in *Aspects of social organization in the New Territories,* pp. 4–9. Hong Kong: Royal Asiatic Society, Hong Kong Branch.
Balfour, S. F.
  1941 "Hong Kong before the British," *T'ien Hsia Monthly,* XI (4,5). Shanghai.
Barnett, K. M. A. (Census Commissioner)
  1961 *Hong Kong: Report on the 1961 census.* 3 vols. Hong Kong: Government Press.
Blackie, W. J.
  n.d. *Report on agriculture in Hong Kong with policy recommendations.* Hong Kong: Government Press.
Blake, Sir Arthur Henry
  1900 "Report of a visit by Governor Blake to the New Territories" (letter to Mr. Chamberlain dated August 16, 1899), in *Correspondence respecting the extension of the boundaries of the Colony.* London: Her Majesty's Government.
Buck, John L.
  1937 *Land utilization in China.* Shanghai: The Commercial Press.
Chang, C. C.
  1930 "A statistical survey of farm tenancy in China," *China Critic,* September 25, 1930, Vol III, No. 39, pp. 917–922.
Chao Yuen-ren
  1947 *Cantonese primer.* Cambridge: Harvard University Press.

Chen Han-seng
  1933 *The present agrarian problem in China.* Shanghai: China Institute of Pacific Relations.
  1936 *Landlord and peasant in China.* New York: International Publishers. (Also published as *Agrarian problems in southernmost China.*)
  1939 *Industrial capital and Chinese peasants.* Shanghai: Kelly and Walsh.

Chi Yu Tang
  1918 *An economic survey of Chinese agriculture.* Ministry of Agriculture and Commerce, 1918, pp. 241–242.

Clapham, J. H.
  1955 *Economic development of France and Germany.* Cambridge, England: Cambridge University Press.

Court, W. H. B.
  1954 *Concise economic history of Britain.* Cambridge, England: Cambridge University Press.

Cressey, George B.
  1934 *China's geographical foundations: A survey of the land and the people.* New York and London: McGraw-Hill Company.
  1955 *Land of the 500 million.* New York: McGraw-Hill Company.

Diaz, May N.
  1967 "Economic relations in peasant society" (Introduction to Part II), in *Peasant society: A reader,* ed. by Jack M. Potter, May N. Diaz, and George M. Foster. Boston: Little, Brown and Company.

Director of Agriculture and Forestry
  1960 *Hong Kong annual departmental report by the Director of Agriculture and Forestry for the year 1959–60.* Hong Kong: Government Press.
  1961 *Hong Kong annual departmental report by the Director of Agriculture and Forestry for the year 1960–61.* Hong Kong: Government Press.

District Commissioner of the New Territories
  1961 *Annual departmental report by the District Commissioner of the New Territories for the financial year 1960–1961.* Hong Kong: Government Press.

Engels, Frederick
  1955 "The peasant question in France and Germany," in *Selected works in two volumes.* Vol. II. Moscow: Foreign Language Publishing House [1894].
  1958 *The conditions of the working class in England.* Oxford: Basil Blackwell [1844].

Fairbank, John K., Alexander Eckstein, and L. S. Yang
  1960 "Economic change in early modern China," *Economic Development and Culture Change,* IX (1):1–27.

Fei Hsiao-tung
  1939 *Peasant life in China: A field study of country life in the Yangtze Valley.* London: Routledge and Kegan Paul, Ltd.
  1953 *China's gentry: Essays in rural-urban relations.* Chicago: University of Chicago Press.

Fei Hsiao-tung and Chang Chih-i
  1945 *Earthbound China: A study of rural economy in Yunnan.* Chicago: University of Chicago Press.

Feuerwerker, Albert
1958 *China's early industrialization.* Cambridge: Harvard University Press.
Firth, Raymond
1951 *Elements of social organization.* London: Watts and Company.
Fong, H. D.
1933 *Rural industries in China.* Nankai Institute of Economics, Industry Series, Bulletin No. 5 (Nankai University). Tientsin: Chihli Press, Inc.
1934 "China's factory act and the cotton industry," *Monthly Bulletins on Economic China,* VII (3) :93–104.
1935 *Rural weaving and the merchant employers in a North China district.* Nankai Institute of Economics, Industry Series, Bulletin No. 7 (Nankai University). Tientsin: Chihli Press, Inc.
1936 "Rural industrial enterprise in North China," *Nankai Social and Economic Quarterly,* VIII (4) :691–772.
Fortes, Meyer
1953 "The structure of unilineal descent groups," *American Anthropologist,* 55:17–41.
Foster, George M.
1961 "The dyadic contract: A model for the social structure of a Mexican peasant village," *American Anthropologist,* 63:1173–1192.
1962 *Traditional cultures and the impact of technological change.* New York: Harper and Brothers.
Freedman, Maurice
1958 *Lineage organization in Southeastern China.* London School of Economics, Monographs on Social Anthropology, No. 18. London: The Athlone Press.
1966a "Shifts of power in the Hong Kong New Territories," *Journal of African and Asian Studies,* I (1) :3–12.
1966b *Chinese lineage and society: Fukien and Kwangtung.* London School of Economics, Monographs on Social Anthropology, No. 33. London: The Athlone Press.
Gallin, Bernard
1966 *Hsin Hsing, Taiwan: A Chinese village in change.* Berkeley and Los Angeles: The University of California Press.
Gamble, Sidney D.
1954 *Ting Hsien: A North China rural community.* New York: International Secretariat, Institute of Pacific Relations.
Gibbs, L.
1931 "Agriculture in the New Territories," *The Hong Kong Naturalist,* II (2) :132–134. Hong Kong.
Groves, Robert G.
1964 "The origins of two market towns in the New Territories," in *Aspects of social organization in the New Territories,* pp. 16–20. Hong Kong: Royal Asiatic Society, Hong Kong Branch.
Hambro, E.
1955 *Hong Kong refugees survey mission. The problem of Chinese refugees in Hong Kong: Report submitted to the United Nations High Commissioner for Refugees.* Leyden: A. W. Sijthoff.
Hayes, J. W.
1962 "The pattern of life in the New Territories in 1898," *Journal of the Hong Kong Branch of the Royal Asiatic Society,* 2:75–102.

Ho, Franklin L.
  1936 "Rural economic reconstruction in China," a preliminary paper prepared for the Sixth Conference of the Institute of Pacific Relations held at Yosemite, California, August 15–29, 1936. China Institute of Pacific Relations.

Hong Kong Government
  1960 *Hong Kong: Report for the year 1959.* Hong Kong: Government Press.
  1961 *Hong Kong: Report for the year 1960.* Hong Kong: Government Press.
  1962 *Hong Kong: Report for the year 1961.* Hong Kong: Government Press.
  1964 *Hong Kong: Report for the year 1963.* Hong Kong: Government Press.
  1965 *Hong Kong: Report for the year 1964.* Hong Kong: Government Press.
  1966 *Hong Kong: Report for the year 1965.* Hong Kong: Government Press.

Hoselitz, Bert F.
  1960 *Sociological aspects of economic growth.* Glencoe: The Free Press.

Hou, Chi-ming
  1965 *Foreign investment and economic development in China 1840–1937.* Cambridge: Harvard University Press.

Hsu, Francis L. K.
  1948 *Under the ancestor's shadow: Chinese culture and personality.* New York: Columbia University Press.

Hu Hsien-chin
  1948 *The common descent group in China and its functions.* New York: The Viking Fund, Inc. (Viking Fund Publications in Anthropology, No. 10.)

Institute of Pacific Relations, Research Staff of the Secretariat
  1939 *Agrarian China: Selected source materials from Chinese authors.* London: George Allen and Unwin, Ltd.

Kautsky, Karl
  1898 *Die Agrarfrage.* Stuttgart.
  1931 *Bolshevism at a deadlock.* Translated by B. Pritchard. London: George Allen and Unwin, Ltd.

Kroeber, A. L.
  1948 *Anthropology.* New York: Harcourt, Brace and Company.

Laidler, Harry W.
  1920 *Socialism in thought and action.* New York: The Macmillan Company.

Lang, Olga
  1946 *Chinese family and society.* New Haven: Yale University Press.

Lenin, V.
  1946 *Capitalism and agriculture.* Little Lenin Library, Vol. 30. New York: International Publishers.

Levy, Marion J., Jr.
  1949 *The family revolution in modern China.* Cambridge: Harvard University Press.

Lichtheim, George
  1961 *Marxism, an historical and critical study.* New York: F. A. Praeger.

Lin Yi
   1963   *A short history of China: 1840–1919.* Peking: Foreign Language Press.
Lin Yueh-hwa
   1948   *The golden wing: A sociological study of Chinese familism.* New York: Oxford University Press.
Lockhart, J. H. Stewart
   1900   "Report by Mr. Stewart Lockhart on the extension of the Colony of Hong Kong," in *Correspondence respecting the extension of the boundaries of the Colony.* London: Her Majesty's Government.
Marx, Karl, and Frederick Engels
   1955   *Selected works in two volumes.* Moscow: Foreign Language Publishing House.
Meyer, Alfred G.
   1957   *Leninism.* Cambridge: Harvard University Press.
Mitrany, David
   1951   *Marx against the peasant.* Chapel Hill: University of North Carolina Press.
Murdock, George P.
   1949   *Social structure.* New York: The Macmillan Company.
Nash, Manning
   1955   "Some notes on village industrialism in South and East Asia," *Economic Development and Cultural Change,* 3:271–277.
National Agricultural Research Bureau, Ministry of Industries
   1935   *Crop reports,* III, April 15, 1935, No. 4. Nanking, China.
Ong Shao-er
   1955   *Chinese farm economy after land reform.* Technical Research Report, No. 34, Air Force Personnel and Training Research Center, Lackland Air Force Base, Texas.
Potter, Jack M.
   1967   "Peasants in the modern world" (Introduction to Part V) in *Peasant society: A reader,* ed. by Jack M. Potter, May N. Diaz, and George M. Foster. Boston: Little, Brown and Company.
Pratt, J. A.
   1960   "Emigration and unilineal descent groups: A study of marriage in a Hakka village in the New Territories," *The Eastern Anthropologist,* XIII (4).
Redfield, Robert
   1941   *The folk culture of Yucatan.* Chicago: University of Chicago Press.
   1956   *Peasant society and culture.* Chicago: University of Chicago Press.
Rostow, W. W.
   1960   *The stages of economic growth: A non-Communist manifesto.* Cambridge and New York: Cambridge University Press.
Shephard, Bruce
   1900   "Memorandum on land system," in *Report on the New Territory during the first year of British administration,* Appendix No. III, pp. 266–269. Hong Kong Government Printer.
Skinner, G. William
   1964   "Marketing and social structure in rural China, Part I," *The Journal of Asian Studies,* XXIV (1):1–43.

Szczepanik, Edward
  1956   *The cost of living in Hong Kong.* Hong Kong: Hong Kong University Press.
  1958   *The economic growth of Hong Kong.* London, New York, and Toronto: Oxford University Press.
Tawney, R. H.
  1929   *A memorandum on agriculture and industry in China.* Honolulu: Institute of Pacific Relations.
  1932   *Land and labour in China.* New York: Harcourt, Brace and Co.
  1939   "Introduction," in *Agrarian China,* Institute of Pacific Relations. London: George Allen and Unwin, Ltd.
Topley, Marjorie
  1963   "Hong Kong," in *The role of savings and wealth in Southern Asia and the West,* Richard D. Lambert and Bert F. Hoselitz, eds, pp. 126–177. Paris: UNESCO.
  1964   "Capital, saving and credit among indigenous rice farmers and immigrant vegetable farmers in Hong Kong's New Territories," in *Capital, saving and credit in peasant societies,* Raymond Firth and B. S. Yamey, eds. Chicago: Aldine Publishing Company.
Tregear, T. R.
  1955   *Land use in Hong Kong and the New Territories.* Hong Kong: Government Press.
Wakeman, Frederic, Jr.
  1966   *Strangers at the gate: Social disorders in South China, 1839–1861.* Berkeley and Los Angeles: The University of California Press.
Ward, Barbara E.
  1954   "A Hong Kong fishing village," *Journal of Oriental Studies,* I (1).
  1959   "Floating villages: Chinese fishermen in Hong Kong," *Man,* LIX, Article 62.
  1965   "Varieties of the conscious model: The fishermen of South China," in *The relevance of models for social anthropology,* ed. by M. Banton. London.
Wolf, Eric R.
  1955   "Types of Latin American peasantry: A preliminary discussion," *American Anthropologist,* 57:452–471.
  1966   *Peasants.* Englewood Cliffs, New Jersey: Prentice-Hall, Inc.
Wong
  n.d.   "The New Territories." (Unpublished manuscript, in Chinese.)
Yang, C. K.
  1959a   *The Chinese family in the Communist Revolution.* Cambridge: The Technology Press.
  1959b   *A Chinese village in early Communist transition.* Cambridge: The Technology Press.
Yang, Martin C.
  1948   *A Chinese village: Taitou, Shantung Province.* London: Kegan Paul, Trench, Tribner and Co., Ltd.

Index

Agriculture: growing season, 7; relatively few engaged in, 44; rapid transition to vegetables, 57; traditional system of, 57–60; stages of development, 60–62; field size and distribution, 62–66; types of crops, 66; technology and implements, 67–75; types of fertilizer, 71; insecticide as important innovation, 72; and farm animals, 73; and irrigation, 74; labor as the most important factor in production, 75; rice yield estimates, 82–83; estimates of expenses and profits, 84–85. *See also* Vegetable gardening

Ancestral lands: establishment of, 23; purposes of, 23–24; as key to lineage segmentation, 26; Six Families, 81; manager of, 104–107; educational stipends from, 108; two categories of, 108–109; unequal benefits from, 109–111; distribution of income from, 112–113; used for private benefit, 113–115. *See also* Land

Animals (farm), 73

Associations: in Ping Shan, 28; functions of Vegetable Marketing Organization, 59; Agricultural Aid Association, 72; reasons for joining Vegetable Marketing Organization, 91–94; land owned by, 95; money loan associations, 156; rice loan associations, 156

"Boat People," 11

Buck, John L.: survey of rural industry, 186–187; on land ownership, 188

Cantonese, 11

Chen Han-seng: on industrialization of China, 177; on Chinese tobacco industry, 182–183

Chia-chang (elders), 102–104

Clan. *See* Lineage

Commerce: small-scale at village level, 48; villagers as middlemen, 48–49

Dau-chung (land-measurement unit), 62

Economic change. *See* Industrialization; Agriculture; Ping Shan

Economics, anthropological approach to, 1–2

Education: organization at village level, 29–30; parents' attitude toward, 41; traditional forms of, 55; stipends from ancestral lands, 108; family expenditures for, 143; as social security for parents, 155

Fei Hsiao-tung: on Western influences in China, 178; on ill effects of treaty ports, 181–182, 201–202; on concentration of land ownership, 182; on effects of industrialization on Kaihsienkung, 196–197; on four village types, 198–200; critique of his methodology, 200–203

Fong, H. D., on China's rural industries, 177–178

Ha Fu: as serf-like group, 19; origin, 20–21; traditional duties, 20–21; social mobility, 21; example of life style among, 52; house ownership by, 98

Hakka: origin, 11; in New Territories, 11

Hang Mei: as dominant village in Ping Shan, 18–19; as representative of old landlord village, 41; distribution of family incomes in, 133–140. *See also* Ping Shan

Ho, Franklin L., on industrialization of China, 177

Hoklo, 11

Hong Kong: population, 6; Japanese occupation, 8–9; reliance on mainland for food, 58–59

Hou Chi-ming, on Chinese handicraft industries, 186

213